MW00527994

Urban Gothic of the Second World War

Urban Gothic of the Second World War

Dark London

Sara Wasson

First published 2010 by
PALGRAVE MACMILLAN

Palgrave Macmillan in the UK is an imprint of Macmillan Publishers Limited, registered in England, company number 785998, of Houndmills, Basingstoke, Hampshire RG21 6XS.

Palgrave Macmillan in the US is a division of St Martin's Press LLC, 175 Fifth Avenue, New York, NY 10010.

Palgrave Macmillan is the global academic imprint of the above companies and has companies and representatives throughout the world.

Palgrave® and Macmillan® are registered trademarks in the United States, the United Kingdom, Europe and other countries.

ISBN 978–0–230–57753–4   hardback

This book is printed on paper suitable for recycling and made from fully managed and sustained forest sources. Logging, pulping and manufacturing processes are expected to conform to the environmental regulations of the country of origin.

A catalogue record for this book is available from the British Library.

A catalog record for this book is available from the Library of Congress.

10 9 8 7 6 5 4 3 2 1
19 18 17 16 15 14 13 12 11 10

Printed and bound in Great Britain by
CPI Antony Rowe, Chippenham and Eastbourne

In loving memory of my mother, Frances
author, teacher, and gleeful spirit

Contents

List of Illustrations

Acknowledgements

The author wishes to thank the Carnegie Trust, the Mario Einaudi Centre, Cornell University Clare Hall Fellowship to Cambridge University and Edinburgh Napier University's Centre for Literature and Writing, for research grants which facilitated this project. Many thanks are due also to the inspirational work of Linda Dryden, Emily Alder, Benjamin Brabon and Stéphanie Genz. I also thank Jacqueline Rose, Mary Jacobus, Douglas Mao and Molly Hite, who supervised the projects of which this is the shadow sibling, the dark inverse. I also thank the students of Edinburgh Napier University's 2008–09 module *Cities: Real and Imagined* for your energy and enthushiasm; it was a pleasure to work with you on literary representations of the city. Most of all, I thank my husband Graham, for his patience, wit and generosity.

The author and publisher wish to thank the following for permission to reproduce copyright material:

N. Elizabeth Cullis for p. 9 from Mary Désiree Anderson, *Bow Bells are Silent*, Williams and Norgate (1943).

BBC Written Archives Centre, Caversham, for E2/131/22, Memo from European News Directorate, 19 April 1945.

Curtis Brown Group Ltd, London on behalf of the Estate of Elizabeth Bowen, for pp. 581, 598–9, 610, 628–9, 631, 637, 650, 661–5, 666, 677, 729–31, 757, *Collected Stories*, Vintage (1982); pp. 17, 23–4, 27, 34, 47, 49, 51–2, 55–8, 60–1, 93, 108–110, 128, 142, 145–6, 152, 159, 162, 168, 174–6, 195, 207, 256–8, 263, 275, 311–13, *Heat of the Day*, Jonathan Cape (1949), reprinted Penguin (1962). Copyright © Elizabeth Bowen.

Alison M. Speirs and the Imperial War Museum for permission to quote from the Papers of Mrs Kathleen Church Bliss, Department of Documents, Imperial War Museum, London.

John Fuller for Roy Fuller, "The Growth of Crime" and "The Middle of a War," *Penguin New Writing* 13 (June 1942): 83–6.

The Trustees of the Imperial War Museum for permission to quote from the Papers of Miss I.H. Granger and the Papers of Mr F. Sittner, Department of Documents, Imperial War Museum, London.

Sebastian Yorke for the epigraph and pp. 11–15, 21, 33–4, 36–7, 40–4, 48, 55, 68–9, 75, 84–5, 95–7, 100–2, 107, 111, 140, 162–3, 167, 169,

176, 180–2, Henry Green, *Caught*, Hogarth (1943; reprinted Augustus Kelley 1970).

David Higham Associates for pp. 1–5, 12, 14–22, 34–5, 38–9, 65–6, 73–5, 78, 82, 85, 97–100, 104, 106–7, 123, 129, 137, 140, 175, 194, 227, 231, 234, 236, Graham Greene, *The Ministry of Fear*, Random House (1943).

Sir Simon Gourlay for permission to quote from the Papers of Mrs I. S. Haslewood, Department of Documents, Imperial War Museum, London.

Pollinger Ltd, the Estate of Hilda Doolittle and New Directions for p. 496, Hilda Doolittle, *Collected Poems 1912–1944*, New Directions (1983).

Blackstaff Press on behalf of the Estate of John Hewitt, p. 71, *The Collected Poems of John Hewitt*, ed. Frank Ormsby, Blackstaff Press (1991).

A.M. Heath & Co. Ltd for pp. 8, 11, 13, 15, 19–20, 22, 25, 43, 47, 74–6, 78, 115, 119, 127–30, 133–4, 136, 150, 163–4, 180, 185, Inez Holden, *There's No Story There*, Bodley Head (1944); pp. 9, 21, 24–5, 28, 30–1, 36–8, 40, 42–3, 47, 56, 59–60, 66, 75, 109, 122–4, *The Night Shift*, Bodley Head (1941). © Inez Holden.

A.M. Heath & Co. Ltd, for F. Tennyson Jesse, "Note to Isolationists 1940" (1940, reproduced in *Chaos of the Night*, Ed. Catherine Reilly, Virago, 1984). © F. Tennyson Jesse, 1940.

David Higham Associates and Peter Owen for pp. 15, 18–20, 54–63, 124, 129–32, 136–8, 140–1, 143, 145–6, Anna Kavan, *I Am Lazarus*, Peter Owen (1945); pp. 6, 31, 102–3, 118, 122–4, 166, 175–7, 179–80, *Sleep Has His House*, Cassell (1948), reprinted Picador (1973).

David Higham Associates for p. 74, Margery Lawrence, *Fourteen to Forty-Eight*, Robert Hall (1950).

Macmillan & Co. Ltd for p. 4, Sylvia Lynd, *Collected Poems of Sylvia Lynd*, Macmillan (1945).

Curtis Brown Group Ltd, London, on behalf of the Trustees of the Mass Observation Archive, University of Sussex, for Mass-Observation, "Tube-Dwellers" (1943) and "Women and Morale" (1940). Copyright © The Trustees of the Mass Observation Archive.

The Museum of London for *New Homes Rise from London's Ruins*, Poster Accession number 95.249. © Museum of London.

The National Archives for quotations from the following papers of the Public Record Office: a paper of the Ministry of Information Planning Committee dated 25 July 1941, PRO INF 1/251; memorandum dated 14 May 1940, PRO FO 371/25189/462 (W 7984/7941/49); minute dated 10

September 1942, PRO FO 371/30917 (C 7853/61/18); minute dated 21 April 1940, PRO FO 371/24472/11 (C 5471/116/55); minute dated 26 Dec 1940–11 Jan 1941, PRO FO 371/433/25242/433 (W 12715/38/48). © Crown copyright.

Jon Stallworthy for Wilfred Owen, "Mental Cases," from *The First World War Poetry Digital Archive*, University of Oxford (www.oucs.ox.ac. uk/ww1lit); © The Estate of Wilfred Owen.

Poems and drawings of Mervyn Peake reproduced by kind permission of the Estate of Mervyn Peake. Mervyn Peake, *Shapes and Sounds* (1941), poems pp. 22, 83–4, 88–9, 95–6, 103, 123, 130–1, 133–4, 137, 170, 178–201, *Poems*, ed. R.W. Maslen, Carcanet (2008), and the manuscript of the Gormenghast play adaptation in the Papers of Mervyn Peake, box 7.iii. © Mervyn Peake.

The Piper Estate and The National Gallery of Canada for John Piper, *House of Commons 1941: Aye Chamber* (1941). Held at the National Gallery of Canada, Ottawa. Gift of the Massey Collection of English Painting. © The Piper Estate. Photograph © The National Gallery of Canada, Ottawa.

David Higham Associates and Random House for p. 12, Anthony Powell, *The Soldier's Art*, Heinemann (1966).

Carcanet Press and the Estate of Anne Ridler for pp. 2, 9, Anne Ridler, *The Shadow Factory*, Faber (1946)

Tate Gallery, London for Graham Sutherland, *Crucifixion* (1946). © Tate Gallery. Photograph copyright © Tate, London 2008.

Every effort has been made to trace rights' holders, but if any have been inadvertently overlooked the publishers would be pleased to make necessary arrangements at the first opportunity.

With regard to the Papers of Miss E. Nelki, S. Rothwell, Miss V. Reid, E Pollak, P. Fleiss and Professor R. Jacobstahl, held at the Imperial War Museum, London, every effort has been made to trace copyright holders and the author and the Imperial War Museum would be grateful for any information which might help to trace those whose identities or addresses are not currently known.

1
Introduction: The Urban Gothic of the British Home Front

> All the world was dipped in a livid, unearthly reful-
> gence, theatrical yet sinister, a light neither of night or
> day, the penumbra of Pluto's frontiers.
> > Anthony Powell, *The Soldier's Art* (12)

> In London now Death holds high festival.
> The clustered candelabra of the flares,
> High in the darkly thrumming vault of heaven
> . . . I have seen Death hold festival to-night,
> With hideous beauty of dark ritual.
>
> > Mary Désirée Anderson, "Blitz" (20–1)

This book explores what might be termed a Second World War Gothic in the literature of Britain's home front. No existing work identifies a Gothic of the Second World War, yet this period richly repays the labour, not least for the way that these works in the Gothic mode sub-vert mythologies of nation that are still influential today.[1] Anna Kavan, Mervyn Peake, Elizabeth Bowen, Roy Fuller, Henry Green and others present counter-stories to the dominant national mythology of British survival and emotional resilience. In the texts of this book, Gothic tropes and forms mark moments of fracture in the national mythologies of wartime home, city and fellowship.

This book thus offers two arguments to extend existing Gothic criticism. First, that the texts of wartime London are a rich resource for critical exploration, despite the absence of critical work on a Second World War Gothic to date. Secondly, that the Gothic narrative strands and tropes of these wartime texts do not speak to fractured modern subjectivity in general, but rather speak to specific forms of fraught subjectivity generated by the material circumstances of the home front. The domestic arena was veined with xenophobia, a relentless propaganda machine, proliferating regulation, and the personal sufferings of those separated – sometimes permanently – by war: evacuees from parents, soldiers from partners, kin from kin, "enemy aliens" from loved ones. These wartime literary texts construct the city as a hallucinatory, claustrophobic and labyrinthine realm, writing topical anxieties into the wartime streets.

Scholars of the Gothic grapple with the challenge of definition each time they ply their trade. The Gothic is more than an uncanny ambience or the presence of ghosts, more than the "hobgoblin machinery" of vampires, demons and castles (Norton vii). The Gothic novel of the later eighteenth century was a particular literary form, but even then, there was substantial diversity among texts tagged with the label. The Gothic has become increasingly diverse in the intervening centuries, the machinery updated for each new moment. Ever since the early nineteenth century the Gothic has been less a genre than a mode of writing, "a mode that exceeds genre and categories" (Botting, *Gothic* 14). The present book follows contemporary critical consensus by defining the Gothic mode as having two core characteristics: a particular emotional colouring of the narrative filter, and a preoccupation with certain relationships to space.

Warped affect is pivotal to most discussions of the Gothic. Andrew Smith insists that the Gothic label cannot be invoked except for texts which "substantively refer to a world of horror" (84); David Punter contends the Gothic is inextricable from paranoia (*Terror* 2: 184); Fred Botting notes that the Gothic is a mode where "[i]magination and emotional effects exceed reason" (*Gothic* 3). In the modern Gothic, the world, be it supernatural or natural, is witnessed through a lens of terror, anguish, paranoia or a perverse emotional deadness. Madness, dread or despair colour Gothic narratives, even in third person narration; sanity and clarity are fragile in these realms.

In the Gothic mode, that intense affect accompanies a particular experience of spatiality. Chris Baldick argues that the Gothic "combine[s] a fearful sense of [historical] inheritance ... with a claustrophobic sense of enclosure in space, these two dimensions reinforcing one another to produce an impression of sickening descent into disintegration" (xix). While the claustrophobic settings of eighteenth-century Gothic are primarily castles, monasteries, convents or forests, as the nineteenth century progressed these settings found their modern corollary in the burgeoning metropolis. Industrialisation and increasing urbanisation made cities a surrogate for the gloomy fastnesses of earlier Gothic, for as Botting says, "the modern city combined the natural and architectural components of Gothic grandeur and wilderness, its dark, labyrinthine forests suggesting the violence and menace of Gothic castle and forest" (*Gothic* 2). In the same way that the location of menace changes, so does the nature of the threat: while earlier Gothic generates a thrill of fear with ghosts or demons, the metropolis evokes the horrors of human violence and corruption, terrifying enough without necessarily needing a supernatural edge. The city's anonymity enables sexual and criminal transgression. Literary representations of the city reflect the anxieties that circulate around class and capital and the city's diurnal duality is recruited to represent interior psychic dramas. Disorienting, labyrinthine and claustrophobic cities are evocative settings for the Gothic.

The extending of "Gothic" from genre to mode has spawned a profusion of hyphenated Gothics in recent years, including Victorian Gothic (Wolfreys and Robbins), Gothic modernisms (A. Smith and J. Wallace), postmodern Gothic (Grunenberg), contemporary Gothic (Bruhm), "AfterGothic" (Botting) and more. Many scholars have welcomed the application of Gothic studies to new texts and periods. In the inaugurative edition of *Gothic Studies*, for example, Jerrold Hogle welcomes critical work which "combines ... the rediscovery of literature and art that have largely unnoticed Gothic dimensions with revelations about the broader cultural context(s) in which such ... work participated" ("Past" 6). Critics apply the term to a profusion of artifacts spanning centuries, and books (like this one) historicise literary Gothic for particular moments. Yet such hyphenation does have perils. Some applications are criticised for being too cavalier in assuming that the presence of a ghost or an "uncanny" moment qualifies a text as "Gothic." Andrew Smith and Alexandra Warwick, among others, criticise indiscriminate applications of the Gothic label, urging literary critics to inform their discussions with contemporary Gothic criticism (A. Smith 83; Warwick, "Feeling Gothicky" 9). A second risk of hyphenation is the temptation to generalise about human subjectivity across a wide range of historical periods, to argue that Gothic forms signify a fraught subjectivity universally typical of late capitalism: such generalising is critiqued by Warwick ("Feeling Gothicky" 10), Alex Link (518), Roger Luckhurst (528, 533) and Punter ("Ghost of a History" ix). Faced with the peril of such broad generalisation, Gothic studies increasingly welcomes studies of historicised, particular Gothic, literary criticism examining how Gothic modes are inflected for particular times and places. Increasingly, critics call not only for historicised but *localised* Gothic: in a 2002 discussion of trends in Gothic criticism, for example, Luckhurst recommends that Gothic criticism heed the way location functions in Gothic texts: "it is worth recalling that ghosts are held to haunt specific locales, are tied to what late Victorian psychical researchers rather splendidly termed 'phantasmogenetic centres'. This might suggest that the ghosts of London are different from those of Paris, or those of California" (542).

Wartime London was peculiarly rich as a "phantasmogenetic centre," for it saw Gothic tropes become literal. People were buried alive in their own homes, night streets turned into a bizarre dreamscape where "banshee" sirens wailed and death howled down in the form of wailing bombs, shelterers took refuge in open coffins and even familiar structures hid new and unexpected horrors, like the ice cream vans commandeered to carry human blood. Corpses, shop mannequins and butcher's meat lay scattered in streets, all queasy doublings of the living. Black rubber gas masks resembled "a growth of black fungus" (Struther 63) and people sheltering asleep in the Tube were "like the dead laid out in a room" (Piette, *"London's Burning"* 43). The nineteenth century saw many attempts to tame London as a space: sewers removed filth, electric light brightened the whole metropolis, and the vast distances of the city were mastered by the London underground and a mass transit network.[2] All these masteries of the city cracked during the Second World War.

London's urban Gothic

The iconic position of London has been established in Gothic studies, particularly with respect to literature of the end of the nineteenth century and the last decades of the twentieth. The closing years of the nineteenth century were particularly fertile for dark fantasies, with Robert Louis Stevenson, Arthur Machen, Bram Stoker and others imbuing London's streets with menace. Stevenson's *The Strange Case of Dr Jekyll and Mr Hyde* (1886), for example, presents nineteenth-century urban geography as facilitating depravity. Bram Stoker's *Dracula* (1897) depicts a vampire entering London with a view to taking over the British empire, and Arthur Machen's *The Great God Pan* (1890) presents London as a "city of nightmares" (79) in which a demonic woman corrupts young gentlemen. The city's duality of wealth juxtaposed with poverty made it a potent symbol for the dual human "self" contemporaneously proposed in psychological texts (Dryden 262). Similarly, the writing of Gothic London from the 1970s onwards has received attention from scholars exploring how Iain Sinclair, Peter Ackroyd and Neil Gaiman envision the modern metropolis (e.g. Lurkhurst; Link).

The Second World War is another iconic moment for that iconic city, also worthy of critical attention. Yet strangely, there is to date a dearth of critical material exploring the urban Gothic of the Second World War London. As it happens, Second World War London shared several of the sociohistorical features that made *fin-de-siècle* London so productive of Gothic. Both eras shared a preoccupation with the prospect of apocalyptic future war and a sense of the human subject as permanently embattled in interior struggle with irrational impulses. Furthermore, just as late nineteenth-century Britain was preoccupied with images of racial degeneration, that rhetoric returns in the war: when people fled to the tube platforms for shelter against raids, official writing began to apprehensively contemplate the risk of such underground shelterers degenerating into troglodyte beings. In Second World War texts, tropes and preoccupations of *fin-de-siècle* Gothic are inflected for a new moment.

H. G. Wells is a key figure in bridging *fin-de-siècle* Gothic and that of the Second World War. His novels *The War in the Air* (1908) and *The War of the Worlds* (1898) depict a devastated London and air attack in terms that prefigure the Blitz. In *War in the Air,* multiple nations invent aerial combat simultaneously, triggering global war and the collapse of civilisation. *War of the Worlds* features Martian invaders who destroy earth's towns and consume humans alive. Wells's descriptions of future war are examples of invasion fiction, a literary genre popular in the late nineteenth and early twentieth century, and other classics of this genre, too, saw their visions partly realised on Britain's Second World War home front.[3] The genre often dwells on technologies of destruction, and Wells's novels are no exception: the London of *War in the Air* is damaged by bombing and that of *War of the Worlds* by a trio of Martian weaponry (gas warfare, Heat-Ray and mechanical attack). Superior to humans in technology, the Martians reduce humanity to scrabbling fugitives. London is decimated in particular by gas, the "Black Smoke" which is "death to all that breathes" (88). Decades after the novel was published, gas became a primary dread of the 1939 civil defence preparations (Ziegler 16). Although gas attacks did not materialise, both these novels accurately foreshadow the emptiness, darkness and strange sounds of the Second World War cityscape. The narrator of *War of the Worlds* is appalled by the "gaunt quiet" that fills London's deserted streets, a city "condemned and derelict" (167, 164). Such a description echoes the loneliness that haunts *fin-de-siècle* writing as a whole. As Warwick notes,

these texts of future war are haunted by a sense of "post-imperial desolation and the sense of being the last person alive" ("Lost Cities" 83).

Like *fin-de-siècle* London, London on the eve of the Second World War
was imagined to be in the shadow of Apocalypse. Air attack destroys
not only soldiers and civilians, but also the very social fabric of a city.
Wells accurately predicts that air attacks can devastate a place, but cannot occupy it or quell resistance (*War in the Air* 278). As a result, war is
prolonged, triggering social devastation, famine and pestilence.[4] *War
of the Worlds* depicts similar social disintegration: after mere days of
Martian attack, the social body of Britain disintegrates and begins to
decay, "losing coherency, losing shape and efficiency, guttering, soften-
ing, running at last in that swift liquefaction of the social body" (*War
of the Worlds* 92). In his emphasis on the grim aftermath of invasion,
Wells echoes a theme of much invasion fiction, for the abiding image
of the genre is the fragility of all civilisation. After the chaos of war,
civilisation declines with shocking rapidity into pockets of small-scale
farming, squalour and superstition. Richard Jefferies's *After London*
(1885) imagines wilderness reclaiming urban terrain, and that fantasy
became strikingly literal in 1944, a few years after the bombing of the
central City of London. The great fire raid of 29 December 1940 almost
annihilated the central City in a blaze which has been described as the
closest Britain ever came to the firestorms of Dresden and Hamburg
(Ziegler 144), and by 1944, the wreckage was overgrown with flowers, and deer and hens were taking refuge in the ruins. R. S. Fitter and
J. E. Lousley saw "the profusion of wild flowers, birds and insects to
be seen on the bombed sites of the city is now one of the sights of
London," and they record "269 wild flowers, grasses and ferns, 3 mam-
mals, 31 birds, 56 insects and 27 kinds of other invertebrates" (3). The
wonder receiving most comment was the plenitude of blossom. H.V.
Morton marvels, "The speed with which vegetation draped itself over
the bomb damage surprised many people. Where did the flowers come
from?. . . . Had the seeds always been blowing about, but had they been
unable, in that wilderness of stone, to find anywhere to germinate and
grow?" (43). Churches, printers' shops, antique stores and entire streets
became wilderness, and the visions of Wells, Jefferies and others were
partly realised on the streets of the wartime city.

When the Blitz did begin, Wells's novels were regularly invoked in
descriptions. Bryher, for example, titles her wartime memoir *The Days of
Mars* on the grounds that the period seemed like science fiction (Lassner
147). In fact, Wells's writing gained such credibility that in 1938 the
British government invited him to act as a consultant in planning for

civilian responses to air bombardment. His predictions were bleak. In *The Fate of Homo Sapiens* (1939) Wells admits he has lost hope in humanity's ability to forestall disaster:

> The material and moral destruction of the war will certainly be enormous. The population stratum of military age will be largely killed, mutilated, poisoned or mentally unbalanced, and after it will come a generation or so, which has been more and more under-nourished, under-educated, demoralised and mentally distorted. ... There will have been a great burning and smashing up of human habitations which no one will have had energy to replace, and such a destruction of beautiful buildings, works of art, and irreplaceable loveliness of all sorts, as will make the feats of the Huns and Vandals seem mere boyish mischief. (290)

In the damaged postwar world, Wells argues, cities will become places of cruelty and peril: "More and more will the world be for the tough, for the secretive, the treacherous and ruthless. Cities will be dangerous labyrinths" (308).

Even in Wells's earlier writing, London can be malignant. In the epilogue to *War in the Air,* a character tells his grandson Teddy – born after the War – about the supernatural horrors that lurk in the abandoned metropolis, where skeletons lie in the silent houses. "'They say there's a 'og man [pig farmer] in Beck'n'am what was lost in London three days and three nights. 'E went up after whiskey to Cheapside, and lorst 'is way among the ruins and wandered. Three days and three nights 'e wandered about and the streets kep' changing so's 'e couldn't get 'ome'" (269). Maliciously mutable, this London contorts itself to trap humans as prey. As night falls, the unlucky hog man finds himself no longer alone. The grandfather continues the story:

> "It was as still as death all day long, until the sunset came and the twilight thickened, and then it began to rustle and whisper and go pit-a-pat with a sound like 'urrying feet. . . . A sound of carts and 'orses there was, and a sound of cabs and omnibuses, and then a lot of whistling. Shrill whistles, whistles that froze 'is marrer. ... They was the ghosts of them that was overtook, the ghosts of them that used to crowd those streets ... they was all painted skulls ..." (269–70)

Past auditory geographies haunt the desolate space. The hog man fortunately remembers some words from scripture, and the ghosts flee.

Wells's aim in this epilogue is primarily to make us aware of the way in which the loss of civiliation would cause human beings to degenerate into superstition, but it is interesting to compare the hog man's fantasy with the final fancy of the narrator of *War of the Worlds*, a man who is – like Wells himself – an accomplished scholar and writer of scientific and philosophical articles. This credible and scholarly narrator has a vision of a phantasmic London similar to that of the unlettered hog man:

> I go to London and see the busy multitudes in Fleet Street and the Strand, and it comes across my mind that they are but the ghosts of the past, haunting the streets that I have seen silent and wretched, going to and fro, phantasms in a dead city, the mockery of life in a galvanised body. (180)

Although the invading Martians have died, this narration does not end in triumph. The narrator intuits that humans are doomed creatures, fated to be supplanted as rulers of earth.

Such dread of civilisation failing was paralleled by fears of racial degeneration. Increasing recognition of Charles Darwin's model of human evolution had raised awareness that humankind is always in the throes of mutation, either progressing in sophistication or dismally degenerating into subhuman forms. The latter trajectory preoccupied *fin-de-siècle* Britain, and cities were seen as fostering illness which could lead to collective racial decay. Max Nordau's *Degeneration* (1892), for example, sees the city as fatal site of racial decline, arguing that cities trigger degenerative change:

> The inhabitant of a large town, even the richest, who is surrounded by the greatest luxury, is continually exposed to unfavourable influences which diminish his vital powers. ... He breathes an atmosphere charged with organic detritus; he eats stale, contaminated, adulterated food; he feels himself in a state of constant nervous excitement, and one can compare him without hesitation to the inhabitant of a marshy district. (35)

Drawing on Bénédict Morel's *Traité des Dégénérescences* (1857), Nordau compares the physiology of town-dwellers with that of people living in rural fever districts. He suggests that the town-dweller born and developed in such a swamp-like environment matures into a subhuman creature, and "the entire being presents a strange and repulsive mixture of incompleteness and decay" (36).

Nordau's views were not unique. An 1885 issue of the medical journal *The Lancet*, for example, asserts:

> He who would find the centres of decay in a nation, still on the whole robust and active, must seek for them at the points of social tension [urban centres]. The proofs of pressure, starvation, and atrophy, of vice and of brutal reversion, and of their results are all to be found there. ("Review of [James Cantlie's] *Degeneration Amongst Londoners*" 264)

London evoked particular alarm, as one of the largest cities in the world. Such degeneration has two aspects, physical decline and the hereditary transmission of such weakness to offspring. James Cantlie combines both strands in his pamphlet *Degeneration Amongst Londoners* when he asserts that Londoners "are town dwellers, and thereby, a doomed race. Without infusions of new blood in a few generations they die out" (qtd. in Warwick, "Lost Cities" 86). Wells depicts cities as hotbeds for infection. The Purple Death of *The War in the Air* is particularly contagious in cities (253) and his non-fiction 1939 *Fate of Homo Sapiens* presents urban settings as rife with disease. "Mankind which began in a cave and behind a windbreak will end in the disease-soaked ruins of a slum" (311).

Fears of degeneration surged forth in new guises in 1939, when impending war forced the government to contemplate the likelihood that people would seek shelter from raids by going underground. The few Zeppelin air raids of the First World War saw over 300,000 Londoners take shelter in the London underground system, and in 1939 government authorities expected new raids would see people do the same. Government reports speak apprehensively of the risk of deep shelter mentality (Ziegler 10), the notion that that extended subterranean sojourns would corrupt the British race like the Morlocks of Wells's *Time Machine* (1895) who are unable to emerge into daylight. Anxieties clustered around these "pathetic, lump-like, and yet breathing figures waiting hollow-eyed or in their public sleep" (FitzGibbon 136). Constantine FitzGibbon notes that there were dreads that "Crowded shelters, besides being a perfect breeding place for various physical infections, would encourage every form of mass hysteria from defeatism to panic" (15). This physical decline is described in terms of evolutionary degeneration: official reports warn that tube shelterers may transform into "timorous troglodytes" (T. O'Brien 342), evolutionary precursors to *Homo sapiens*. This language is echoed in Edith Sitwell's poem

"Lullaby," in which an ape encourages a child to regress to a subhuman condition, and the American poet H.D. describes herself and fellow sufferers on the British home front as degenerating into the lower orders of animals: "We've grown alike, slithering ... / grey faces, fish-faces, frog gait, / we slop, we hop" (Hilda Doolittle, "May 1943" 496). People sheltering in the tube are often described as abandoning the proprieties of civilisation (Mass Observation, "Tube-Dwellers" 102). The language of evolutionary deterioration and a sense of moving into a prehistoric past abounds in wartime writing. Evelyn Waugh, for example, describes blacked-out London as strangely ancient. "Time might have gone back two thousand years to the time when London was a stockaded cluster of huts down the river, and the streets through which they walked, empty sedge and swamp" (*Men* 23). Just as *fin-de-siècle* Britain was preoccupied with images of evolutionary degeneration, so too does that rhetoric run through wartime writing.

In another way, also, the Second World War seems to mark a return to an earlier time. For many, World War II was a dread continuation of the First (Lassner 12, 53, 104, 141). Diarist Stanley Rothwell, for example, dreams that he sees the dead of the First World War return:

> I thought of the boys who had been sacrificed in 1914–1918. ... All night I tossed and turned in my bed, I could not sleep, I could hear the trains in the distance. ... I could swear I was sweating blood as I saw a Ghost army marching, faces down and silent, just the tramp, tramp, tramp of their boots in the road, they wore grey greatcoats and were led by some monstrous figure. (12)

The next day, he sees his dream come true on Charing Cross Road: "behold we saw the Ghost army of my dreams in reality and in every detail led by one lone figure on horse back, it was a division of the Guards that I believe fought the rear guard action that protected the evacuation from Dunkirk, I believe that they were wiped out almost to a man in that action" (12). Elizabeth Bowen's wartime fantasies also suggest a continuum between the wars. Her short story "Songs my Father Sang Me" (1945) opens with two lovers talking in a night club during the Blitz. The man recognises the dance tune as "pre-war," but his partner corrects him: "'It's last war'" (*Stories* 650). He replies, "'Well, last war's pre-war'" but the very discussion makes us wonder if that is actually true – might wartime occupy a different time continuum than peace? Similarly, in Bowen's story "The Demon Lover" a ghost from the First World War returns, and Columbia's 1944 horror film *Return of the Vampire* depicts the return of a vampire which had been sealed in a London tomb in 1918. During the Blitz twenty years later, a bomb destroys his prison, his corpse is discovered and assumed to be a civilian casualty, and is reburied in a London cemetery – from which he rises to roam the streets anew.[5] Much of the literature examined in the following chapters posits a continuity between the two combats, a way in which the First World War never quite ended on a certain imaginative plane. To a generation who had seen the slaughter of the Somme, the Second World War seems dread repetition, humanity locked into a cycle of violence. This structure typifies Gothic anachronism, in which horrors from the past return.

The Gothic of the two wars differs in the way it locates its horrors. While the First World War's iconic locus of dread is the trenches, that of the Second is the damaged city, not the blood and mud of Passchendaele, but an imperial metropolis made suddenly uncanny, primitive, and hostile.[6] In this way the Second World War Gothic reactivates the urban preoccupations of the *fin-de-siècle*. Stephen Spender notes,

> In this war, by "War Pictures" we mean, pre-eminently, paintings of the Blitz. In the last war we would have meant pictures of the Western Front. ... The background to this war, corresponding to the Western Front in the last war, is the bombed city. (5–6)

World War II was not the first war to see bombing of the British home front: previous wars had a few Zeppelin air raids, tube shelterers, rationing and a mild blackout (Ziegler 9–10; "War Doesn't Change") but despite these diluted precedents, World War II was indisputably the first to see widescale bombing of British cities. As it happens, First World War trenches saw their own dark parody of urban terrain in that some soldiers named trenches after streets back home, the names of British streets presiding over avenues of decaying corpses in walls of mud. Paul Fussell notes these trench names often had "a distinctly London flavor. *Piccadilly* was a favourite; popular also were *Regent Street* and *Strand*" (42–3). In the Second World War, those original streets become implicated in new horrors.

The very sensory environment of the home front came to exemplify Edmund Burke's eighteenth-century redefinition of the sublime. Burke argues that any sense of the sublime is fundamentally rooted in danger and a sense of the fragility of the human organism. Rather than seeing the feeling of the sublime as something evoked by beauty, Burke argues it is evoked by a sense of mysterious powers beyond ourselves, a sense triggered by "Vacuity [emptiness], Darkness, Solitude and Silence" (65). All three were plentiful in blacked-out London.

Light was the first casualty of the home front. Until the late nineteenth century, London was lit unevenly, wealthy quarters benefiting from gas lamps and (later) electric light while poorer quarters lacked such luxuries. Darkness saw crime prosper, and the closing decades of the century saw impassioned pleas for increased lighting. In October 1881 the *Star* newspaper declaimed: "The cry of the East End is for light – the electric light to flash into the dark corners of its streets and alleys, the magic light of sympathy and hope to flash into the dark corners of wrecked and marred lives" (qtd. in Curtis 263). Since dark streets meant increased crime, peril and transgression, light is described in the language of salvation.

The 1939 blackout saw such redemptive light vanish. First enforced at sunset on 1 September 1939, it lasted for over five years (the "dim-out" lightened the darkness in September 1944, and blackout ended completely in April 1945). The blackout was conceived to prevent bombers having clear targets. Neon signs were forbidden, traffic lights were reduced to slits, street lights were dimmed, house windows were covered, and car headlights were screened.[7] The sheer profundity of the darkness amazed people. Waugh, for example, describes it as a "baffling midnight void" (*Men* 23) and Mary Désiree Anderson describes the darkness as "a time of dread" and a "shuddering" beast of prey(9). Richard Brown Baker describes being in a crowd at night in Piccadilly on a Saturday night: "It seemed to me sinister to have so many people shuffling around in blackness" (qtd. in Ziegler 312). Kathleen Raine describes "the sense of phantasmagoria which was cast over our blacked-out cities, making familiar places seem strange, and strange sights and scenes familiar" (Martin 47). The strangeness was intensified by the way the night-time city lost its three-dimensional depth. Wartime streets, dominated by featureless black bulks, mimic the nineteenth-century streets of James Thomson's *City of Dreadful Night*, a place of "soundless solitudes immense/Of ranged mountains dark and still as tombs" (ll. 43–5). London became a city of implacable silhouettes.

What light remained merely made the city even stranger. Vera Reid describes how blue "blackout" light bulbs created "a dim twilight that gave the scene a sense of unreality" (7) and while the city below was implacably dark, the sky became filled with light and unnatural colour. Searchlights and incendiaries transformed the sky, and lexis of the spectral gathers around this illumination. Haslewood describes the searchlights that scoured the sky as "crossing and recrossing in ghostly silence" (1) and Sylvia Lynd sees the lights as funereal, producing "A grey stone forest where dark night has been. [...] / As if all living trees were dead / And pale marmoreal branches raised instead" (4). The lights could also seem disturbingly alive. Mary Désirée Anderson describes the "moonbeam tentacles" of searchlights (20) and Margery Lawrence imagines them as a "monstrous garden in the sky," "blossoms, hideously fair, / Sprawling above the shuddering citadel!" (74).

Dryden notes that darkness facilitated crime in the nineteenth-century city (257–8) and certain transgressions also flourished in the wartime gloom (see Chapter 2). In addition to real dangers, the darkened city elicited fantastical fears. Many writers imagined the night to have a new, strange life of its own. A writer for Mass Observation, for example, notes that "Nothing, no amount of experience, makes you really used to the black-out. ... [T]he consciousness of it, waiting for you, out there, behind the black material on the window, is a threat" (*War Begins* 187). Darkness is personified as hungry and living. For some, the wartime quenching of urban light symbolised a fading of civilisation; as *Picture Post* noted grimly in December 1940, "In capital after capital in Europe, the lights have been going out" ("New York" 13).

Equally ominous were the silence and emptiness, potent catalysts of Burke's sublime. Apart from raids, when sirens, incendiaries, and high explosives made the city a chaotic orchestra of sound, the city was uncharacteristically quiet.[8] The Control of Noises (Defence) Act of 1940 reconfigured the soundscape so that air-raid sirens would not have misleading competition. Unauthorised sirens, factory sirens and whistles were forbidden, and after June 1940 even Church bells were outlawed unless improvised alarms. The silence was intensified by the sudden emptying of London. Three million children and mothers were evacuated from the capital in three days, and four hundred thousand pets and zoo animals were euthanised at the outbreak of war (Gardiner 70; Ziegler 74). "Enemy aliens" were interned and conscription increased apace.[9] Although London's population revived during bombing lulls, the city as a whole remained unusually empty for the duration of the war, Ziegler noting that wartime London became "a place of unwonted silence" (67). This muted city mimics the nineteenth-century streets of James Thomson's *City of Dreadful Night*, where the inhabitants endure

> The silence which benumbs or strains the sense
> Fulfills with awe the soul's despair unweeping:
> Myriads of habitants are ever sleeping,
> Or dead, or fled from nameless pestilence! (ll. 46–9)

The threats were no longer nameless in 1939.

After air raids began in 1940, other masteries were challenged. While the nineteenth century had brought light, sewers, and transport infrastructure to the city, the Second World War partially reversed all these triumphs. Tube stations were hit, such as the stations at Marble Arch, Trafalgar Square, Sloane Square and Balham. Sloane Square tube station was simply "carved ... out of existence" by a 2000 lb bomb (Haslewood 41). One ARP worker involved in the raid on Balham tube station describes the Thames burying screaming people in rushing water and sludge (qtd. in Ziegler 117). Water and mud were no longer neatly channelled and tamed. Nor did sewers remain intact. In September 1940, bombardment damaged London's sewage system, flooding the Thames with human waste (Calder, *People* 171).

Transport infrastructure also crumbled. One's mental maps of a place are always underscored by knowledge of the time it will take to cross a distance, and by 1939, technological advances and infrastructure changes had transformed the way people engaged with London's terrains. Three technologies in particular had tamed London's vast distances: the motor car, the mass transit system and the telephone. Transport changed the city-dweller's impression of urban vastness; as Venturi, Brown and Izenour note in their analysis of Las Vegas, certain spaces are customarily approached and passed through by car (75). In wartime London, such travel became increasingly difficult, for petrol was rationed, roads and vehicles were damaged, and after November 1940 cars were no longer manufactured for civilian use (Haslewood 38). As a result, people became increasingly conscious of the city's vast size as insurmountable. Charles Graves, a transport historian, suggests that "London without its rumbling red omnibuses, its clanging trams, its rushing Underground trains, its gliding trolleybuses, its streamlined coaches and its moving staircases – such a London would be almost uninhabitable" (7) and damage to the transport infrastructure indeed made it hard to live in the ways Londoners had come to take for granted. As a character says in Jane Nicholson's novel *Shelter* (1941):

> Bricks and mortar are not the only things the blitz has destroyed; we have lost our sense of time. ... You look across barricades of rope at long sections of West End thoroughfare down which there is no traffic. You appreciate for the first time the breadth and architecture of streets that have meant nothing before but a traffic jam. (100)

Telephone networks, too, become increasingly unreliable, and people became conscious of the city's recalcitrant distances. Another character muses,

> We have got in the habit of ringing up all our friends to know if they're "all right'; now this diversion ceases, as most of us are off the air. Some of us set out nobly to see for ourselves, and a journey that took fifteen minutes by bus is now three-quarters of an hour, on foot, by bus, and by taxi. We dial hopefully the outer darkness of the suburbs. (122)

A character in Graham Greene's *Ministry of Fear* (1943) muses as he telephones a friend, "It was always questionable in these days whether a telephone bell would ring at all, because overnight an office might have ceased to exist" (75). He finds a friend listed in phone book, but "That meant nothing ... the Blitz was newer than the edition" (85). The telephone's technology of sensory extension fails with the Blitz, and people are thrown back on the limitations of their bodies. Fragile and limited human organisms, deprived of such prosthetic extensions, struggle with the expanse of the city. The nineteenth century's hard-won masteries of the city begin to break.

Fractured narrative, fractured nation

The aforegoing summary of some of Britain's home front wartime challenges may sound oddly bleak, given the way British national discourse usually constructs the war as a time of resilience and camaraderie. The role that Blitz history has taken in the popular imaginary is famously explored in Angus Calder's *Myth of the Blitz* (1991). Calder uses "myth" here in Roland Barthes' sense, denoting not deception but the way a culture empties certain icons into simplified signs, "abolish[ing] the complexity of human acts, it gives them the simplicity of essences" (143). Barthes uses "myth" to denote the way cultures leach complexity from events, effacing the messy counter-stories which do not fit myths' reassuring simplicities.

   The Blitz myth is a potent shorthand for collective courage, generosity and fellowship. Calder notes that the account of the Blitz in the British cultural imaginary "involves heroes, suggests the victory of a good God over satanic evil, and has been used to explain a fact: the defeat of Nazism" (*Myth* 2). The Blitz myth asserts that wartime was a time of golden togetherness. In Phyllis Bottome's novel *London Pride*

(1941), for example, a group of strangers sharing a shelter sing "Home, Sweet Home" to raise their spirits during a raid:

> Walls might go up, roofs might go, the prized possessions of a lifetime might be burned or broken up, but something within the people's hearts grew stronger through the harsh and noisy hours. ... They felt that those who shared their danger with them – were their brothers. (109)

This notion of people feeling brotherly and sisterly kinship with strangers invites comparisons with Benedict Anderson's descriptions of a nation as an "imagined community," "imagined because the members of even the smallest nation will never know most of their fellow-members, meet them, or even hear of them, yet in the mind of each lives the image of their communion" (*Imagined* 6). A nation can thus be defined as a collective in which members share a sense of connection with other members, even if those people will never be met. Benedict Anderson describes this emotional bond as a "deep horizontal comradeship" (*Imagined* 7). In this model, nationality and national identity are "cultural artifacts of a particular kind" (*Imagined* 4), constructed with the help of texts and phenomena that give people a sense of horizontal kinship with imagined fellow members of their nation.

Anderson saw print capitalism as nurturing this sense of horizontal connection. Newspapers and novels create a sense of lives simultaneously unfolding alongside each other, and such representations of people living parallel lives leads, in time, to a conception of the nation as a unified collective, "a solid community moving steadily down (or up) history" (*Imagined* 26). He argues that before the era of print capitalism, time was seen instead in the religious terms of prophecy, destiny and Messianic fulfilment (*Imagined* 23–4). In such a view of time, the nation is not seen as moving through history in a linear progression, but instead as a glorious entity spanning all historical periods with a single story of destiny, triumph and prophetic fulfilment. In describing the shift from prophetic time to linear time Anderson controversially co-opts Walter Benjamin's notion of "homogeneous, empty time ... arked not by prefiguring and fulfilment, but by temporal coincidence, and measured by clock and calendar" (*Imagined* 24). This new non-religious sense of time, argues Anderson, underpins a new sense of community across all the members of a nation, a harmonious web of imagined fellowship.

Anderson's notion of the imagined community connects with popular depictions of the Blitz in two ways. First, home front discourse was abundant in expressions of such "horizontal kinship." Secondly, since the war ended narratives of Blitz heroism have become a significant component of the British nation's discourse of itself as a united collective moving through history. Emotion is central to Anderson's definition of a nation, for a sense of national affiliation involves "affective bonds" between oneself and the rest of the imagined community (*Imagined* 64). Such a surge of affect was widely noted during the Blitz in what Elizabeth Bowen calls, "[t]he war-warmed impulse of people to be *a* people ... the curious animal psychic oneness, the human lava-flow" (*Heat* 275, emphasis in original). There is indeed an element of truth to the grand story of community spirit and jovial defiance. In the propaganda film *London Can Take It* (1940) American journalist Quentin Reynolds declares: "A bomb has its limitations ... It cannot kill the unconquerable courage and spirit of the people of London. London can take it." Anecdotes abound of laconic Cockney responses to bombing. One barber's shop which had lost its entire façade, for example, added the sign: "OPEN AS USUAL – CLOSE SHAVES A SPECIALTY" (Woon 127). But stories of bravery and togetherness leave little room for the experience of those who had to fight for spaces on the tube platforms, or who felt visceral disgust at seeing public shelterers in the "tube," or wardens and police who squabbled over who had authority over a bombed street, or the many victims of bombing who then became victims of looting (Ziegler 148–50; S. Jones 11–16; Haslewood 37). Anguish, too, was far more widespread than the Blitz Myth would have one believe. Blitz exhilaration often gave way to a seemingly nonchalant calmness, but both almost invariably yielded, in turn, to grief and disorientation (FitzGibbon 118). Calder notes:

> To judge from certain versions of the blitz, it was a mean and pusillanimous Londoner indeed who did not emerge from the debris with a wisecrack on his lips. ... But it was something close to hysteria which produced many of the gay remarks, and those who made them might be found, a few hours later, sobbing uncontrollably in the rest centres. A true, if chilling, anecdote illustrates this condition. One elderly woman refused to leave her stewpot and stayed on in her house in a huge area of devastation. A stretcher-bearer, to humour her, asked to taste her cooking, and found the pot was full of plaster and bricks. (*People* 187–8)

Reid describes a man reduced to madness by the destruction of his entire street (141), I. Haslewood recalls the brave leader of her stretcher squad collapsing and saying he could not go out into the hail of bombs (8) and H.D., who lived in London during the Blitz, laments the "tensions and tiredness and distress and distorted values and the high pitched level" (*Gift* 216). Ackroyd notes that "Some citizens were hysterical, filled with overwhelming anxiety, and there were several cases of suicide" (738). Wartime camaraderie did not dissolve human fear and grief.

Class conflict, too, was not erased by wartime camaraderie. Peter Conway declares that the home front saw differences between people erased: "Before the war, they had just been units, each living in his own house or flat or rooms – or even part of a room. [...] They were welded by the fires of horror into a unity. They forgot petty differences and saw only the big, inescapable truth of life and living" (8–9). Such warming narratives downplay the reality of continuing class inequities during the Blitz. Yet Bluemel notes that "The myth of blitz unity tends to obscure the history of class conflict early in the 1940s, when people in the East End were paying with their lives for the government's decision to shelter the rich rather than the poor" (128): here, Bluemel refers to a constellation of flaws in the government's civil defence procedures which arguably benefitted the middle-class over the working-class. Before the war, for example, much work went into producing prefabricated Anderson shelters which middle-class families could use in their gardens; since many working-class families lacked gardens, they could not benefit from these, and the under-table Morrison shelters and flimsy public shelters that many had to use as a result often had grave safety deficiencies, collapsing on shelterers on several occasions. In addition, class divisions were very marked in public shelters (Hewison 37).

Any nation's stories of itself will inevitably be partial. Ernst Renan notes that national consciousness requires selective forgetting of facts that do not mesh with the nation's favoured narrative (11) and Robert Miles notes that nation building requires "historical amnesia. ... Nothing must contradict this narrative ... especially ... evidence of past diversity, heterogeneity, and conflict" ("Abjection" 53). The lacunae of the Blitz mythology have been explored by Calder, Stuart Hylton, Clive Ponting and Steve Jones, but the myth is resilient and continues to attract defenders. Robert Mackay and Jean Freedman, for example, defend the truth in the myth, citing significant evidence of generosity and upstanding citizenship, and they are indubitably correct that the Blitz myth of fellowship was echoed in the lives of many and that counter-stories to the dominant tales of Blitz goodness were rare. This present book, however, explores exactly those shabby counter-stories. Some people felt, for example, that their own fear was a shameful contaminant. One brave ambalance-driver recalls her own experience:

> Fear. Paralysing physical fear. It grips you and you feel contaminated, unclean. ...
> Couldn't go among other people and let them catch it too. ...
> I felt ashamed. ... It's like a sinister vibration which shatters you to pieces inside. Was quite incapable of movement though I wanted to get away before the others were affected. Like a leper. (Reid 153)

This driver's actions during the war were consistently brave and heroic, but even she experiences the shame of dread, and she uses the trope of infectious disease to convey shame at her own terror. People whose wartime experience did not match the myth could see themselves as sick or deviant. The following chapters explore how the wartime city is marshalled in literature to express such inadmissible experience.

Benedict Anderson's emphasis on the nation as a site of warm, horizontal connections has been criticised for downplaying the way in which any nation features inequalities: some people are always effaced, exploited or persecuted. This lacuna is clearest in his appropriation of Walter Benjamin's concept of "homogeneous, empty time." John Kelly notes that Benjamin actually coined the phrase to denote the contemptible delusion that one is part of a benevolent social unit progressing together through history: Benjamin sees the notion of a historical continuum as a device for oppression, trying to maim the revolutionary classes' ability to overthrow a dominant order (Kelly 865). Benjamin deplores homogeneous empty time and indeed all sense of a continuum of history; rather, he wishes to shatter all continuums of history and fill empty time with the shock of a revolutionary present. He contrasts homogeneous time with "The awareness [among activists] that they are about to make the continuum of history explode [and which] is characteristic of the revolutionary classes at the moment of their action" (*Illuminations* 261). In Benedict Anderson's hands, the concept of homogeneous time becomes emptied of such oppression, becoming a serene phenomenon underpinning a fraternal national sentiment.

Rather than being a solid community, however, a nation is always an asymmetrical collective, and critics have identified asymmetries that complicate imagined community. Homi Bhabha argues that we see the nation differently if we look at it from the perspective of the equivocal position held by "colonials, postcolonials, migrants, [and] minorities"

("DissemiNation" 315). Such outsiders cannot so readily access the horizontal kinship of the privileged who can easily self-identify with the nation's stories of itself. Such outsiders recognise that nations are not only collectives of horizontal kinship, but are also entities that constrain and regulate movement: "the worn-out metaphors of the resplendent national life now circulate in another narrative of entry permits and passports and work permits that at once preserve and proliferate, bind and breach the human rights of the nation" ("DissemiNation" 315). This perspective leads Bhabha to challenge Benedict Anderson's "homogeneous, empty time" – he argues that the contemporary time of a nation is not so neatly tamed into a single story. Rather, Bhabha contends that any national narrative always functions in a kind of "double-time," where past and present meet in complex relationship. On the one hand the people of a nation "are the historical 'objects' of a nationalist pedagogy" in the sense that they are taught to accept a hegemonic narrative of the nation's past progress. In this view, the nation's story unfurls through history like Anderson's "solid unit," historical events building on events and accumulating into a narrative of progress. On the other hand, the people of a nation are also agents who imaginatively insert themselves into national story, and Bhabha calls this second dimension of nation the performative ("DissemiNation" 297). The passive pedagogical and active performative elements are always slightly at odds with each other, particularly in the case of outsiders, those who "speak the encrypted discourse of the melancholic and the migrant" ("DissemiNation" 315). Bhabha invokes Freud's notion of the uncanny to analyse the ways in which the perspective of exiles, migrants, and the dispossessed unsettle the dominant narratives of any nation.

Bhabha agrees with Anderson that a nation is a constructed artifact – indeed, he goes further, suggesting that it is helpful to think of a nation as a constructed *literary* artifact. However, Bhabha finds different meaning in narrative form than does Anderson. While Anderson looks at novels and sees narratives contributing to a sense of fellowship, Bhabha sees "metaphoric displacements, sub-texts and figurative stratagems" (Introduction 2). In other words, Bhabha recognises that narratives are incorrigibly fractured, equivocal creations, and he argues that it is these qualities that makes narrative such an accurate metaphor for nation.

Bhabha's model of nation as ambivalent narrative is particularly salient for this book. One of the earliest needs of Britain at war was to define Britishness, and many publications leapt to specify national identity and traditions. Titles like *The English People* and *The Character of England* abounded (Richards and Aldgate 45) and despite the paper restrictions Collins produced short booklets defining aspects of British art.[10] Such projects tend to elide Britishness metonymically to mere "Englishness," in an example of the selective elaboration that nationhood requires, and Irish, Welsh and Scottish citizens were often misrepresented as equivocal towards the war effort. In particular, citizens of Northern Ireland were sometimes assumed to be collectively in support of the IRA, partly due to the violence which characterised 1939 in the months before war was declared. The first bomb to explode in London after war was declared was claimed by the IRA (Ziegler 77).[11] In Wales and Scotland a minority spoke out against conscription into the English war (Calder, *Myth* 66–9), pointing out that the Westminster government did not accord the other nations of the United Kingdom the same support as Westminster accorded to England. Although most members of the Union seemed to support the war, some recognised that the "buried nationalities" of Scotland, Wales and Ireland, in Tom Nairn's phrase, were still marginalised by England and its imperial capital (Calder, *Myth* 66; Nairn 168, 195).

In addition, home front discourse repeatedly positioned British Jews as "foreign" and other, even when those in question had sacrificed blood on British fields of combat. 1930s Britain saw long-standing anti-Semitism develop along a range of different trajectories, most notoriously in fascist movements (Thurlow xvii). The most notorious of the fascist groups was the British Union of Fascists (BUF) under the leadership of Oswald Mosley who made anti-Semitism central to his message from 1935 onwards, but anti-Semitism was also a significant driver for the Imperial Fascist League, the British Fascists, the Britons Society, the Nordic League, the Militant Christian Patriots, the White Knights of Britain and more.[12] None of these movements had massive membership – the likely maximum enrollment of the BUF was 40,000 – and fascist parties never won any seats in Parliament (Thurlow 101–2; Lunn and Thurlow 9–11; Calder, *People* 79). Nonetheless, although the groups were small, their influence was toxic. Jews in East London, for example, suffered attacks and window-smashing in a faint echo of Germany's *Kristallnacht* (Calder, *People* 164). Further, many non-Fascists were also anti-Semitic, and Andrea Loewenstein argues that "The English liberal ideology prevented overt violence against the Jews in England but encouraged less open, more passive forms of prejudice which were in the end equally lethal" (42–3).

Anti-Semitism remained surprisingly rife in wartime Britain (Thurlow 117). Even after the outbreak of war made people more aware of Nazi persecution of Jews, people often did not associate anti-Semitism with

Nazism (Calder, *People* 498). British propaganda did not emphasise Nazi anti-Semitism until late in the war. The outbreak of war actually saw popular British hostility to Jews increase: George Orwell wrote in 1945 that "anti-Semitism is on the increase ... it has been greatly exacerbated by the war, and ... humane and enlightened people are not immune to it" ("Anti-Semitism" par. 2). Several reasons have been put forward for this paradoxical response. First, Mass-Observation noted that after allegations of Holland's undoing by an alleged Jewish-dominated "Fifth Column" in May 1940, anti-Semitic feeling began to be expressed far more openly (Mass Observation, "Recent Trends"; "Public Opinion"). Fear of a fifth column caused German and Austrian Jews to be treated as doubly suspicious, and several blitz attacks were interpreted as guided by Jewish intelligence (Ziegler 238). The German Jewish Aid Committee in Britain urged new arrivals to never speak German in public (Wasserstein 83), fascists wrote "This is a Jewish War" on London walls and shelters saw displays of anti-Semitism (Calder, *People* 167). As food and resources grew more scarce and rationing tightened, many people levelled a flurry of accusations against Jews as black-marketeers (Wasserstein 107); Zelma Katin recalls, "Jews were blamed for the war, black markets, high prices, and most other universal ills" (72). Allegations that Jews were black marketers reached such a pitch that the government formally investigated, discovering the accusations to be groundless (H. Smith 11). Jews experienced substantial hostility on the British home front.

Even news of the Death Camps did not always soften anti-Semitism. In September 1942 the *Manchester Guardian* described Theresienstadt (Calder, *People* 499) but British government officials were at first inclined to downplay the stories of Nazi atrocities as "rather wild," suggesting that "As a general rule Jews are inclined to magnify their persecutions" (The National Archives PRO FO 371/30917 C 7853/61/18; FO 371/24472/11 C 5471/116/55). By December 1942 the evidence was too substantial to dismiss, but even then, some doubted the genocide until the liberation of the camps in 1945 (Wasserstein 155–60). Some people even felt more enraged against Jewish people the more they heard of the camps, and Orwell records an "[i]ntelligent woman, on being offered a book dealing with anti-Semitism and German atrocities," saying, "'Don't show it me, *please* don't show it to me. It'll only make me hate the Jews more than ever'" (par. 2, his emphasis). Chilling jokes were told about Jews being sent the gas bill for the death chambers (Lassner 274n10) and Alexander Ratcliffe, the leader of the British Protestant League, became one of the first to deny the holocaust atrocities, claiming the film footage was faked (Hannan 22). People marked as "other" were typically denied a full place in the horizontal bonds forged by wartime experience.

Justin Edwards defines a nation as "not just a sociopolitical fact, but also a ghost story. A way of 'storying' or talking about ourselves . . . always haunted by the spectre of the Other" (xix; cf. Schmitt 14, 74; Brabon 45). Doubling, temporal dislocation, narrative disjunction and tropes of haunting gather around these shadowy figures on the margin of the nation. Glennis Byron notes that the Gothic is about the ways we say "we are not this," and the Gothic mode can express such estrangement. As Punter argues, "Gothic is a mode – perhaps *the* mode – of unofficial history" (*Terror* 2: 187). Yet I do not imply that unofficial history is straightforward or single, nor do I imply a simple binary between "false" dominant narratives of the home front and "true" subversive narratives of the same. The shadowy figures in these texts do not offer a straightforward alternative narrative of the nation at war; rather, they offer a plurality of alternative stories, a plurality simultaneously inhabiting and complicating dominant narrative.

These texts are not merely subversive of dominant home front narrative; I agree that "it is no longer adequate – if it ever was – to consider Gothic solely under the rubric of the counter-cultural or the subversive" (Punter and Bronfen 7). The Gothic elements in these wartime texts can also signify conservative impetuses. Eighteenth-century Gothic regularly tames subversion into an enlightenment narrative, ending by re-asserting conventional family structures and the power of modernity to vanquish the ghosts of the past. These wartime Gothic narratives can do similar work, taming the Gothic by building it into stories of familial and national stability. The Gothic can never be recruited to one stable political project, be it subversion or conservativism; nonetheless, the darker, less hopeful texts excavated in this book often subvert dominant myths. Howard Wollman and Philip Spencer have warned that although "imagined community" is a useful concept, it is sometimes used as a substitute for analysis. In particular, they call for literary scholars analyzing nation to not stop at identifying an imagined community, but to "focus ... on the discursive strategies at work in defining what the nation is and what the nation is not, on who they include and who they exclude" (9). This book responds to that call, examining the contradictory discourses which underlie national story.

Any project such as this must be wary of the suspect iconicity of the "London Blitz." From the vast industry of films, books, and museum re-enactments of London as blitzed city, one might think that the capital was the only British city bombed during the Second World War. Yet numerous other cities were seriously damaged – Glasgow, Liverpool, Plymouth, scores of others – and as for the midlands city of Coventry, its centre was so thoroughly destroyed on 14 November 1940 that a new word temporarily entered the language to denote utter destruction: "coventration."[13] A similar lacuna prevails with regard to the Allies' sustained bombing of German territories and it must be said immediately that the most devastated cities of World War II were *German* cities, including the tragedies of Berlin, Lubek, Dresden, and Hamburg.[14] Calder notes, "The [Blitz] Myth could not accommodate acts, even would-be acts, of killing of civilians and domestic destruction initiated by the British themselves, however they might be justified strategically" (*Myth* 43). Churchill had already forged an impression of Britain as heroically enduring the atrocity of civilian bombardment – St. Paul's Cathedral riding a sea of flames – so British bombing of Germany had to be downplayed. This lacuna does frightening political work because it elides horrors that should not be forgotten, not least, the firestorms of Dresden and Hamburg. It would be impossible to give a thorough discussion of literary representations of all damaged European cities during the war, and such a discussion would also risk eliding differences in the country's narratives of nationhood. However, in none of the discussion which follows do I wish to imply that Britain had a monopoly on suffering. I concentrate on London not because London was the only place to suffer – far from it – but because the sprawling metropolis dominates the artifacts of the time, and both then and since was taken to be emblematic of wider suffering (e.g. Sansom, *Blitz*). Most significantly, London had for centuries been an imperial centre, and both in 1939 and today is marked with traces of its imperial legacy. As such, the city was – and is – a nexus in a complex mesh of national fantasy.

London was emphasised, then, but which London? The metropolis defies definition. The different towns that comprise Greater London have distinct characters which intensified when blackout and petrol rationing made movement difficult. Graham Greene describes this phenomenon in his novel *The Ministry of Fear* when his protagonist breakfasts in a café on Clapham High Street:

> London was no longer one great city: it was a collection of small towns. ... So special characteristics developed, and in Clapham where day raids were frequent there was a hunted look which was absent from Westminster, where the night raids were heavier but the shelters were better. ... Gray's Inn and Russell Square were noted

for more of a reckless spirit, but only because they had the day to
recover in. (73)

London's numerous villages experienced very different Blitzes. The
heterogeneity of London's spaces is echoed by the heterogeneity of the
war years. Home front experience was divided into distinct stages, from
the inactivity of the "Phoney War" of the first months when the only
markers were blackout and an increasing web of government regulation,
to the hallucinatory vividness of the first "Blitz," to the desolate years
of the "lightless middle of the tunnel" (Bowen, *Heat* 93) when the war
seemed unending, to the sudden devastation of the "Little Blitz" V1 and
V2 rocket attacks of 1944 and finally to the last months in a "whole
world ... gone shabby" (Mellor, "Brandt's Phantasms" 93). I comple-
ment study of the war period with scrutiny of the immediate postwar
years, in which "the deep bruises that the war inflicted" began to come
to the surface (J. Lehmann, "Foreword" 7). I argue that Gothic tropes
and narrative modes are deployed to express specific material realities
in wartime London.

However, despite the large body of critical work which finds value
in historicising Gothic, some critics challenge the act of finding *any*
significance in Gothic texts. Critiques of efforts to unpack signification
in Gothic writing are not limited to the way that twentieth-century
criticism sometimes too glibly discerns repressed sexual material in
Gothic fiction (Botting, "Unconscious"); even the act of finding economic or material resonances in a Gothic texts has been challenged.
Roger Salomon, for example, criticises theorists of the Gothic who try to
"explain away" its horrors, to "impose on it [horror] some single, clear
and rational meaning – critics, in this case, playing that well-known
Western role variously called detective, scientist, doctor (especially psychiatrist)" (17) and George Haggerty laments the "rage for explanation"
that besets critics, particularly those eager to unmask hidden meaning
(*Gothic Fiction* 42). In many cases the one thing which horror signifies
is the experience of something that cannot be signified at all. Chapter 6
and my Afterword confront this unpalatable fact.

This book deploys a range of theory. For much of the twentieth
century, Gothic criticism revolved around identifying the "hidden,"
especially the return of repressed and threatening aspects of the self.
Over the decades, the Freudian model of repression has been joined by
other discourses of the hidden, like contemporary trauma theory and
Julia Kristeva's theories of abjection. There are problems with using psychoanalysis or its derivatives to explain Gothic, not least the fact that

psychoanalysis is arguably itself a Gothic fiction, albeit a hundred years late to the party (Castle; Botting, "Gothic Production"; Warwick, "Feeling Gothicky" 10; Mighall xii; Ellis 13; Kilgour 220; Miles, *Ann Radcliffe* 108). Nonetheless, recent Gothic criticism treats psychoanalysis as a valuable hermeneutic provided that the work is historically aware and does not blithely generalise psychoanalytic models across all cultures and times. I approach the "hidden" of wartime texts through a trifold combination of socio-historical discussion of the wartime context in which these texts appeared, post-structuralist theories of national identity as ambivalent narrative, and cautious use of psychoanalytic hermeneutics (particularly of the uncanny, abjection and trauma). This book combines literary criticism of wartime Gothic with awareness of social history and local specificity.

Chapter 2 explores two wartime incarnations of the literary trope of the *flâneur*, a figure famously rendered in Charles Baudelaire's nineteenth-century poetry. Baudelaire's *flâneur* is a poetic visionary strolling through the city and consuming the visual pleasures newly possible in nineteenth-century cities. Henry Green's novel *Caught* (1932) and Roy Fuller's wartime poetry challenge the *flâneur's* position as detached and masterful spectator. While nineteenth-century *flânerie* made intellectual order out of city spectacle, these wartime texts present commodity spectacle as maddening. The texts' Gothic tropes and narrative textures mark moments of fracture in capitalism's grand narratives.

Chapter 3 examines two traditional tropes of Gothic: the struggle to escape a confining space and the effort to decode mysterious signs. Both tropes become disturbingly relevant for many marginalised people in wartime Britain, particularly refugees, other immigrants, and people marginalised due to troubled mental health. Anna Kavan's short story anthology *I Am Lazarus* (1945), her novel *Sleep Has His House* (1948) and Greene's *The Ministry of Fear* (1943) depict the wartime city as prison, in which victims suffer under capricious, malicious authorities. In these texts, human bodies are constrained by terrible codes and prohibitions.

Chapter 4 builds on the discussions of the previous chapter, examining how spaces of industry construct otherness during World War II. Government propaganda, radio broadcasts, film and workers' diaries present factory labour as community-building and personally enriching, but novels by Inez Holden, Anne Ridler and Diana Murray Hill use the Gothic mode to depict wartime industry as a site of loneliness and alienating work. The Gothic has, since its inception, expressed class anxieties and conflicts as well as intrapsychic ones. In the texts of this chapter, the Gothic mode enables commentary on the darker realities of industry during and directly after the war, depicting working spaces as fraught with gendered violence both physical and psychological.

While Chapter 4 scrutinises gender and the Gothic in wartime workplaces, Chapter 5 examines gender and the Gothic in domestic interiors. The Gothic characteristically constructs homes as places of alienation, hallucination, haunting and madness. In the case of period fiction of Second World War Britain, the domestic Gothic subverts a key national myth of the war: the notion of the home as a war front, literally and figuratively, on which Britons would fight with a sense of national identification with the war effort. Bowen's fiction narrates wartime domestic interiors as places of twofold strangeness, terrains occupied by an alien and malevolent intelligence in which linear time collapses. Her uncanny houses undermine the dominant wartime narrative of heroic domestic endeavour, for Benedict Anderson's theory of the nation as "imagined community" assumes a particular notion of time: members of the nation have a sense of simultaneous lives continuing alongside their own, even if those fellow-members of the nation are merely imagined and never met. The texts of this chapter challenge such comforting narrative structures, for their time is frozen, distorted or usurped by the past.

The final chapter examines the conjunction of nation and the abject through the writing of John Piper, Graham Sutherland and Mervyn Peake. Julia Kristeva's concept of abjection has been pivotal to Gothic Studies, and recent criticism has applied abjection in analyzing national discourse (e.g. Miles "Abjection"; Hogle "Gothic Ghost"; Edwards 53). To date studies of abjection and nation have tended to focus on eighteenth- and nineteenth-century Gothic, but the concept is similarly useful in analysing twentieth-century conjunctions of Gothic and nation. This chapter contributes to such work by examining the way that literary depictions of the corpse subvert the neat memorialising performed by the British nation-state. Specifically, in the wartime writing of Piper, Sutherland and Peake, corpses are not tamed by redemptive stories of national triumph.

The texts of this book exemplify subjective fracture, incompletion, and anguish – indeed, the Gothic can be defined in terms of these formal qualities. As such, these texts of wartime Gothic are not only of historical interest, but also of profound contemporary value in that they present alternative ways to respond to collective agony. The Afterword examines the new ethics of mourning advocated in recent studies of nation and memory. Normative mourning – working through grief, accepting loss, and ultimately finding solace – is increasingly seen as ethically suspect, in that it may comply with state policies and actions which enabled the deaths to occur. In response to this dilemma, critics have recently called for a more ethical "resistant mourning" which discerns political value in incomplete mourning, fractured subjectivity and ongoing emotional anguish. This chapter suggests that Gothic literary forms are valuable in that they do not subsume loss and death into a neat narrative of healing and survival.

Overall, this book moves from city streets (Chapter 2), to hospitals and prisons (Chapter 3), to factories (Chapter 4), to homes (Chapter 5) and finally to morgues (Chapter 6). The city of each location is, in the words of Peake, "half masonry, half pain" (*Poems* 88).

2
Nightmare City: Gothic *Flânerie* and Wartime Spectacle in Henry Green and Roy Fuller

Europe's cities changed dramatically after the industrial revolution. New kinds of buildings were designed, most famously the shopping Arcades with wide central passages lined on both sides by shops. As the middle-class grew richer, new diversions emerged, particularly cafés and other semi-public spaces. These new spaces offered what Christopher Prendergast calls "a special kind of visual field, peculiarly open to the mobile gaze and unforeseen encounter" (3). The eighteenth century had seen literary depictions of watchful walkers savouring the city's sights (Mazlish; Parsons, *Streetwalking* 18–19) but the nineteenth-century changes saw a new aesthetic and a new subject position: the *flâneur*, the stroller who savours urban spectacle.

Although Charles Baudelaire himself does not use the term *flâneur*, his collections *Les fleurs du mal* (1857) and *Le spleen du Paris* (1869) catalogue the various urban spectators that have come to define the category: the passionate artist, the wistful poet, the exhibitionist dandy, the detective, the journalist, the criminal and the "rag-picker" or harvester of trash. The definite article is misleading, for Baudelaire offers not one *flâneur*, but several, noting that these "independent, intense, and impartial spirits ... do not lend themselves easily to linguistic definitions" (*Selected* 400). Benjamin seeks to clarify Baudelaire's classifications, but the *flâneur* remains a complex and contradictory creature. Nonetheless, four qualities of the watchful walker have acquired the label of *flânerie* through decades of critical commentary. The *flâneur* savours the spectacle of the city, has a fraught relationship with capitalism, craves to be amidst crowds but feels solitary within them, and does imaginative work on what he sees on the streets.

Today, literary analysis of urban representation often tends to distance itself from the concept of *flânerie*, with its outdated focus on the privileged perspective of an individual. Instead, recent criticism is increasingly influenced by what Mimi Sheller and John Urry call the "mobility turn," a developing body of theory which seeks to articulate how multiple members of a society move through and use urban (and other) spaces in a complex variety of ways. Despite *flânerie's* anachronistic emphasis on the privileged perspective of a poetic individual, however, it remains a useful literary framework for one particular kind of investigation: exploration of the fantasies that commodities accrete in particular late capitalist contexts.[15] Benjamin is the most famous critic to note the provocative connections between Baudelaire's sociohistorical milieu and the new form of urban spectatorship he espoused Hailing Baudelaire as "A Lyric Poet in the Era of High Capitalism," Benjamin discerns in Baudelaire's *flâneur* the attributes which characterised the commodity in nineteenth-century Paris (55). This chapter examines two Second World War texts in search of fractures in capitalism's grand narratives of consumption, arguing that these texts reveal some of the secret suffering underlying commodity circulations in mid-twentieth-century Britain.

The *flâneur's* use of the city

Flânerie relied on new architectures of commodity display, and Baudelaire's *flânerie* delights in urban spectacle: "it is as though an ever more luminous light kept making each object glitter with an ever more dazzling splendour ... as though the heat, making the perfumes visible, were drawing them up to the sun like smoke" (*Spleen* 10). Synaesthesia subsumes other senses to vision. Similarly, "Parisian Dream" is a fantasia of the city's visual delights, sound fading as the poem progresses: "These marvels all were for the eye, / And there was nothing for the ear" (*Flowers* 51). For the *flâneur*, Benjamin notes, "the joy of watching is triumphant" (*Baudelaire* 69). He dismisses the city of Brussels on the grounds that it lacks enough shop windows: "There is nothing to see, and the streets are unusable" (qtd. in Benjamin, *Baudelaire* 50).

Yet although the *flâneur* looks at commodities, he is not an eager consumer. Baudelaire scorns bourgeois aspirations. The narrator of his prose fragment "The Temptations of Eros, Plutos and Fame" encounters a Satanic personification of capitalism:

> He was a man of vast proportions, with an eyeless countenance. ... [H]is skin was gilded ... with masses of little hurrying figures, representing numerous forms of universal misery. There were lean

little men who hung themselves from nails, there were the deformed skinny little gnomes whose supplicating eyes begged more eloquently for alms than their trembling hands. ... The gigantic Satan tapped his immense belly with his fist, and there came from it a prolonged metallic jingling that ended in a vague groaning, as of many human voices. (*Spleen* 41–2)

This revolting apparition embodies the exploitations that underpin capitalist economy, for, like the ancient god Moloch, his belly is swollen with the people he has devoured. Baudelaire condemns anyone who seeks profit in a world governed by such a divinity. On the other hand, the *flâneur* needs money. Horner and Zlosnik note that he "is often a journalist as well as an artist [which] suggests his capitulation to market forces despite his abhorrence of them" ("Nightwood" 87). Baudelaire feels horror at the pettiness of working life: "Time reigns, he has resumed his brutal tyranny. And he pokes me with his double goad as if I were an ox ... 'Sweat, slave! Man, be damned, and live!'" (*Spleen* 7).

In addition to feeling alienated from paid work, the *flâneur* is alienated from other people. In Baudelaire's prose fragment "The Stranger," the narrator is asked if he loves his father, mother, sister or brother, and he replies, "I have neither father, nor mother, nor sister, nor brother." When asked if he loves his friends, he replies "Now you use a word whose meaning I have never known" (*Spleen* 1). Benjamin argues that this isolation is not idiosyncratic, but symbolic of the cultural malaise of capitalist alienation (*Baudelaire* 77). Benjamin reads the *flâneur* as damaged by the abstractions that ensue after labour is commodified. For Marx and Benjamin, empathy is one of the casualties of capitalism (Maslish 46). The *flâneur* is not only scornful of – and yet anxious about – the need for money in a capitalist system, but also emotionally wounded by the alienation inherent in this form of political economy.

In the face of such aching emptiness, the crowd gives the *flâneur* solace. A *flâneur* does not look in order to select items to purchase and triumphantly bring into a bourgeois interior. Rather, he looks in order to imaginatively occupy that which he sees. "The poet enjoys the incomparable privilege of being able to be himself or some one else, as he chooses. Like those wandering souls who go looking for a body, he enters as he likes into each man's personality" (*Spleen* 20). Yet the unwitting people and objects which the *flâneur* consumes in this way are co-opted without respect. As such, the *flâneur* is condemned by critics who rightly read his voyeurism as a colonizing act (Wolff; Pollock, "Vicarious Excitements"; Buck-Morss; Walkowitz; Wilson 5).

The dubious ethics of the *flâneur's* gaze are readily unmasked when one considers the object which his eye most often seeks: purchasable women. Rachel Bowlby observes, "*flânerie* involved a certain conception of the woman as being herself part of the spectacle, one of the curiosities in which the *flâneur* will want to take an interest in the course of his walking" (*Still Crazy* 6); women were to be looked at, not to look. The *flâneur* is thus rightly described as masterful and arrogant. He not only visually consumes people, but classifies them and weaves his own explanations for what he sees. Baudelaire notes admiringly that, "All the materials [he sees], stored higgledy-piggledy by memory, are classified, ordered, harmonised" (*Selected* 402). That alone would not seem inappropriate, were it not that the *flâneur* is convinced of the intrinsic merit of *his* classifications over those of others. He is a prince, the "maker of the order of things" (Tester, Introduction 7). Much literary criticism of *flânerie* emphasises its mastery.

Gothic *flânerie*: psychological disintegration

Yet the *flâneur* is also vulnerable. Baudelaire regularly figures the *flâneur* as addicted to the crowd as if to narcotics, craving "a singular intoxication" and "mysterious drunkenness" (*Spleen* 20–1). Like the vampire, the *flâneur* needs the life of others and suffers a damned, unquenchable thirst. The *flâneur's* possession of another is thus not merely colonising mastery, but also has connotations of self-abandonment and loss. Not only a sovereign, he also has aspects of the drug addict, the criminal, the tramp and the melancholic. The narrator of Baudelaire's "Epilogue" to *Paris Spleen* is drawn to criminal denizens of the city, declaring, "Infamous City, I adore you! Courtesans / And bandits, you offer me such joys, / The common herd can never understand" (108). The *flâneur* is not only a master, but an addict "half in love with easeful death" (Keats l. 52), drawn to the darker side of the metropolis and longing to be annihilated. The *flâneur's* stance of mastery readily gives way to Gothic nightmare, hallucinatory and despairing.

These shadow sides of *flânerie* have often been downplayed in literary criticism which has tended to primarily approach the *flâneur* through a gendered binary in which *flâneur* is masterful watcher and woman mere passive object.[16] The paradigm of *flânerie* held little room for women other than as commodities, but some modernist women writers, notably Virginia Woolf and Dorothy Richardson, depict women walking city streets and weaving them into narrative. The walking and watching of the *flâneuse* is often presented as less arrogant, less tyrannical, than that of the *flâneur*, but here, too, we encounter an ambivalent position, one in which a watchful walker surveys and organises the scene while partially surrendering to it. Woolf's essay "Street Haunting" (1927) describes walking through London for the pleasure of it, under the pretext of buying a pencil (like Baudelaire's *flâneur*, this streetwalker also writes). She shares many of the qualities of the *flâneur*: she delights at being reduced to the visual sense, "an enormous eye" (318). Yet her eye cannot skim unaffected over sights of suffering: after glimpsing a dwarf-woman in a shop, the narrator discerns deformity in all she sees (320). Both *flâneuse* and *flâneur* are vulnerable to what they see.

"Bright, dead Dolls": *flânerie* and wartime London

Wartime London has been hailed as multiplying opportunities for wandering watchers. Fires drew crowds (Ackroyd 739) and were hailed as spectacles of "violently beautiful flames" (D. Johnson 157). Louis MacNeice admits that taking a stroll after one particular destructive air raid, he "could not help – at moments – regarding it as a spectacle," and he admires "the shifting pattern of water and smoke and flame ... as subtle as the subtlest of Impressionist paintings" ("Photographs" 11). The blackout, too, produced visual marvels. Chiang Yee recalls, "I have often been out during the black-outs in order to find pleasure out of the darkness. The slender red, green and yellow crosses of the traffic lights never fail to thrill me" (32) and photographer Bill Brandt is similarly enchanted by the blacked-out city, avering that "The dark-ened town, lit only by moonlight, looked more beautiful than before or since" (30). In addition to spectacle, the wartime city offered the furtive sexual satisfactions of *flânerie*. Cartoons and gramophone record sleeves presented the blacked-out city as a site for sexual dalliance and a para-doxical abundance of voyeuristic possibility (Opie 6–7). Some people experienced the blacked-out streets as an especially sexually-charged terrain, Bowen speculating that the darkness "brought out something provocative in the step of most modest women; Nature tapped out with the heels on pavement an illicit semaphore" (*Heat* 145). In both vivid spectacle and sexual possibility, then, wartime London can be read as particularly fruitful for *flânerie*. In addition, Deborah Parsons suggests that the Blitz arguably offered new opportunities for *flâneuses* in that it forced women out of their houses to become "the wandering 'I/eye'" and to discover the city on their own terms ("'Souls Astray'" 28). This argument downplays, however, the challenges the wartime metropolis posed to anyone who savoured walking in the city and watching its wares. Obstacles included damage to streets, restrictions on light and scarce commodities.[17]

Warwick notes that "the sense of the incipient destruction of the physical environment is a strong and characteristic Gothic device, from the castle of Otranto through to the house of Usher" ("Lost Cities" 79) and this trope became very real in the wartime metropolis. The first German bombs fell on Greater London on 8 June 1940, in open fields at Addington. 16 August saw the first raid on the urban area, with fourteen fatalities, but Londoners were hardly inspired with terror by the event – it even drew sightseers (Ziegler 108–10). The raids worsened after 24 August, and from 7 September 1940 to 1 January 1941 London was bombed for fifty-seven nights. The final massive raid of this first "Blitz" happened on 10 May 1940, damaging Westminster Abbey, the Law Courts, the War Office in Whitehall, the Royal Mint, the House of Commons, the Tower of London and the British Museum, where 250,000 books were destroyed (Calder, *People* 214). Two thousand fires were started, killing 1,436 people and leaving 155,000 families without gas, water or electricity, and it took eleven days to quench the flames (Gardiner 105). Raids diminished in intensity after that, only to resume in June 1944 with the V1 doodlebugs, pilotless planes packed with high explosive and designed to crash (Ziegler 282–95). September 1944 heralded V2 supersonic rockets that could annihilate entire streets (Ziegler 296–9). Throughout the extraordinary months from August 1940 to May 1941, and again during the V1 and V2 attacks of 1944, the city became shockingly mutable. In this regard, Peter Adey identifies a "fluid urban traumatic" in which "the urban environment was 'unmade' and urged into violent motion" (par. 2). FitzGibbon recalls, "Night after night. ... London was vanishing" (173). The metropolis became fragile, disintegrating in a nightmare made real.

The darkness, too, unsettled people's relationship with their city and capital. Prewar urban illumination had become closely tied to rhetorics of nationhood. In 1938, for example, *Picture Post* ran a photo-essay showing Piccadilly Circus by night and declaring "THE HEART OF THE EMPIRE IS ... ADVERTISEMENT. Flashing lights – the hundred sounds of traffic, all the activity of commerce and enjoyment" ("In the Heart" 23). 1942 saw a series of advertisements for Mazda light-bulbs in the magazine *Lilliput*, each quoting extracts from Victorian novels about light and implicitly linking urban illumination with English nationhood. One such advertisement depicts Charles Dickens's Nicholas Nickleby riding a cab through streets lit with street-lamps, alongside the quotation, "Nicholas Nickleby and sons ... rattled on through the crowded streets of London, now displaying long double rows of brightly-lit lamps." This caption is followed with the slogan "Mazda: The Nation's Light" (Mazda xxvii). The advertisement confirms a nexus between illumination and the nation, an association rendered fragile by the black-out.

Air raids even produced grim parodies of commodity display. Even MacNeice, who relishes the impressionistic quality of fires after raids, sees the architecture of display become tragic:

> There was one narrow street that in the sun had the air of a bazaar – bales of coloured cloth piled high on the pavements. But when you got near you saw it was not a bazaar at all; no, it was just salvage. And you felt you mustn't stare: these things weren't meant to be seen in this way, any more than the pictures still hanging in the disembowelled parlour of the shining white bath that stands on the edge of an abyss. ("Photographs" 12)

Expecting a marketplace, MacNeice finds devastation, and he deploys metaphors of bodily dismemberment to convey the shock of the damage. Similarly, Bottome's *London Pride* depicts a fire in a West End department store as a final blaze of commodity splendour, the flames holding the "whole contents of the great shop in one last orgy of advertisement. Thousands of garments of all shapes and colours shone for a last time in a burst of glory" (85). Yet this parody of a sale ends in abject filth, the commodities sinking into "sour smelly ashes" (85). A parallel metaphor is evoked by the John Lewis store in Oxford Street, a "charred skeleton with blackened walls and gaping windows and rust orange girders and its wax models lying like corpses on the pavement" (Ramsey 2: 109). Shop mannequins reminded onlookers of corpses, and vice versa. Anthony Jacobs recalls seeing the bombing of an expensive restaurant, the corpses of wealthy patrons laid out on the pavement:

> they lay quite still in their beautiful dresses, beautiful colors, covered in sawdust – sawdust which must have fallen on them when the bomb had exploded down below, and this dust gave them a kind of unreal sheen, they looked like beautiful dolls that had been broken and the sawdust come out ... bright, dead dolls with dust on them. (FitzGibbon 265)

Corpses lie like "bright, dead dolls," like vivid shop mannequins in a parody of life. Each of these three metaphors – a building disemboweled, a burning shop in a final sale, and human corpses as shop dolls – conveys the increasing fragility of architectures of display. Wartime London not only facilitates new opportunities for wandering watching, but also sees threats to consumer confidence.

The two literary texts of this chapter feature watchful protagonists strolling the city. Green's novel and Fuller's poems see *flâneurs* become less sovereign than victim; they are destroyed by what they see. Their increasing delirium unmasks the brutalities that have always underpinned capitalist consumption. In their disintegrating psyches we see the multiple sufferings underlying the cult of the commodity: alienation and the exploitations of empire. As such, these texts give a snapshot of a particular moment of crisis.

Henry Green, *Caught*

Green's novel *Caught* has two protagonists. Richard Roe is an upper-middle class volunteer firemen in London's Auxiliary Fire Service. His wife is recently dead and his young son, Christopher, has been evacuated to stay with Roe's sister-in-law in Wales. As an auxiliary fireman he is under the command of the novel's second protagonist, Pye, a working-class Regular (professional) fireman. The novel traces their respective disintegrations, Roe into "nervous debility" (172) and Pye into madness and suicide.

The work has several features of the Gothic mode, including anguished affect, a tortured narrative structure and a claustrophobic sense of being locked into a grim trajectory of degeneration. This is a cruel world where people are as destructive as fire (94) and even children are brutal: little Christopher kills mice with a spoon (189).[18] The city of this novel is seen through a filter of despair and threat. We hear, for example, that as evening draws in, "the melancholy light, as it failed, seemed to stretch long as grey elastic" (36) and the anti-bomber aircraft barrage balloons are "the colour of the blade of a knife" (37). Roe flinches from "the menace in that highly polished sky which they felt might, at any moment, fall flat, and across which the stars began to skate or slither" (43–4). This city evokes paranoia. Discussing late nineteenth-century London, Warwick has suggested that the spatial arrangement of Baudelaire's Paris enabled spectatorship in a way that even nineteenth-century London never could, and she argues that "London does not produce ... the man in easy mastery of his surroundings, but rather his negative double, the person in paranoid relation to his environment" ("Lost Cities" 82). Paranoia and vulnerability similarly characterise the wartime city, but with an additional charge of dread, for the opening months of the war were a particularly disorienting, unreal period. The "Phoney War" ran from 3 September 1939 to 8 June 1940, the months between the declaration of war and the first air raids (Ziegler 40–64). Lyndsey Stonebridge notes this period was an: "interminably anxious space" (49).

The wartime city becomes a place of strange rituals and delirious nocturnal visions. When Roe tries to sleep in the Firemen's shelter, two barge in and instigate a bizarre cockroach race with hammers:

> [I]n a deep violet light from three coloured bulbs invisibly wreathed with footrot, two Regular firemen, one with a twenty-eight-pound hammer, the other with a crowbar, racing cockroaches along a course they had prepared between Auxiliaries rolled in blankets on the floor out of which, as though about to rise from the dead, came heads and shoulders. (44)

Night shifts are troubled with nightmare and delirium, with the firefighters "asleep, yet groaning and calling out" (55).

In this troubled terrain, the characters suffer multiple estrangements. First, their urban space is alienated from nature: one character is reduced to making artificial flowers from sardine tins (51). Secondly, characters are alienated from each other. When Roe takes his colleague Hilly out for a date they witness:

> the spectacle, dreary, commonplace and sad, of dim lit faces leaning two by two towards each other beside pink-shaded table lamps, solid, rosy, not so young couples endlessly talking, talking within their little coral pools, in half whispers, waited on by those hopeless, splay-footed, black-coated waiters. (100)

Even the city's spaces of recreation are funereal. Furthermore, in this city, people do not connect. Both Roe and Hilly are constantly conscious that they are lying even to themselves. When Roe speaks to Hilly, "a sensation that he was being false attacked him" (101–2) and when he kisses her "'Oh darling,' he said, low and false, 'the months I've waited to do that'" (111). When Hilly hears herself reply, "she knew that she was lying" (100). Pye is similarly tormented: he lies on his bed with his head near a telephone, "a myriad anguished conversations held ... within the black, shining, idle handle" (84). Bystanders debunk the myth of wartime togetherness: when Richard says to a fellow fireman, "'it brings people together, there's that much to a war'" a nearby woman interjects wryly, "'When it doesn't put blue water between'" (48). Finally, the protagonists are alienated from themselves, in psychological disequilibrium: Roe collapses from nervous exhaustion after repeated raids and Pye commits suicide after hallucinatory experiences in the city. In depicting their respective deteriorations, Green makes repeated use of the trope of coloured light as seductive and maddening. I will now explore what this trope represents through the course of the novel, and then demonstrate how the trope deftly unmasks the shadow history of the commodity.

Perilous light

Key to the *flâneur's* pleasure is the displayed commodity, revealed thanks to architectural innovations of shopping arcades, plate-glass storefronts, superabundant shop-lighting and artificial street-lights. Prendergast notes that: "[T]he presence of light itself, both natural and artificial (at first the gas lamps, later electric light), came to be seen as one of the most precious commodities in the city" (31–4). Commodities could be made even more enchanting if drenched in light.[19] Poets wrote ecstatic descriptions of the play of light and fairy-tale light-shows captivated hundreds of Parisians. In Baudelaire's *flânerie* the city's light delights spectators. By contrast, in Green's novel of wartime London, illumination bewilders and misleads.

Benjamin notes that the commodity has power; it "whispers to a poor wretch who passes a shop-window containing beautiful and expensive things" (*Baudelaire* 55). Illuminated commodities transfix two characters early in the novel. Roe's son Christopher is kidnapped from a London department store while dazed by the store's dramatic lighting, and when Roe visits the store he is affected in a similar way. The shop windows are stained glass, and artificial arc lights shine through the glass to drench the store's contents in vivid colour "like seeing the toys through Christmas cracker paper" (15). Both Roe and Christopher are spellbound. Yet this light is not benign. The outside lamps "cast the violent colors of that glass over the goods," "aggressively" steeping the customers in its glow under the "dominion of the glass" (11, 13–14). This forceful light has an agenda:

> The walls of this store being covered with stained glass windows ... the body of the shop was inundated with colour, brimming, and this colour, as the sea was a predominant part of each window, was a permanence of sapphire in the shopping hours. Pink neon lights on the high ceiling wore down this blue to some extent, made customers' faces less aggressively steeped in the body of the store but enhanced,

or deepened that fire brigade scarlet to carmine, and, in so doing, drugged Richard's consciousness. (12–13)

The light-saturated commodity is narcotic. For father and son, "it was the deep color spilled over these objects that, by evoking memories they would not name, and which they could not place, held them, and then led both to a loch-deep unconsciousness of all else" (12). The hypnotic light satisfies a profound craving in them. When the kidnapper approaches Christopher, the shop's illuminations conspire to bewilder the child:

> He became dazzled by the pink neon lights beyond her features. Caught in another patch of colour, some of her chin was pillar-box red, also a part of the silver fox she wore. ... [S]he caught full at him with her eyes that, by the ocean in which they were steeped, were so much a part of the world that his need had made ... that he felt anything must be natural, and was ready to do whatever she asked. (14)

In the novel's first use of its title, the spectator is "caught" in coloured light which dangerously misleads.[20] Christopher and Richard are not sovereign spectators, but captive, the light-transfigured commodity entrancing them and demolishing their independent will.

In other passages, coloured light takes on the power to derange. During Roe's fireman training he is required to climb forty feet up inside Tewkesbury Abbey, and in the light of the stained glass windows:

> he had that terror of the urge to leap, his back to deep violet and yellow Bible stories on the glass, his eyes reluctant over the whole grey stretch of the Abbey until they were drawn, abruptly as to a chasm, inevitably ... that height calling on the pulses and he did not know why to his ears, down to dropped stone flags over which sunlight had cast the colour in each window, the colour it seemed his blood had turned. (11–12)

Here, the coloured light is associated with cowardice and a temptation to suicide (12). Similarly, the blue-violet interior bulbs used in the firemen's night shelter are figured as damaging human vitality.[21] "A man's face, in that profound, dim blood of the [violet] flower, was dead white" (44). The garish lighting of another room is similarly unwholesome: the faces below are "one hundred watt shadow-carved faces ... purple shadows hacked out beneath their eyebrows, chins and noses by the naked, hot spotlights in the orange ceiling" (68–9). This light "carves" human flesh and "hack[s] out shadows." The coloured lights of this wartime metropolis are inimical to human life.

Critics have sought to decipher the narrative logic whereby this trope of light becomes so perilous and compelling, beginning with its first appearance in the shop window. Rod Mengham argues that this shop light represents longing to reunite with the lost mother's body. "The oceanic blue, colour of the amniotic sea of oblivion ... fascinates the boy who has lost his mother" (76). It is depicted in liquid terms – it "inundate[s]" the "body" of the shop, it "brim[s]," and it all stems from a stained-glass image of the sea painted on the shop window. Yet reading this passage as marking a longing to regain a lost mother downplays the *particular* images the coloured light casts on the people it enchants. Although this coloured light takes both Christopher and Richard to "a loch-deep unconsciousness of all else," it does not do that by annihilating all difference between self and object, but rather by depicting stories: specifically, stories of travel and empire. The scenes painted on the shop's stained-glass windows depict ships setting sail from docks:

> The walls of this store being covered with stained glass windows which depicted trading scenes, that is, of merchandise being loaded on to galleons, the leaving port, of incidents on the voyage, and then the unloading, all brilliantly lit from without, it follows that the body of the shop was inundated with colour. (12–13)

In this passage, the dangerous coloured light becomes associated with one of the *flâneur's* favourite spectacles: signs of imperial trade. For the more traditional *flâneur*, such spectacle is a source of pleasure, but in these wartime texts such spectacle serves as an unsettling reminder of London's ebbing glories.

London's imperial legacies

Flânerie was always an imperial project, for the streets of the nineteenth-century city saw empire become emporium.[22] As Shields notes, "For the metropolitan citizen not involved in questions of colonial administration on an everyday basis, the most direct expression of empire is through the commodity" (74–5). Benjamin himself participated in such consumption, collecting engravings of exoticised immigrants. Such spectacle could give the wandering watcher a sense of mastery over the empire's colonies and dominions.

Second World War London had a complex relationship with imperialism. On the one hand, the colonies were often depicted as willing allies, contributing troops and supporting Britain's war effort. Lawrence James notes that in 1938, the British public typically saw the Empire as "a valuable asset of which the British people could feel proud" (450). The Empire Marketing Board, founded in 1926, was still working to increase British domestic awareness of the empire and foster British pride in it; among other things, the Board circulated imperial artifacts around schools to impress youth with a sense of the value of Britain's imperial possessions, and produced Empire-themed "annuals" for children (L. James 444–5; R. Johnson 165). Similarly, films, both educational and commercial, repeatedly presented colonial subjects as appreciating and respecting the Empire (L. James 450). The Second World War saw such domestic celebrations of empire multiply, particularly after air raids began in 1941. A "War Weapons Week" was combined with a day celebrating Empire, and Britain's civil defence forces were involved in parades (Calder, *Myth* 54). On the other hand, the imperial yoke was slipping. By 1939 the British empire was no longer the dominant force it had been a century earlier, and even the concept of empire had become diluted, erstwhile colonies increasingly recast as dominions or members of the Commonwealth, categories implying more autonomy (L. James 385, 415). Although decolonisation did not begin apace until after the Second World War, even in 1939 the Empire was fading.

Given this ambivalence, Jane Jacobs has argued that it can be helpful to approach twentieth century and contemporary London as a post-imperial city, a metropolis shot through with traces of its imperial past:

> In contemporary cities people connected by imperial histories are thrust together in assemblages barely predicted, and often guarded against, during the inaugural phases of colonization. Often enough this is a meeting not simply augmented by imperialism but still regulated by its constructs of difference and privilege. (4)

The post-imperial as a category is similarly fruitful for the Second World War metropolis. Three post-imperial signifiers are scattered throughout *Caught* in addition to the "storied sea" of the shop windows: a jazz club, an imperial statue amidst a blaze and a docklands inferno.

Roe frequents the jazz club with his girlfriend Hilly. The décor of "dark palm leaves" (107) recalls the southern lands from which these Black migrant musicians come, and again, coloured light transforms the public space. Spotlights with coloured filters single out the singer, and violet-shaded table lamps adorn each table, so that Roe watches the singer through "the steep purple left behind by that beam of intense blue light ... a shiny film of dark blue, so that he might have been looking through Christmas cracker paper" (111). Like the shop illuminations, this light casts a story of departures:

> the spot light spread a story over her body ... as she pretended to remember the south, the man who had gone, as she held all theirs with her magnificent eyes guardedly flashing, solely turning from one couple to another, then again dropping her voice, almost sighing, motionless, while beads of sweat began to come like the base of a tiara on her forehead. (111)

This description invites comparison with Baudelaire's litany to an exoticised lover: "On the burning hearth of your hair I breathe in the fragrance of tobacco tinged with opium and sugar; in the night of your hair I see the sheen of the tropic's blue infinity; on the shores of your hair I get drunk with the smell of musk and tar and the oil of coconuts" (*Spleen* 31). Exotic female others were of particular interest to Baudelaire's *flâneurs,* who encountered such women on streets and in cabarets (Shields 66). Yet crucially, what *Caught's* wartime post-imperial auditors savour about her song is not only its evocation of sensuous pleasure, but also its diasporic melancholy. The hearers identify with her longing and fall into a wistful trance: "the blues negroes played were to foreigners in a foreign land of the still farther south which, with simplicity, became everyone's longing in this soft evening aching room; bottles on tables held stifling moonlight from that south" (107). In the minds of the hearers, the singer's nostalgia merges with their wartime emotional wounds to form a generalised melancholy. What differentiates this melancholy from the generalised languor of nineteenth-century *flânerie,* however, is the extent to which those experiencing it are convinced they will collectively die very soon. These dancing couples sense they have mere months "to live, and chew, and love not very much, before it might be they would have to be dug out of the heaped ruins" (108). Even the women, not conscripted, are aware they could die in war: "In the hard idiom of the drum these women seemed already given up to the male in uniform so soon to go away, these girls, as they felt, soon to be killed themselves, so little time left, moths deathly gay, in a daze of giving" (49). These patrons of the jazz club do not expect to emerge unscathed from the war, and their melancholy underpins their strange self-identification with a song of nostalgia for a homeland lost through diaspora.

Heroic statues commemorating martial triumphs are another characteristic feature of the imperial metropolis. Immediately after war was declared many statues were evacuated or protected with special shelters (Ziegler 54, 318). Those which remained were anachronistic emblems of empire. Roe encounters an unprotected statue "which still looked blindly on, in the centre of a London square. ... Against this livid incandescence stood the old war horse, pitch black, his bronze rider up, pitch black, both, as always, facing south" (95). These imperial streets have become "twin approaches to a palace in a story, the story of ruin" (95), a fantastical world in which bombs "float swaying down like pearls on fire, dropped by magic" (96). The marker of imperial triumph – the charging horse facing southwards – is "blind" in this transformed world of flame. As the firefighters seek to erect dams against the blaze they find themselves using the statue as a reference point: "it was not until [Roe] ... was back among dams that had been erected on each side of the bronze horse, black on one flank, rose coloured on the other towards the now spreading fire beyond the gas mains, it was not until then that he was frightened" (96). Yet although the firemen use the statue as a bulwark, it cannot protect. Ambulance men carry a stretcher bearing a "twisted creature" coughing up "a last gushing, gout of blood"; policeman carry an arrested looter, "most of his clothes torn off, heels dragging, drooling blood at the mouth, out on his feet from the bashing he had been given" (97). The triumphant statue is incongruous in this world of unheroic death.

A similar post-imperial moment occurs at the climax of the novel when Roe recalls the first fire he attended at the London Docklands. The docklands were a crucial site of imperial power. Jonathan Schneer notes the Docklands were "the nexus of imperialism" (14) and Jane Jacobs observes that "the East End docks handled goods traded between core and periphery and factories turned raw materials from the periphery into products for local and international consumption" (73). The docks are a liminal terrain, where exotic and domestic meet and mingle. In 1900 the London docks were the world's largest, but by 1939 the docks had lost much trade to other British ports (Schneer 42). Nonetheless, the docklands remained iconic, an emblem of imperial migration and labour. Over the ten miles of London docklands,

> the world performed daily a symbolic obeisance to the British Empire, when East End "dock rats" unloaded from ships holds and

then trucked along quays and stacked in warehouses behind them the tokens of Africa, Asian, Latin American, Middle Eastern, and Antipodean submission, the riches extorted from imperialised peoples. (Schneer 39)

The Blitz saw numerous such riches disintegrate in flame, never more dramatically than on the night of 10 September 1940 when St Katherine's Docks became an inferno. Ziegler notes that these docks were "annihilated in an extraordinary blaze. Flames roared 200 feet high, and every warehouse was destroyed in less than four hours" (122–3). Haslewood describes what she saw at Surrey Docks after a similar conflagration: "there was really nothing left of the docks at all except skeletons ... a dead forest of distorted and mangled steel girders, and these lifeless shells standing gauntly" (44).

In *Caught*, the dockland inferno renders British heroism trivial. Fire reduces warehouses containing imports to "a broken, torn-up dark mosaic" (180) and ships' goods become "an upthrusting mountain of fox-dyed smoke" (182). Firemen often saw products becoming physically dangerous, for pepper fires "load the surrounding air heavily with stinging particles," rum fires are "torrents of blazing liquid pouring from the warehouse doors," and rubber fires produce "black clouds of smoke so asphyxiating that it could only be fought from a distance, and was always threatening to choke the attackers" (Ministry of Information, *Front Line* 25–6). In a striking twist, the products of imperial exploitation now threaten the heart of the empire. Similar startling visions of transmuted goods fill Sansom's short story "Fireman Flower," in which firemen wade hip-deep through the commodities of empire: the ensuing gas disorients the protagonist, the burning commodities lulling him into dangerous actions like a somnambulist (132, 133, 139–41). Similarly, in an article titled "Polychromatic Bombing," the Overseas Service describes how such materials transform in flame:

Oil, petrol, rubber, grain and chemicals all have their particular characteristics when they are set on fire. ... Burning crude oil has a brilliant golden glare. ... When rubber begins to burn it gives off an enormous amount of thick, black, rolling smoke. ... (587)

In the paradoxical wartime context, instead of urban light illuminating treasures from the empire, the light testifies to the destruction of those treasures. Just as imperial products are destroyed, so too is heroic British labour rendered diminutive. Roe tells his sister-in-law that as the firemen and their taxi laboured through the massive flames, "Our taxi was like a pink beetle drawing a pepper corn. We were specks" (179).[23] The blazing fire in the docklands sees an imperial nexus disintegrate and heroic effort dwarfed.

Fuller's poem "The Growth of Crime" (1942) depicts a similar faltering of imperial confidence. It opens with a sailor walking around the docklands. A thalassocracy, Britain's imperial might was underpinned by maritime strength, and even today one of the nation's most popular songs avers that "Britannia rules the waves." Yet in Fuller's poem, the docks are a place of menace:

> Bounding the town is the acid sea
> Which nibbles the plates of the plying ships;
> ... suspended on summits curled like whips,
> And from rigging and gun, like a leaky house,
> ... the grey sea drips. (84)

This "acid" sea dissolves both the land and the ships that traverse it, and its waves hold the ships in attitudes of violence, "curled like whips." This sea is active and malignant, and a ship is no match for it because rigging and gun are "leaky" and cannot withstand the insidious waves. A similar dread of the sea characterises Fuller's poem "The Middle of a War" (1942):

> The ridiculous empires break like biscuits.
> Ah, life has been abandoned by the boats –
> Only the trodden island and the dead
> Remain. (86)

Ships are no salvation and all that remains of the imperial project is corpses and earth. In these wartime texts, empire is no longer intact.

Hallucinations of women in urban space

In the same way that this wartime novel unsettles the *flâneur*'s imperial confidence, so too does it complicate his customary encounters with women. Green's protagonists and Fuller's sailor encounter eerie traces of women in the city which usurp the sovereignty of their spectatorship.

Waiting in a bleak asphalt parking lot while training in London, Roe encounters his dead wife strangely embodied across the cityscape. He stands with his fellow firemen:

> They were mute in a vast asphalted space. The store towered above, pile after dark pile which, gradually, light after light went darker than the night that was falling and which he dreaded. For twenty minutes at dusk the scene was his wife's eyes, wet with tears he thought, her long lashes those black railings, everywhere wet, but, in the air, the menace of what was yet to be experienced, the beginning. (37)

Roe's lost beloved becomes the city terrain, but this personification is odd. First, she is formed out of empty space, and second, her ghostly presence is depicted as assertive and seductive, leading him into wild desire: "he could not leave her alone when in an empty room, but stroked her wrists, pinched, kissed her eyes, nibbled her lips while, for her part, she smiled, joked, and took him up to bed at all hours of the day, and lay all night murmuring to him in empty memory" (33). Later, "he clutched at her arm, which was not there, above the elbow" (34). Rather than being a sovereign spectator with a mastering gaze, Roe is a captive to this female presence, unable to resist the vivid hallucination of her embodiment across the urban space.

Pye, too, experiences hallucinatory encounters with women. As the novel progresses, we realise that a horror lurks in his sexual history. Wartime sandbags and blackout remind him of his first sexual experience:

> in moonlight, in colour blue ... oh my God he said to himself as he remembered how she panted through her nose and the feel of her true, roughened hands as they came to repel him and then, at the warmth of his skin, had stayed irresolute at the surface while, all lost, she murmured, "Will it hurt?" Oh God she had been so white and this bloody black-out brought you in mind of it with the moon, this blue colour, and with the creeping home. (40–1)

Again amidst disorienting coloured light, Pye half-forces his partner to submit. The reader gradually realises that the transgression was more than force, for his partner was his sister. As he crept home afterwards:

> he had seen another shadow moving in front towards their bit of garden at the back, creeping as he was but lower, more like a wild

animal, heavier in shame because a woman, and, as he saw with a deep tremor, his own sister, out whoring maybe as he had been, up now from off her back no doubt. ...

He called to mind how disgusted it had made him, the sight of his sister, like a white wood shaving. ... (42)

He feels contempt for the woman, abject as a "white wood shaving," but represses knowledge of his crime until years later. Pye eventually realises his transgression when her psychiatrist asks him why he thinks his sister never married:

with a shock that took all his breath, Pye saw the dry wood shaving creep, bent in the moonlight ... it might have been his own sister he was with that night ... [I]n the blind moonlight, eyes warped by his need, he must have forced his own sister. (140)

Both are tormented by the experience, Pye "suckling on an ulcer the sickly, sore-covered infant of his fears" (169) and his sister maddened by the incestuous rape, "(... the senseless nightingale, the whining dog, repeating the same phrase over and over in the twining briars of her senses)" (42). In his guilt, Pye imagines visiting his sister in the asylum, using Gothic tropes to convey his horror:

he saw himself groping to a vast pile that was raised black against him, for by now it was night and no gleam could escape into the darkness from this tiered tomb which shut those inside from the sky. He found he was under a large hall of bars that cast over him a zebra light. ... Looking up, he could see Amy on the third floor of the cage, hanging to bars like they do in pictures, dressed all in yellow. (85)

In this fantasy, Pye sees his sister suffering as a result of his action, caught behind bars in a vast prison or sarcophagus. In this carceral environment, the trope of coloured glass returns again, alongside the consequences of his transgression. When he finally visits the asylum, he discovers it has "violet-coloured glass" (137).

In his final disintegration, Pye walks through the streets of London seeking a prostitute and savouring any spectacle the blackout permits. Yet despite this position, so like that of *flânerie*, he is unable to imaginatively master what he encounters. Instead, his past transgression comes to claim him, and he staggers through the streets in increasing disorientation.

Coloured light returns when he passes "dark sapphire shadows exactly laid by houses" (162) and the moon casts "deep gentian cracker paper shadows off his uniform" (163). Amid distorted illumination, he sees purchaseable women on display in a newly hallucinatory way:

> the tart, stood back in the doorway, shone a copper beam from the torch she carried, full on her left breast she held bared with the other hand. She murmured "Hullo love." Longingly he ogled the dark purple nipple, the moon full globe that was red Indian tinted by her bulb. ... She laughed into a cough and then, when she snapped down the light, was again, and at once, indigo, and the door against which she stood. (163)

Pye sees a strangely-coloured fragment of a woman, a hallucinatory new commodity for a wartime *flâneur*. This woman's body is rendered exotic by the light, but she is not a mere spectacle: she has agency and controls the display. After this glimpse Pye begins to fantasise that every doorway hides somebody. "He crossed quickly into that bounded sea of shadow. He grew furtive. He imagined women where none were. He spoke suggestively to gentian hooded doorways" (167). Wandering disoriented through urban squalour, Pye imitates the walkers of Thomson's *City of Dreadful Night*: "They often murmur to themselves, they speak / To one another seldom, for their woe / Broods maddening inwardly" (ll. 64–7). The light changes from being the *flâneur's* source of power to being a source of active harm. When he walks back into the light, he becomes "a drowned man walking" (167). This light is murderous. Like Roe, Pye loses control of the fantasy, no longer a sovereign spectator.

Fuller's poem "The Growth of Crime" offers useful parallels to Green's novel. The sailor protagonist seeks a prostitute, and initially the scene recalls the stroll of the Baudelairean *flâneur*, savouring the squalor of an illicit part of the city. "Out of the squalid window gleam / Curved surfaces of skin and red" (83). But after a prostitute invites him in, his experience rapidly becomes nightmarish:

> "Come in, come in." The voice is plucking
> Softly the horizontal air.
> The searchlights start to stain the night,
> A trembling hum is everywhere.
> He imagines the see a film of blood,
> Lopped bodies the shadows on the stair. (84)

Her soft invitation competes with the hum of attack planes approaching the city, and as the sounds of war become audible he begins to see gruesome visions and to experience profound detachment from his own body. "This sordid boneless oyster flesh / Is one of his symbols; the cave, the flask" (84). His detachment from his own body transmutes into a revulsion from hers – "The woman's shape beneath the sheets / Is a gross and convoluted bloom" (84). The woman's body becomes a threat and sexual desire transforms into something more terrible:

> Some secret lives behind the brambles,
> The wine brims up and can be spilled,
> Madness and hatred grow in a night:
> Strumpets are lonely and can be killed:
> Nothing reminds him of day and its reason. (84)

At the close of the poem, the sailor is in the grip of homicidal paranoia:

> The common objects of the room
> Glow like the rows of watching faces
> In a theatre's powdered violet gloom. ...
> The empty bottles point their fingers,
> The idiot clothes lie on the floor. (84)

Amid coloured light, the verses end with a sense that objects are alive and menacing, and he is no longer watcher but watched.

Monstrous city

In Green's novel, Pye's inability to master the spectacles of the city are echoed by other moments in the text which present the wartime city as a monstrous space, overwhelming and inexpressible. *Flânerie* involves doing analytic work on what is seen, classifying spectacles into taxonomies which tame the city's complexity. The wartime city resists such projects. In the epigraph to the novel Green declares that in this book "only wartime London is real." But the "reality" of the wartime city is recalcitrant, and Green's very language continually foregrounds the inadequacy of words to communicate the anguish of the period.

Texts in the Gothic mode characteristically feature convoluted narrative structure (Sedgwick, *Coherence* 20; Botting, *Gothic* 2; Tropp 8) and *Caught* is no exception. In this novel, the actual Blitz firescape is approached through tortuous narrative structure and multiple parenthetical interjections. The first two chapters of *Caught* create the "reality" of 1940s *London* by describing a halting rural encounter between father and child. This oblique approach cannot be explained by the novel's chronology of events because the first four chapters are written from a standpoint after November 1939 (which is when 48-hour leaves began to be permitted at all), while the London chapters (five to fourteen) open with a temporal leap backwards to begin in August 1939. Opening the novel with a description of a mid-war visit to an evacuated child in the countryside means the book is dislocated not only geographically but also temporally.

The narration is complicated further by extensive parentheses which contradict Roe's narration, particularly during his climactic narration of the docklands fire. Richard tells his sister-in-law, for example, that the fire seemed like " 'a huge wood fire on a flat hearth,' " but the parenthetical narration informs us it was more like a glowing wall mosaic (180). The bracketed sections are also temporally disjointed from Richard's reverie. This discrepancy could be interpreted as signifying the difficulty of imagining another person's experience in a world where people will always be separated by poignant disjunctions, yet interpretting these passages as merely symbolising the impossibility of communication does not do justice to one of the oddest qualities of *Caught*. The parenthetical text is not presented as merely one of many versions with equal weight – rather, it has a fundamental authority.

> "The first night" he said, "we were ordered to the docks. As we came over Westminster Bridge it was fantastic, the whole of London seemed to be alight."
>
> (It had not been like that at all. ...) (176)

The authority of the extended parenthesis – "It had not been like that at all" – implies that there *is* a way to express the event. Salomon notes that narratives of horror "insist on the truth of some (now rewritten) record, while ... 'distrustful' even of the implications of the act of recording" (125). Similarly, *Caught*'s parenthetical structures suggest that there is in fact a reality to be reached, even if not one that a human mind can bear.

Cathy Caruth argues that the defining element of a traumatic event is that it could not be witnessed fully at the moment of experience

(*Unclaimed* 7) and Dori Laub describes a trauma as "a record that has yet to be made":

> While historical evidence to the event which constitutes the trauma may be abundant and documents in vast supply, the trauma – as a known event and not simply as an overwhelming shock – has not been fully witnessed yet, not been taken cognizance of. (57)

The paradox of this impossible knowledge is that although the event could not be comprehended at the time, it is remembered with shocking exactitude. Unable to forge delicate strands of logic to link the memory with the rest of one's history, the psyche is helpless to master the memory. Instead, the memory masters the mind, returning willfully in unbridled literality. While the *flâneur* deliberately organises his images of the city into narratives over which he has control, these users of the wartime city are in the grip of forces larger than their conscious mind. Horrifying visions are similarly the climax of Fuller's "Growth of Crime," in which the sailor's sexual desire triggers gruesome hallucinations and ultimately homicidal madness. As his sanity collapses, this wandering watcher undergoes an atavistic awakening:

> The time is the endless hinge of night,
> The opening, slow and living the door.
> He pits his face near hers as though
> To see the grinning, yellow core. (84)

Watching a Blitz conflagration, Cyril Connolly declared "It's the end of capitalism. It's a judgement on us" (Orwell, "Diary" 468). The home front did not see capitalism crumble, but it did see the shadow side of the commodity unmasked. The light which made the *flâneur's* confident work possible is shown to be deceptive and dangerous, and wandering watchers are no longer autonomous, but vulnerable. This brings us to Anna Kavan's and Graham Greene's fictions of the carceral city, where the city's users are not only spectators but are themselves spectacle, surveilled subjects within a terrible system.

3
Carceral City, Cryptic Signs: Wartime Fiction by Anna Kavan and Graham Greene

Punter suggests that Gothic fiction "deals with those moments when we find it impossible, with any degree of hope, for our 'case to be put'" (*Pathologies* 5). Such helplessness dominates the texts of this chapter, which represent the subject positions of immigrants, refugees, psychiatric patients and other outsiders in an environment organised by war. As such, this chapter grapples with wartime adaptations of two traditional Gothic tropes: imprisonment and the struggle to decipher elusive signs. Anna Kavan's short story anthology *I Am Lazarus* (1945), her novel *Sleep Has His House* (1948) and Graham Greene's *The Ministry of Fear* (1943) construct the wartime city in terms of a carceral logic. This city is a menacing labyrinth in the grip of authorities who manipulate signs that fearful inhabitants cannot decipher. Both authors update key Gothic tropes for a period when confinement of outsiders took on dark new forms.

Barbed wire and locked doors: internment camps and asylums

Imprisonment by a diabolic villain has been a staple of Gothic since the eighteenth-century novel (Hurley 191). Trapped, the Gothic victim struggles to make sense of her plight by reading the signs around her: hieroglyphs, letters, omens.[24] Victor Sage suggests that the preoccupation with reading signs is symptomatic of the increasing dominance of a Protestant world view, in which the onus was on the worshipper to actively decipher and interpret text and symbol (xvi). The Gothic sees these efforts repeatedly flouted, signs remaining opaque and thus menacing.

While the eighteenth-century Gothic primarily saw confinement occur within convents, castles and dungeons, the nineteenth century saw the dread locus now became any place where bodies are disciplined and constrained, including hospitals, schools, orphanages, prisons and asylums. The carceral spaces of traditional Gothic can be approached through Michel Foucault's concept of a "heterotopia," a place which follows different rules from the world outside it, a site in which "all the other real sites that can be found within the culture, are simultaneously represented, contested, and inverted" (par. 14). Botting notes that the castles, dungeons and labyrinths of eighteenth-century Gothic are het-erotopias in the sense that they were spaces under which daylight laws no longer held sway, where victims "are subjected to vicious, illegitimate and tyrannical authority" ("Gothic Production" 29). Wartime Britain was rich in heterotopias of deviation aiming to house, restrain and reform individuals deemed deviant from the norm. This chapter examines two such heterotopias: internment camps for enemy aliens, and psychiatric institutions. Kavan's and Greene's texts engage what we might call a carceral imaginary, a culture's pervading constellation of images cluster-ing around the concept of involuntary confinement by the state.

The work of grappling with prohibitions became grimly salient on Britain's Second World War home front. World War I had already seen an unprecedented increase in the extent to which every person in the coun-try was surveilled and regulated, A. J. P. Taylor noting that an inhabitant of Britain had numerous freedoms before the First World War:

> He had no official number or identity card. He could travel abroad or leave his country for ever without a passport or any sort of official permission. He could exchange his money for any other currency without restriction or limit. He could buy goods from any country in the world on the same terms as he bought goods at home. (1)

These freedoms were not restricted to those born in Britain. Immigrants could enter and leave without restrictions (Taylor 1). World War I changed much: people were conscripted, food was rationed, employ-ment laws were introduced, lighting was controlled, alcohol consump-tion was regulated, and even clocks were changed. A. Taylor observes, "The state established a hold over its citizens which, though relaxed in peacetime, was never to be removed and which the Second World War was again to increase" (1–2). When World War II loomed regula-tion again proliferated, classifying a host of new behaviours as crimes (Mackay 128).[25] Nonetheless, Britain's prison population dropped with the onset of war, 5,000 prisoners being discharged immediately. These prison releases were not due to "a patriotic outbreak of law-abiding citizenship" (Hylton 186) but rather due to the government's desire to intern aliens in their cells instead.

When the Second World War loomed, Britain's intentions had been noble with regard to non-nationals.[26] World War I had seen mob violence against – and mass internment of – enemy aliens, and ministers were keen to avoid both this time around; in addition, unlike many European countries Britain accepted German and Austrian refugees, despite the fact that Britain had passed a legislative order in 1920 which removed the right of persecuted aliens to seek refugee status in Britain (Fraser 40, 59). On the other hand, the government was not eager to see unbridled immigration by refugees, and their ambivalence was manifest in Britain's immigration policy. Britain did not recognise Jewish refugees as a persecuted category, caps were set on the number of refugees admitted, and Jewish organisations were required to financially support refugees (Lassner 206; Loewenstein 55). Loewenstein notes that, "Between 1939 and 1941, Hitler was eager to expel the Jews from the Third Reich. The governments of Great Britain and the United States, while all the time professing their deep commitment to and sympathy for the refugees ... shut their doors, and the Jews were killed" (42).

For aliens who did succeed in entering Britain, the government initially tried to develop a nuanced classification system to reduce the number interned. Category A aliens were overtly hostile to the Allies, and were interned immediately. Category B aliens could not conclusively demonstrate sympathy with the war effort or were too infirm to be interned, and were initially subject to curfew, travel restrictions and a ban on possessing a radio, British maps or any means of transport. Category C aliens had lived in Britain at least six years and had demonstrable reasons to support the Allies; initially they experienced no constraints (Leicester Joint Refugee Commission; Calder, *Myth* 110–11, *People* 130–3). However, as the war progressed, each category experienced harsher restrictions. On May 1940 the Joint Intelligence Committee recommended "all enemy aliens, both male and female, between the ages of 16 and 70" be interned immediately (Wasserstein 80). As a result, May 1940 saw many category B aliens sent to the camps, and July saw many from category C interned too (Nelki 2; Hylton 12–13). Regardless of category, all aliens were rapidly hedged around with a multitude of proliferating documents and regulations.[27]

Popular bias against aliens was fanned by persistent rumours of a treacherous "fifth column" embedded within Britain, comprised of aliens and British people secretly supporting the Nazi cause.[28] Although no evidence was ever found that it existed, even military authorities lent it credence, Churchill himself denouncing "this malignancy in our midst" (Calder, *People* 134). Mass-Observation discovered in a 1940 survey that the bulk of British people did not initially feel that aliens were a threat, but public sentiment darkened as the war progressed and by July 1940 43 per cent of respondents to a poll felt all aliens should be interned (Calder, *Myth* 117). Such bias was echoed in the highest echelons of British policymaking, not least in Churchill's declaration to his Cabinet that, "A very large round up of enemy aliens and suspect persons [is desirable] ... it would be much better that these persons should be behind barbed wire" (Hylton 11). Churchill's call was arguably partly motivated by concern for aliens' welfare, but distrust of aliens characterises much ministerial discourse of the war. Neville Bland (Minister for Holland) was particularly unhelpful, blaming a Fifth Column for Holland's collapse and warning that "Every German or Austrian servant, however superficially charming and devoted, is a real and grave menace ... satellites of the monster [Hitler]" (TNA PRO FO 371/25189/462 [W 7984/7941/49]). By May 1940 Churchill declared in favour of deporting all internees, and when Italians became enemy aliens Churchill decreed "Collar the lot!" (Lafitte xiv).[29] In total over 27,200 enemy aliens were interned on the British home front (Hylton 19).

The camps were often sites of profound physical and psychological suffering.[30] Since initial plans had only provided for category A aliens to be interned, accommodation became difficult after category B and C aliens also joined. The conditions at Warth Mills internment camp illustrate the resulting squalour of some camp conditions. 500 men were crammed into a filthy, rat-infested mill, kept on a starvation diet and even deprived of light (Hylton 17–18). Thousands were deported, some dying due to submarine attack or inhumane conditions on board. Some invalids were interned despite ill health (Hylton 16–17; Wasserstein 67). Families were often separated, Livia Laurent recalling, "We were pushed, counted, torn apart" (366). Many camps banned radios and newspapers, a profound cruelty when refugees yearned for news on the fate of their loved ones on the Continent. Suicide attempts followed such media deprivation (95). To add insult to injury, refugees and overt Nazi sympathisers were initially kept in the same camps. Jewish refugees were mocked at prayer with chilling songs such as "Let the Jews' blood drip from our shining knives" (Spier 131). Internment camp authorities did not always defend the refugees (Lafitte 99; Nelki 3) and many suffered greatly as a result. Erna Nelki recalls that at her camp, "Despair, unhappiness and insecurity dominated. One woman even walked into the sea and committed suicide" (4).

Nelki notes that the consequences of the British government's alien internment policy unwittingly partially echoed some cruelties of anti-Semitic continental regimes, for: "Once again Jews were made outcasts of society which caused much despair, unhappiness and personal tragedies" (12). Many survivors of Nazi concentration camps were incarcerated anew when they reached Britain's shores.[31] One eye-witness of forced deportation saw 1,580 refugees herded onto lorries like cattle. "Many of the old men fell on the ground and kissed it. They pleaded with tears before the police officers ... to have pity on them, that they had already passed through Dachau and Buchenwald. And the officers paid no heed to them" (TNA PRO FO 371/433/25242/433 [W 12715/38/48]; qtd. in Wasserstein 67). Internee Ernest Pollak describes being stripped naked, treated as a prisoner and threatened with violence, and his camp commandant even echoed dehumanizing Nazi language of "vermin," calling the internees "black snakes on a rock" and warning Jews that they must be more clean or they will get lice ("Departure" 40, 50).[32] With regard to Warth Mills, an official from the Ministry of Information noted that some suicides had already survived Hitler's concentration camps. "'Against [Hitler's camps] ... they held out, but this camp has broken their spirit.'" G. M. Trevelyan wrote to *The Times*, "The Nazis keep their concentration camps for their enemies; we use them for our friends" (qtd. in Hylton 1).

Popular sentiment became increasingly hostile to aliens as the war progressed. Some newspapers demanded that concentration camps be explicitly established, and one even argued that aliens should wear special armbands like the Nazi badges (Hylton 8–9). Some British local authorities even asked refugee communities to pay to dispose of the corpses of refugees who committed suicide (Lafitte 147). Public opinion shifted in July 1940 with the sinking of the *Arandora Star*, on which 1500 aliens were being deported, some being famous opponents of Nazism (Calder, *People* 132). Francois Lafitte's scathing exposé *The Internment of Aliens* (1940) evoked further public outrage. As a result, at the end of 1941 the government recognised new legal categories of people who could be released: those persecuted by the Nazis, those who had fought Hitler or Mussolini, those who had given distinguished service in science or arts and those infirm or aged over 70 (Wasserstein 96; Nelki 11; Hylton 21). Yet internment cannot be lightly dismissed. It was a harrowing period in which many refugees experienced profound distress. Major Cazalet declared in the House of Commons in August 1940 that "No ordinary excuse, such as that there is a war on and that officials are overworked, is sufficient to explain what has happened. ... Horrible tragedies, unnecessary and undeserved, lie at the door of somebody" (Lafitte vi).

Gothic tropes flicker throughout refugees' representations of their own experience. P. Fliess, for example, describes his experiences interned in Britain and then transported to a camp in the Commonwealth. His fellow captives have "yellow faces, more death's-heads than faces" (42). R. Jacobstahl notes that his fellow inmates in camp move and talk "in an atmosphere of haunted unreality, [in which] vision and sound were distorted ... [M]en were barely themselves, nor was I myself" (10). Pollak creates a nightmare dream-sequence in which images of the menacing camp authorities interweave with images of his dying brother:

> Black uniforms, brown uniforms are marching past, growing bigger and taller, a formidable human tank, they are marching on to me. ... And the barbed wire has clasped me from all sides clutching me. ... Rows and rows of brown and black monsters are approaching me again, and there lies my brother on his white bed, feebly waving his white hand.
>
> Muddy boots will stamp on my fists clenched round the wire. ...
> "We have been ordered to intern you."
> "Silence please." (*Dreams*)

This poetic prose fragment conveys the disorientation, vulnerability and grief which characterised much internee experience. MacNeice describes refugees as the "disinterred," exhumed but still dead ("Refugees" 164). As internee Friedrich Sittner sombrely recalls, "one grows strange behind barbed wire."

Psychiatric hospitals were another carceral institution affected by the War. The First World War had seen the new diagnosis of "shell-shock" for psychological damage sustained in war and a range of medical procedures were developed in response.[33] As war loomed again, the government and medical establishment feared that psychiatric casualties would be three times as plentiful as physical casualties (Titmuss 338–9), Calder noting dryly that if the projected numbers had been true, "everyone in London would have very soon been either mad or dead" (*People* 223). These fears proved unfounded for, surprisingly, mental health seemed to improve during the Blitz. Psychiatric admissions fell and some neurotics recovered (Titmuss 347–8; Harrisson 305–6; Calder, *People* 223; T. H. O'Brien 532, 540). Such recoveries have been explained with reference to the way war unites people in adversity, giving useful tasks and clear emotional foci – enemies to hate, victims to pity. The most famous proponent of that view is F. A. E. Crew (K. Jones, *History* 227, 379n4) and Richard Titmuss echoes him, arguing that to many the Blitz meant "less social disparagement ... useful work and an opportunity to play an active part in the community" (347). Kathleen Jones, however, offers a less rosy explanation for the drop in psychiatric admissions:

> War-time economy establishes an unusual series of priorities. The fitness ... of the men in the Services is a top priority; next comes the well-being of productive workers. The mentally ill come a long way down the scale. ... The available beds are overcrowded, there are fewer doctors and nurses to give treatment, and the general emphasis is on giving treatment only where absolutely necessary. (*History* 229)

In other words, the drop in classifications of people as mentally ill may be due in part to doctors' reluctance to send patients into an environment where they would not be well-treated. Her argument is supported by the fact that psychiatric patients on the home front had a singularly bleak experience.

In the First World War, home front asylum conditions had been appalling (K. Jones, *History* 228–33). Overcrowding caused many deaths from tuberculosis and dysentery (Crammer; Brooking 10; Carpenter 9) and staff allegedly used sedatives and laxatives to tranquillise patients into obedience (Lomax; Brooking 10). Exposés by doctors like Montagu Lomax led to outcries for mental health reform, which triggered official inquiries culminating in the Mental Treatment Act of 1930 (K. Jones, *History* 232–50).[34] Despite such efforts, however, 1939 saw most wards permanently locked and patients' lives highly circumscribed (Brooking 11).

At the beginning of the Second World War several mental hospitals were immediately commandeered for new purposes, and as a result, overcrowding again became widespread and standards slipped (K. Jones, *History* 270). Tuberculosis increased so sharply that by 1942 the percentage of infected psychiatric patients was 15 times above the national average (Cherry 209). Steven Cherry admits:

> In many respects the experience of mental hospitals and their patients in the Second World War resembled that of the asylums and their inmates in the First World War. ... [T]he essentials of accommodation, food, care and attention, and recreational space for patients

were pared down. … Deprivation was one part of the war experience in which mental hospital patients fully participated. (208)

Overcrowding and TB meant the ominous "return of the locked door, of inactivity, of isolation" (K. Jones, *History* 270).[35]

Incarcerated people such as internees and psychiatric in-patients are people at the fringes of society; they are "the minority, the exilic, the marginal" (Bhabha, "DissemiNation" 300). Gothic narrative modes can convey the wartime experiences of these minorities. In the texts of this chapter, denizens – not "citizens" since deprived of rights and fellowship – try to negotiate the cruel wartime carceral city by deciphering cryptic signs. In Kavan's work, protagonists decipher textual clues in an attempt to escape cruel authorities, while in Greene's, the protagonist decodes uncanny auditory phenomena in an attempt to elude the murderous plans of a controlling organisation. Both depict the city as carceral heterotopia.

Anna Kavan

Born Helen Woods to wealthy expatriate parents in 1901, Kavan's early life was characterised by isolation. Her parents spent little time with her even as an infant, and at the age of six she was sent to boarding school in America where she was often left alone in the school on holidays (Reed 15–17). At the age of eighteen she married, and her husband took her to Burma where he held a post in colonial administration. She hated her domineering husband and took refuge in writing semi-autobiographical fiction under her married name, Helen Ferguson. The marriage disintegrated within two years, after which Helen returned to Europe, became addicted to heroin and entered a relationship with artist Stuart Edmonds. They lived in rural Britain for much of the 1930s until the relationship faltered under the pressure of their mutual addictions, his to alcoholism and hers to heroin. She attempted suicide twice and underwent the latest psychiatric treatments for addiction and depression, and after her second suicide attempt was admitted into a Swiss sanatorium in summer 1938.

The woman who emerged was Anna Kavan. She changed her name by deed poll to the name of a defiant, unconventional character in two of her earlier books published as Helen Ferguson, *Let Me Alone* (1930) and *A Stranger Still* (1935). At the same time, she altered her appearance from brunette girl-next-door to skeletal metallic blonde, an appearance she maintained until her death in 1968 (Zambreno par. 7). Her friend Rhys Davies recalls her radical transformation:

> I failed to recognise the woman running to me ... Helen Ferguson had vanished. This spectral woman, attenuated of body and face, a former abundance of auburn hair shorn and changed to metallic gold, thinned hands, restless, was so different. ... [L]ater I came to understand why she called one of her Anna Kavan books *I Am Lazarus*. She herself had returned from an abeyance of personality in the shades. (Reed 47–8)

While Helen Woods Ferguson had been an obedient daughter and a stifled wife, Kavan was a new creature, independent, unnerving and defiant of convention. In the same way that Kavan broke free of her original identities, she broke free of traditional literary forms, switching to experimental prose.

Kavan's new life was an exercise in deliberate engagement with otherness. The seeds of this estrangement were already there even in the experience of the child Helen Woods – born to expatriates, moved around the world and repeatedly neglected. Years later, she suggested that the wet nurse who accompanied her to Britain "hated the cold and transmitted this aversion in her breast milk" (Zambreno par. 8), a whimsical hypothesis that illustrates Kavan's profound sense of her body being veined through with a sense of estrangement from Britain. Helen Ferguson, too – her identity after marriage – was continually aware of otherness: for the two years of her marriage, she lived with her husband in British-ruled Burma, where she quickly came to abhor colonial condescension to the colonised (Stuhlmann 58). Her self-chosen identity was founded on resistance and isolation. After her marriage ended she claimed her freedom by restlessly wandering the world. Her chosen name sounds eastern European, and her first book as Kavan – *Asylum Piece* (1940) – is set in a Swiss sanatorium full of people from a range of nations which Jeremy Reed notes "gives its author a peculiarly anational feel, as though in reinventing herself she no longer owned to a specific nationality" (49). Kavan was an outsider by choice (a restless world traveller), by birth (never feeling at home in her ostensible homeland) and by medical category (a registered heroin addict for over thirty years and regularly incarcerated in psychiatric institutions). Similarly, her protagonists are outsiders rendered "other" by national position, by madness, or by falling prey to callous bureaucracy.

Given Kavan's dramatic life, it is perhaps not surprising that most critics approach her writing as autobiographical, taming her disturbing prose by viewing it as representative of her experience of addiction and her unusual life.[36] Jane Garrity goes beyond seeing Kavan's work as representative of her idiosyncratic experience, suggesting that it "interrogates the issue of what constitutes 'psychic normalcy' specifically for women within an increasingly alienating and fragmented social context" (254). Kavan's writing unquestionably features potent representations of subjective female experience. I wish, however, to enrich such discussions by also examining the context which saw these texts emerge, and which glimmer dream-like behind Kavan's use of Gothic tropes. Kavan's writing can be read as a hallucinatory refraction of some of the authoritarian pressures that convulsed the home front.

Forced narcosis: "The Palace of Sleep"

All fifteen stories in her collection *I Am Lazarus* (1945) depict madness, and five deal specifically with suffering in psychiatric hospitals. Ripa Yannick has observed that madness tends to be described from the perspective of outsiders looking on rather than from the perspective of those experiencing it directly (5) but these stories by Kavan take readers into the latter world of humiliation and agony. For much of the nineteenth century and the first decades of the twentieth, psychiatry had been limited to "warehousing" patients, but by 1939 psychiatry had been revolutionised by new treatments of which much was hoped: electroconvulsive shock treatment, lobotomy, and chemically-induced prolonged narcosis (semi-coma) (Shorter 208; Angel 44). Kavan's story "The Palace of Sleep" describes narcosis, which Kavan herself experienced several times (Reed 34, 99).

Using prolonged sleep to treat psychoses was arguably pioneered by Jacob Klaesi, who used a drug called Somnifen.[37] Others used bromides, insulin injection to artificially induce hypoglycaemic coma, or paraldehyde, the latter causing the stench that characterised sleep wards (Shorter 209). Narcosis rapidly gained currency with psychiatrists Harold Palmer and Francis Braceland hailing it in 1937 as of proven value in everything from neurosis to manic depression to schizophrenia. The first British psychiatrists to use insulin coma were William Sargent and Russell Fraser of London's Maudsley Hospital, who began using it in November 1938 after the Munich Crisis, when the Second World War loomed (Showalter, *Female Malady* 205). Later, narcosis was shown to have high mortality rates, and to be better at sedating patients than healing them (Angel 43–4). Significantly, although medical reports assume that the recipients are unconscious throughout, narcosis was often a distressing state of semi-consciousness, a "hideous sleep" from a "poisoned needle" (Kavan, *Lazarus* 15).

Kavan's story describes a doctor touring a narcosis ward. His benevolent host calls the narcosis wing a peaceful "palace of sleep" (*Lazarus* 18) but the visitor is unnerved:

> The wide corridor was coldly and antiseptically white, with a row of doors on the left and windows on the opposite side. The windows were high and barred, and admitted a discouraging light that gleamed bluishly on the white distemper like a reflection of snow. (*Lazarus* 18)

This place is chill, its corridors "coldly" white, its light "bluish," and the coldness recalls what Simone Buffard has called *le froid pénitentiaire*, a "carceral iciness," a sense of isolation and coldness (Fludernik and Olson xxvii). Yet the horror of this place is not only confinement in an institution, but confinement in darkness and speechlessness. He sees one patient's heroic efforts to fight unconsciousness:

> suddenly a tremor disturbed the immobility of the anonymous face, the eyelids quivered under their load of shadows. The man watched fascinated, almost appalled, as, slowly, with intolerable, incalculable effort, the drugged eyes opened and stared straight into his. Was it imagination, or did he perceive in their clouded greyness a look of terror, of wild supplication, or frantic, abysmal, appeal? (*Lazarus* 20)

Mary Cecil, treated with narcosis several times, recalls that one of the horrors of insulin coma was the struggle to emerge: "I tried to address a nurse who looked in, and to my horror heard only unintelligible sounds. ... I wept with shame" (222). Narcosis patients were rendered speechless and helpless.

Gender is a crucial facet of the iconography of the narcosis treatment, the supine patient of Kavan's story recalling late nineteenth-century imagery of the passive, deathly feminine:

> Under the white bedspread pulled straight and symmetrical, like the covering of a bier, a young woman was lying quite motionless with closed eyes. Her fair hair was spread on the pillow, her pale face was absolutely lifeless, void, with the peculiar glazed smoothness and eye-sockets darkly circled ... [this shape] already seemed to have

forfeited humanity and given itself over prematurely to death. (*Lazarus* 19–20).

Pale, passive, and corpse-like, this representation of the female patient evokes the "cult of invalidism" which Bram Dijkstra has identified in nineteenth-century art, a cult which eroticises women near death and dwells on their immobility and otherworldly mystery (40–1). Kavan's "Palace of Sleep" features a similar deathly feminine. Although Kavan's asylum victims are not exclusively female, a gendered language clusters around the treatment of narcosis. Visual representations of narcosis patients are almost always female, and the majority of people treated with the therapy were female (Showalter, *Malady* 205). In addition, the treatment renders the recipient passive and dependent, in a stereotypically "feminine" position. Showalter argues that psychiatric practices confine resistant female bodies which resist the roles decreed for them by particular societies; with this in mind, narcosis does troubling work, silencing patients with sleep.

Language of religious mystery clusters around the procedure. The patient lies motionless as though on a "bier," the psychiatrist is like a "clergyman," and the eyes of the half-conscious recipient plead in "wild supplication" (*Lazarus* 19–20). Yet as the story unfolds, we become aware that the Palace of Sleep is more unholy than holy. Faced with the corpse-like patient, the lead psychiatrist feels nothing but approval. This story has two horrors: the drugged women imprisoned in sleep, and the untroubled man perpetrating the violation. The visiting doctor, by contrast, recognises the horror. He lingers by the patient, "held by an obscure reluctance to withdraw his gaze from those unclear eyes. And when he finally moved away he felt uneasy and almost ashamed" (*Lazarus* 20). He departs, a reluctant witness, and the story ends inconclusively, in squalour and shame. This new therapy, launched in Britain on the eve of war and conveniently silencing patients in overcrowded sanatoria, is presented as malignant.

"Face of My People": aliens and alienists

While non-nationals are legally known as aliens, the nineteenth century term for a psychiatrist was an alienist, "an intermediary between the social world and the world of the mentally ill. ... He identified the mentally ill, segregated them, and, if possible, later reintroduced them into the community" (Littlewood and Lipsedge 33). The two terms converge in the protagonist of Kavan's story "Face of My People," other in two senses: a refugee and psychologically disturbed.

Known only by his nickname "Kling" – the first syllable of his name, and the only syllable his English acquaintances bother to learn – he has been traumatised by his war labours on the Continent. He dug mass graves and is tormented by the memory of those he buried, "wrecked or fearful or quiet or obscene faces, far too many of them, how he had laboured and toiled till his saliva ran sour, desperate to hide the faces away from the brutal light" (*Lazarus* 58). There is tenderness in these interments; he hides these broken faces from "brutal" light, his digging a futile but loving attempt at protection. In time he becomes obsessed with the burying, "always the compulsive urge in him like a frenzy, to hide the ruined faces away" (*Lazarus* 58).

One face haunts him, the face of an old man whose face he saw destroyed by stones during burial. This face has become the single "face" of the story's title, for he can no longer remember any faces from his homeland apart from that of this shattered corpse (*Lazarus* 58). Witnessing the stones smash that face damaged Kling's mind, triggering somatic symptoms: he felt a stone smash into his own chest simultaneously, which has literally weighed on his heart ever since. "[H]e had seen the falling stone and felt it strike, felt it smash bone, tearing through muscle, sinew and vein to lodge itself immovably in his breast" (*Lazarus* 57). Over time the stone grows larger and heavier, until all feeling is numbed. This numbness is a blessing, for at night when the stone rolls free he sees the dead anew. In Wilfred Owen's phrase, Kling is one of the men "whose minds the Dead have ravished," wracked by guilt at his own survival and tormented by memories of the dead ("Mental Cases" l. 2, 10).

The asylum responds to Kling's plight with impatience, for their priority is getting men back into combat. As Williams, one of Kling's fellow inmates, says, " 'Cannon fodder, that's all they care about. ... Pills to pep you up. Dope to make you talk. Putting chaps to sleep and giving them electric shocks and Christ knows what' " (*Lazarus* 59–60). Williams is correct that the asylum director and nurse savour violent methods for breaking people's minds. The director Dr Pope is as chilling as the "clergyman" director of "The Palace of Sleep." Pope is undaunted when the nurse says Kling has " 'shut himself up like an oyster' ": smiling, the psychiatrist responds, " 'Oysters can be opened.' " "He got up and stood with his back to the window ... framed in dusty blackout material. He had his hands in his trouser pocket and he was still smiling as he went on, 'we might try a little forcible opening on oyster Kling' " (*Lazarus* 54). Blackout material frames him as he smilingly speaks of force, and *le froid pénitentiaire* gleams again in the nurse's "pale, cold" eyes (*Lazarus* 59).

"[F]orcible opening" involves drugging Kling intravenously with sodium pentathol. Again, the blackout material becomes symbolic as Kling awaits their attentions. "The passage was dark because the windows had been coated with black paint for the blackout. Nothing moved in the long, dark, silent passage at the end of which Kling sat alone on the bench" (*Lazarus* 60–61). The doctor looms at Kling after he is injected:

> The hand that had hold of his shoulder gripped hard like a trap, the distorted face looked monstrous, foreshortened and suspended. ... Kling groaned, turning his head from one side to the other to escape from the eyes, but the eyes would not let him go. He felt the strangeness of sleep or sickness or death moving up on him, and then something gave way in his chest, the stone shifted. (*Lazarus* 62)

The drug not only removes Kling's self-protecting illusion of the stone, but also plunges him into a horrifying hallucination:

> all he could see above was a cloud of faces, the entire earth was no graveyard great enough for so many. ...
>
> The old man was there and had been for some time, not sprawled in leaves now but standing, bent forward, listening; and Kling knew that this time something must pass between them. ...
>
> The old man bent over him and blood dripped onto his face and he could not move because of what lay on his breast. (*Lazarus* 63)

Kling speaks, yet both doctor and nurse turn away, for he speaks in another language (*Lazarus* 64). They dismiss Kling at exactly the moment when his defences have been ripped from him, for neither considers there may be value in his using the language of his home country. This story again features two horrors, psychiatristic sadism and the war trauma which damages the protagonist's mind. Kling's suffering is not unique; he recognises the psychiatric institution as a place of live burial for others too. "How many stones there are in this place; so many faces and stones" (*Lazarus* 61). Like the "ruined faces" he interred, the other inmates are also buried.

Kavan felt passionate about the plight of Europe's wartime refugees, particularly after she formed a close attachment with Karl Bluth, a doctor she met in her second psychiatric hospital. Bluth was a German refugee obliged to flee Nazi Germany because of his anti-totalitarian writing, and Reed notes that "Bluth's predicament as a refugee had alerted her to the reality of the death camps, and, more generally, to the disenfranchised, nomadic predicament of Europe's dispossessed" (94, 107). In a book review early in the war, Kavan wrote that the problem of tens of thousands of global dispossessed was "of the utmost urgency to all. ... Any [literary or artistic] representation, any experiment whatsoever, which may shock people into awareness of their responsibility to these undefended ones is of extreme importance" (Kavan qtd. in Reed 96). Kavan speaks urgently here about the need to recognise the damage war wreaks on combatants, exiles and more. The asylum cruelties in these stories are not representative of all wartime psychiatric practice, but rather are nightmarish intensifications of wartime asylums' overcrowding and regimented ethos, coupled as they were with the profound distrust of the foreign Other that characterised popular and governmental discourse. Butler notes that societies imply distinctions between "grievable" and "ungrievable" lives: if some people are never recognised as fully human, then damage to them may not be recognised (*Precarious* 32). Kling is one such marginalised life, Other in multiple senses.

Resisting authority in the carceral metropolis

Like Kling, the protagonist of Kavan's story "Our City" (1945) is doubly vulnerable, other in nation and in madness. The story is a sequence of ten vignettes told by a narrator in the grip of faceless authorities. She has committed some unnamed transgression, and as a consequence is under "two sentences, mutually exclusive but running concurrently: the sentence of banishment from the city and of imprisonment in it" (*Lazarus* 124). This paradoxical combination typifies the law in Kavan's writing as a thing of contradictions and malice. Yet the protagonist is not incarcerated in prison, but in an ordinary apartment; we see no guards, and as the story progresses we realise she is an unreliable narrator. She hears the objects in her domestic interior mock her. The bottles on the dressing table "snigger," "everything in the rooms jeers at me ... The walls shake with laughter" (130,132) and she experiences the searchlights as a bodily attack: "I can feel the broad beams sawing and the narrow beams scissoring through my nerves" (129–30). Her nights are gripped by paranoid fantasy. Like Thomson's *City of Dreadful Night*, her city is

> ... of Night, but not of Sleep;
> There sweet sleep is not for the weary brain;
> The pitiless hours like years and ages creep,
> A night seems termless hell. (ll. 71–4)

Kavan's writing is often approached as a representation of madness, but as I will show, wartime circumstances were such that outsiders would not be delusional to believe that they were controlled by secretive authorities.

The narrator lists three transformations she has witnessed London undergo during the war. First, the city is a giant black octopus, extending black tentacles across the globe to summon her from abroad: "a blackish tentacle was unfurled which travelled undeviatingly across the globe to the remote antipodean island where I imagined myself secure" (124). This wartime city is a Lovecraftian monster. Secondly, the city is a brutal animal trap snapping flesh and bone, with "sadistic jaws which snap upon the delicate leg or paw of some soft-furred wild creature, mangling the flesh and splintering the fragile bones and clamping the victim to a slow, agonising death"; the bomb-damaged skyline even symbolises the city's trap-like quality: "There is even a sort of resemblance between the serrated blade as it must appear shearing down on its prey and the ferocious skyline of the city partially laid waste" (124). Thirdly, the city is a Kafka-esque court, rendering unfathomable judgments on a bewildered citizenry who have no appeal, "a judge, what's more, who not only arraigns the criminal, sets up the court, conducts the trial, and passes sentence, but actually sees that the sentence is carried out" (124). This city is violent and monstrous and there is no appeal against its decrees.

Isolation is the hallmark of the narrator's experience in this wartime urban space. Despite the "Our" of the title, the narrator feels no camaraderie on the home front. Rather, she feels profoundly isolated, and air raids only intensify her loneliness. "I have the impression that I am the only living soul in the midst of this fiendish hullabaloo. Can there really be other human beings out there in the city?" (*Lazarus* 130). The only people with whom she feels any affinity are the foreign soldiers. "I, the city's outcast and prisoner, seemed to feel with these foreigners a connection, sympathetic perhaps, which did not exist where the citizens [of the city] were concerned ... it was all I could do to restrain myself from making an appeal of some kind to them, in my desolation" (136). This narrator describes experience counter to the Blitz mythology of togetherness.

The authorities of "Our City" cannot be challenged. Like the protagonist of Kafka's *The Trial*, the narrator tries repeatedly to make her case, but the only people she can contact are minor officials who never help. "Like a recurrent dream, the following scene repetitiously unfolds itself: I am sitting in a bureau, putting forward my case; it is the nine-hundred-and-ninety-ninth station of my tedious calvary" (137). Language of the sacred again circulates around the authorities: they are those "into whose hands we are committed," who require supplicants to "petition" and sit in "restless vigil" (*Lazarus* 132, 138, 143). Like cruel deities, the authorities require surrender to their capricious will. Kavan's novel *Sleep Has His House* (1948) also features supernatural authorities who delight to induce fear:

> Everything's ghostly and grim and dark, and though there are people present, they seem to be in another dimension. All that's perceptible is a continuous strange stir, as if a crowd of transparent onlookers were seated in thin air, fidgeting and whispering, rustling their spectral papers. ...
>
> [T]he atmosphere generated by these invisible spectators is far from friendly. There's a sort of malicious tittering in the background, a nightmare Alice-in-Wonderland inconsequence, which is most disturbing. The inconsequential element is manifest too in certain architectural caprices and light shifts, whereby the building is given a fluctuating resemblance to a church, a law court, a prison, an operating theatre, a torture chamber, a vault. (102–3)

Architectural caprice is echoed by regulatory caprice, for the authorities of "Our City" continually change their laws. The carceral city is webbed with mutable regulation.

From the perspective of Second World War refugees to Britain, capricious authorities are not mere paranoiac fantasy. Until 1920, Britain's laws showed sympathy for refugees. Under the Magna Carta, aliens were free to enter and depart at will. The Aliens Act of 1905 saw immigration law become stricter, but even then refugees had right of entry and all applicants had the right to appeal (Fraser 37–8, 41–2). The Aliens Restriction Acts of 1914 and 1919 diluted these freedoms, and the Aliens Order of 1920 removed them altogether, repealing right of appeal and rejecting persecution as an eligible reason for refugee status. In practice, refugees did continue to be accepted, and in large numbers: over 70,000 refugees were admitted to Britain in the early war years (Calder, *People* 129–31). Yet aliens in wartime Britain inhabited an extraordinary web of regulation, receiving contradictory instructions and required to fulfill bizarre rituals of officialdom. Isabelle Granger, a schoolteacher and volunteer supporter to refugees, describes the experience of helping aliens with wartime bureaucracy:

> we are conditioned to bolts from the blue – shrieks from a radio, sudden phone calls, appeals that must be answered at once, an important

feeling that if I don't act at once by ringing up a committee in London, or wiring a committee in Vienna, or standing in a queue at an Embassy in order to personally hand in some poor wretch's papers, then something will go badly wrong for somebody. ... It's like living in a lunatic asylum, my head is crammed with shibboleths and rules. (Goodall 221)

Arbitrariness similarly characterised the internment of aliens. Well-intentioned though the 1939 Categories of Aliens were, the tribunals which implemented them proved disastrously capricious in their workings, working to independent criteria which were frequently reactionary. Hylton notes:

One put all domestic servants into category B, while another immediately interned anyone who was a socialist or a communist. Some interned anyone they thought would be vulnerable to blackmail ... others were locked up because they were in sensitive occupations. ... [A] German who spoke no English was examined by a Tribunal which spoke no German, without the benefit of an interpreter. He was immediately interned on suspicion of being foreign. (2–3)[38]

What troubles legal historian C. F. Fraser, however, is that in 1940, "secrecy of proceedings and absolute executive discretion dominate the process" (33) and the laws are wholly mysterious:

[W]e are, in dealing with aliens, "in a domain in which no recognised principles seem to apply." We have no means of knowing the standards, if any, on which the Home Secretary bases his decisions. ... In spite of a carefully prepared approach to the officials of the Home Office, and a special introduction from distinguished Englishmen to the Home Secretary himself, the writer has met with an impenetrable wall of silence. ... An air of secrecy seemed to cloak all the proceedings. Even the methods of the police in gaining information about a prospective candidate for naturalisation were shrouded in mystery. (71)

This passage is dominated by Gothic tropes. The law is "an impenetrable wall of silence," "cloak[ed] in secrecy" and "shrouded in mystery," and we are in "in a domain in which no recognised principles seem to apply." This heterotopic terrain is the terrain of Law, itself Gothic in its "presumed antiquity, its imperviousness to reason, its status as a discourse of mystery, its ability to mortify the body" (Punter, *Pathologies* 21). Garrity argues that Kavan's fracturing of conventional literary form is a manifestation of a desire to reconnect with the maternal body (258). Persuasive though Garrity's argument is, I suggest that Kavan's writing challenges not only language's conventions but also the implacable body of law that shapes the experience of those marked "Other" in the wartime city. Kavan offers "night-time language" (*Sleep* 6) to destabilise that monumental body of texts.

The Liaison Officer in *Sleep* notes that ancient texts declare the existence of the authorities. "Everyone knows that the authorities exercise supreme control over each one of us ... and this is even specifically stated in the writings of our ancient teachers" (166). While Garrity compares these texts to the literary canon which marginalises women (268), this body of writing can also be compared to the body of written law, since law is fundamentally a textual artifact. In this vein, the narrator describes an imposing body of documents:

> The pile is seen from the side, very monumental in the strong light, as if made of stone. The effect is somewhat of a model cenotaph squarely set on the dark featureless plane. ... Cold white light edges the edges of certain projecting forms, striating the black-shadowed perpendicularity. ... (118)

In extreme close-up, this majestic heap of pages is "monumental," and reminiscent of a funerary monument at that. Its "black-shadowed perpendicularity" resembles a cenotaph or gravestone. Later Kavan's protagonist B is interrogated by a multitude of carceral professionals, "doctors, civil servants, professors, government officials ... [and] white-coated workers comparing case notes," all at work on a multitude of "college, hospital, government forms snowing into a pile" (*Sleep* 122), documents classifying and disciplining human bodies. B's anguished self-defence invites us to approach her speech through the lens of refugee experience in wartime Britain. " 'I came as a stranger ... bringing only [myself] a present that I wanted to give you ... Am I accused because you, wanting a victim and not a friend, threw away the only thing which I had to give?' " (*Sleep* 123). Her cry echoes that of internee Pollak, who laments, "We put up a long struggle to maintain this freedom and we were ready to participate in the great fight for the freedom of our land from tyranny, but we were rejected" (*Departure* 2). Kavan's narrator experiences the same rejection: multiple voices intone that "B does not concentrate ... Does not adapt ... Does not co-operate ... Does not compromise ... Not satisfactory ... unsatisfactory ... Does not ... Un ... Dis ... Does not ... Non ... Un ... Not ... Non ... No. ..." (*Sleep* 123–4, ellipses in original). At the same time, however, this list of incoherent negations shows the vulnerability of the law's position: as Punter notes, "[T]he law's victims are always in danger of sliding between its stretching fingers, of reducing the law to a merely sonorous rhetoric which resounds in our ears and signifies nothing" (*Pathologies* 46–7). This catalogue of negations literally signifies nothing.

Kavan's protagonists are not passive and try to read signs within their carceral locales. In the Gothic mode, however, such efforts are doomed to failure. The blurry printing B sees on the chaos of forms, for example, cannot be deciphered (*Sleep* 122). Salomon argues that horror narratives' fascination with hieroglyphs bespeak "the impossibility of deriving significant human meaning from language acts" (94). Salomon's argument is valuable, but these failures of meaning in Kavan wartime prose can be fruitfully historicised beyond reading them as symptomatic of the general fragility of meaning in modernity. Kavan's character B asks in desperation, "Is it my fault that a charge has been laid secretly against me in a different language?" (*Sleep* 123). She seeks to translate the case made against her, and her plight echoes that of much refugee experience in wartime Britain (and indeed since): she is treated as guilty, and proving she is not requires she master an opaque and imperious system. In Second World War Britain, deciphering signs is key to refugee experience both literally (learning language and different cultural practices) and figuratively (interpreting opaque laws governing alien movement).

Similarly, the London of "Our City" abounds in cryptic signs, but efforts to read them are thwarted. Aural signs became particularly salient in home front cities, people coming to value sounds as reliable signifiers of the city's events. Amid blackout and blitz, vision in home front cities no longer had orienting power, so other senses filled the breach. Sounds could identify dangers. The siren itself was a "prolonged banshee howling" (Nicholson 55) and a "melancholy dirge ... like ritual wailings of barbarous obsequies" (Powell 5); bombers had a characteristic throb; breaking glass had a "snake-like sibilance" (M. Anderson 20), incendiary bombs clattered, fire crackled and German bombs wailed since each was fitted with a cardboard siren. People gained new kinds of aural literacy and sound became "a precious index to Blitz events" (Wasson 89). In Kavan's urban Gothic, however, even aural signs are not helpful – in fact, the devastating excess of sound defeats human comprehension. "The noise batters the night with unappeasable fury ... an absolutely inhuman excess of noise" (*Lazarus* 129–130). Such an aural sublime defeats attempts to interpret sound. Increasingly, aural signs are depicted as physically dangerous in themselves. The protagonist of "Our City" feels violated by the clamour and, later, physically threatened by the silence:

> Through the darkness of the blacked-out windows I am aware of an indescribable movement throughout the city, a soundless spinning of motion in the streets and among the ruins, an unseen upward surge of building: the silence industriously, insecurely, building itself up. ... [T]the frail edifice mounts up quickly towards the moon. Soon the precarious work is finished, the whole city is roofed, covered in with silence, as if lying under a black cloche. ... With compressed lips and foreheads lined with anxiety every citizen crouches uneasily, peering up at the transparent black bell of silence hanging over our city. Is it going to break? (*Lazarus* 131)

Here, the silence is figured as performing a work of terrible mystery. Sound and silence are more than mere indexes to events; in Kavan's Gothic fiction, they themselves become threats.[39]

Untrustworthy though aural signs may be, Kavan sometimes depicts the written word as refuge. Throughout *Sleep*, B. is repeatedly seen floating reading within an enclosure, reading: the little girl sits "in a quiet place ... reading a book ... Everything here is springlike and very much simplified; just the grass and the innocent green tree and the child" (*Sleep* 31) and later, the girl is seen reading serenely inside a bubble (*Sleep* 84). Similarly, "Our City" suggests that the written word can be a protector. The ninth section opens by noting that the poet Rainer Maria Rilke's books defended him from the world's casual cruelties and the narrator muses that she, too, has books as bodyguards, "members of a suicide squad who do not hesitate to engage the enormously superior enemy, life, on my behalf" (*Lazarus* 140). But even books ultimately betray the vulnerable narrator of "Our City." She becomes passionately attached to one particular book, a horror story which appalled the public – "I remember the horror the story inspired in the land, and how I wondered that any normal brain could conceive and elaborate so dreadful a theme" (*Lazarus* 140). Yet as time passes and her own plight worsens, she gradually comes to suspect that the book is of unique significance to her:

> How can I describe the profoundly disturbing suspicion that slowly grew upon me. ... [L]ike a latent venom it dwelt obstinately in my

blood, poisoning me with the idea that the story told in the book related to myself. ... [T]he terrible book revealed itself as my manual, tracing the path I was doomed to tread, step by step, to the lamentable and shameful end. (*Lazarus* 140–1)

Rather than the book being a refuge from external control, it becomes an instrument for that control, forcing her to follow a deadly script. The signs that end the story are no more auspicious:

I passed a stranger who glanced coldly at me, and other strangers passed by with cold faces, and still other strangers. Armoured vehicles, eccentrically coloured, stood in an endless chain at the roadside, painted with cabalistic signs. But what these symbols meant I had no idea. I had no idea if there were a place anywhere to which I could go to escape from the strangeness, or what I could do to bear being a stranger in a strange city. (*Lazarus* 145–6)

The isolated narrator finds no fellowship in glances from fellow inhabitants and no meaning in the military sigils which mark the urban space. This story closes in despair and dread.

Raymond Williams notes that bleak literary representations of urban space often contrast cities unfavourably with countryside, implying the latter is less inimical to human life. Yet Kavan offers no such comforting contrast. In fact, she challenges that binary in a subversive Gothic revision of the wartime fantasy of idealised English pre-war idyll:

roses round the door, elm-muffled peaceable strokes of church clock striking the tea hour ... unseen pigeons cooing. ...

Twilight gathers quickly ... roses droop, wither, fall, their petals are blown away; the pigeon coos hoarsen to ominous hooting as a huge spectral white owl with lambent eyes sweeps stealthily past. ...

In deepening darkness dimly seen conspiratorial forms, wearing some kind of horrific disguise-uniform (Inquisition or Ku-Klux-Klan suggestion). ... The Hanged Man swings from a black tree. ...

Mist wraiths coagulate, hover lugubriously, disintegrate, among dark shapes of bushes or tombstones or crouching things. (*Sleep* 175–6)

A military commander appears urging young boys to fight, "hovering batlike and spraying from the poison ducts at the back of his vampire fangs a fine rain of blood" (177). In this dream sequence,

Kavan warps the popular ideal of pre-war England into tortured Gothic. Kavan does not nostalgically idealise a prewar pastoral. Rather, she suggests that prewar idylls already held racism and sadism (the "Ku-Klux-Klan"), laying the ground for a war in which those categorised as Other will be hounded. Kavan's work of fantastical persecution renders wartime oppressions visible, telling the suffering of the marginalised in nightmarish forms.

Graham Greene's *The Ministry of Fear* (1943)

Very different from Kavan's wartime writing, Greene's *Ministry of Fear* deploys the Gothic mode with a conservative agenda. While Kavan uses the Gothic to depict threats to the individual in the form of state and psychiatric cruelties, Greene deploys Gothic tropes to depict threats to the state from fifth columnists. As such, it illustrates that the Gothic mode is not invariably subversive.

Greene's title was inspired by William Wordworth's *The Prelude* (1805–6, rev. 1850) which praises nature's benevolent nurturing of the human mind. Nature is a "ministry" which fosters the human mind "by beauty and by fear" (1805, Book I, ll. 494, 306). For Wordsworth, the ministry of fear is nature's tender way of awakening humans to awe, joy and a sense of all life as interconnected ("Tintern Abbey," ll. 95–103). In Greene's novel, by contrast, the "ministry" is a Nazi group which blackmails British subjects into joining the fifth column (124). Greene's novel is a dark inversion of Wordsworth's vision (Hoskins 34). Contrary to the wartime reality, in this novel fifth columnists not only exist but exist in multitudes; at one point, protagonist Arthur Rowe marvels at their vast numbers, and Anna Hilfe agrees there are "An awful lot. More every day" (104). The novel characterises refugee aliens and their British supporters in stark terms. Although Willi Hilfe is ostensibly a young Austrian refugee and charity-worker, he turns out to be an Aryan nihilist who savours murder, for "wherever men killed his spirit moved in obscure companionship" (227). The British sympathisers are equally villainous. British psychiatrist Dr Forrester defends Nazi euthanasia of the elderly and infirm (194) and Poole, his asylum attendant, is "dark and dwarfish and twisted in his enormous shoulders with infantile paralysis" (15), "deformed" with "simian" arms (14, 22, 131). In the reactionary logic of the novel, Poole's physical deformities echo his deviant ideological position. In a similar way, the Gothic trappings of Lew Landers' film *Return of the Vampire* (1944) are recruited to the wartime narrative of a treacherous fifth column of spies. Bela Lugosi's vampire, Armand Tesla, poses as a German refugee scientist, and his werewolf ally is a fifth columnist embedded in British society for decades then recruited to undermine it from within.

Greene's novel depicts a hunt for photographic film holding photographs of documents describing weaknesses in Britain's defences. Fifth columnists are trying to send the film out of Britain for Nazi perusal, and if they succeed, Blitz wreckage would be nothing by comparison with the resulting annihilation (175). The spies hide the film in a cake and make the cake a prize in a fête competition, which they rig so another spy should win. The collector is meant to get the answer to the competition from the fortune-teller's booth. By sheer chance, Rowe attends the fête and uses the code phrase the fortune-teller is waiting for: he asks her to tell him his future, although that is against the law (fortune-tellers were only permitted to tell the past). She tells him the answer to the cake competition, and he wins the cake. Later, the organisers realise the mistake and try to kill him, but are thwarted when Rowe's home is destroyed in a raid. Bewildered by the assassination attempt, Rowe investigates the charity that organised the fête, run by Austrian refugees Willi and Anna Hilfe. Willi seems eager to help him and takes him to Mrs Bellairs' house in search of clues. While there, Rowe is pressed to attend a séance, during which he is framed for a murder – someone is apparently stabbed with Rowe's knife while the lights are out. In fear he literally goes underground to a public air raid shelter. The next day he is manipulated into helping an old man carry a suitcase into a hotel, then detained in a hotel room. To his surprise Anna Hilfe is there waiting for him: she has come to warn him about the organisation that hunts him. They hear people approach and Rowe opens the suitcase in desperation. It contains a bomb, which explodes and renders Rowe amnesiac for months. He forgets his identity and is confined in a private asylum run by the organisation. When his memory eventually returns, he contacts Scotland Yard, who find his information useful in their search for the film. Rowe tracks down the film to Willi Hilfe's possession, and retrieves it. Hilfe commits suicide, and Rowe becomes romantically involved with Anna.

Narrated thus, the novel sounds like a glib thriller with a happy ending. Yet such a summary misses the strangeness of the wartime city Rowe traverses. Rowe is a haunted man who experiences wartime London as a carceral metropolis, filled with uncanny terrains and cryptic signs. He is an outcast who finds the city hostile and who feels wholly estranged from war camaraderie. In this urban terrain, he feels "directed, controlled, moulded, by some agency with a surrealist imagination" (97).

The threat Rowe fears most is his own pity (19). "People could always get things out of him by wanting them enough: it broke his precarious calm to feel that people suffered. Then he would do anything for them. Anything" (14) – even murder them. As a child, he is unable to bear the sight of a paralysed rat suffering with a broken back, so he smashes the creature's skull in a frenzy (64) and as an adult, he cannot bear to watch his wife die slowly in pain of a long illness, so he poisons her without asking if she wants death. After the murder Rowe is tried in court and briefly incarcerated in an asylum. Even before his crime he was never rich in friends (73) and since then he has been ostracised by all but one. He dreads contact with people he knows, and defines home as somewhere "to shelter from people who might know him" (88).

Although spy novels often feature taciturn, independent heroes, Rowe's isolation is not voluntary. He tries to get involved in the war effort, but is excluded from it:

> God damn it, he thought. ... I've done my best to take part too. It's not my fault I'm not fit enough for the army, and as for the damned heroes of civil defence – the little clerks and prudes and what-have-yous – they didn't want me: not when they found I had done time – even time in an asylum wasn't respectable enough for Post Four or Post Two or Post any number. And now they've thrown me out of their war altogether. (75)

The London he encounters is rife with distrust, with even the waitresses and hotel commissionaires he encounters repeatedly suspicious of him. He is even more isolated than an enemy alien. When he asks Anna Hilfe, a refugee, how to live if he cannot go to his bank, she suggests he ask a friend to cash a cheque for him. He is ashamed to admit he has nobody to ask. "Refugees always had friends; people smuggled letters, arranged passports, bribed officials; in that enormous underground land as wide as a continent there was companionship" (78). Rowe, by contrast, is alone. Amid such solitude, Rowe is imprisoned inside himself: "to go through life without trust ... is to be imprisoned in the worst cell of all, oneself. For more than a year now ... there had been no change of cell, no exercise-yard, no unfamiliar warder to break the monotony of solitary confinement" (38).

Unsurprisingly, then, Rowe experiences wartime London as a prison. The city torments him in that it awakens memories of experiences he shared with his dead wife. "Perhaps if every street with which he had associations were destroyed, he would be free to go. ... After a raid he used to sally out and note with a kind of hope that this restaurant or that shop existed no longer – it was like loosening the bars of a prison cell one by one" (14). His guilt and grief make the city a jail, and he views his carceral London through a filter preoccupied with death. A city office block is a "mechanised mortuary with a separate lift for every slab" (35); the safes in the wreckage of the Safe Deposit resemble "above-ground tombs in Latin cemeteries" (74); the "obliterated acres" of Paternoster Row are a "Pompeiian landscape" (175). Rowe's London is a city of premature endings and finality. Redemptive possibilities are few.

In this grim landscape, Rowe tries to make sense of a multitude of aural signs. As discussed earlier, raids saw hearing become a particularly valued sense, but for Rowe hearing is of little help. When a bomb does devastate his house hearing gives no warning. "They hadn't heard the plane this time: destruction had come quietly drifting down on green silk cords; the walls suddenly caved in. They were not even aware of noise" (21). Hearing is unreliable. In addition, while the narrator of Kavan's "Our City" is devastated by an aural sublime, the protagonist of Greene's *Ministry* is disturbed by an aural uncanny (Stewart). He hears bombers approach seeking him personally, muttering "Where are you?" "like a witch in a child's dream" (18, 22) and in the course of the novel he imagines that he hears his wife's voice from beyond the grave and hears the city's very streets wail in pain.

In these unsettling urban terrains, the Blitzed buildings parallel his personal ruin: "in the strange torn landscape where London shops were reduced to a stone ground-plan like those of Pompeii he moved with a certain familiarity. ... It was as if the ruins were part of his own mind" (34). The damaged city represents his damaged self. Yet this place also functions as a stage on which he tries to take action, to resist despair and strive for comprehension. In the course of the novel, Rowe traverses dream-like terrains resembling prewar countryside, a hotel that is a blend of labyrinth and mausoleum, and a psychiatric hospital. In each, Gothic trappings convey the sufferings of a marginalised man.

Prewar pastoral versus wartime city

The Nazi sympathisers are presented as morally flawed in their inability to cherish particular place: they feel no ties to particular villages or towns (123). Rowe, by contrast, cherishes a particular place, musing "I am one of the little men ... tied to a flat Cambridgeshire landscape" (137). Rowe cherishes not only a particular place, but a particular time: his loved location is distant temporally as well as geographically, for its happiness is irrevocably pre-war. His greatest longing in life is to lose his

memories of his wife and her murder (4) so he prizes a schoolboy pen-
knife and books he read as a child because they hold no adult memories
for him (12). In the course of roaming through the wartime city Rowe
encounters two simulations of his cherished prewar rural life, each triggering nostalgic longing.

Many critics read Rowe's nostalgia as Greene's (Watts; Cuoto;
Spurling) but Greene himself speaks scathingly of nostalgia, particularly that inspired by country life: "it is easy to construct a dream town
where unhappiness has the faded air of history. But to live there you
must build the walls, not round the town, but round yourself, exclud-
ing any knowledge that the eye doesn't take in" ("Conservative" 361).
The Ministry of Fear challenges the notion of a pastoral prewar ideal,
for Rowe's visions of rural bliss mutate into the nightmarish wartime
city. Like Kavan, Greene does not contrast city and country in order to
nostalgically privilege the latter. Instead, he implies that prewar peace
already held the seeds of cruelty.

The first simulation of prewar pastoral Rowe encounters is a "village
fête," that iconic event of the English countryside calendar bizarrely
recreated in a bombed London square. The fête is an archetypal emblem
of English pastoral idyll (DeCoste 435) and it inspires Rowe with wistful
joy, reminding him of fêtes in attended as a child in a Cambridgeshire
village. "The fête called him like innocence: it was entangled in childhood, with vicarage gardens, and girls in white summer frocks, and the
smell of herbaceous borders, and security" (1). This fête functions as a
heterotopia, a zone within which normal rules are suspended: Rowe
steps "joyfully back into adolescence, into childhood" (3). Time often
functions strangely within a heterotopia, and Foucault coins the term
"heterochrony" to describe heterotopias' temporal twists (par. 24). At
first the fête's heterochronies comfort Rowe. He buys a children's book,
enters a competition to guess the weight of a cake, and has his fortune
told – all staple activities of the traditional fête. As the fête progresses,
however, he becomes conscious of reminders of his murderous adulthood. Some houses in the square have been bombed to rubble and
others lack walls; in a less cosy analogy from childhood, he can see a
fire-place "half-way up a wall like a painted fire-place in a cheap doll's
house" (1). The ruined city represents for Rowe his damaged adult life.
"It was as if Providence had led him to exactly this point to indicate
the difference between then and now. These people might have been
playing a part in an expensive morality for his sole benefit" (5). Here
and elsewhere Rowe's loss of innocence is depicted in spatial terms:
he approaches the fête "hesitantly, like an intruder, or an exile who

has returned home after many years and is uncertain of his welcome"
(2). Exiled from innocence, he belongs "to the region of murder – he
was a native of that country" (58). Rowe represents innocence as a
particular terrain. However, closer scrutiny suggests that this prewar-
style fête is not quite so pure an emblem of innocence. This archetypal
fête is a gate to the menacing world that Rowe inhabits for the rest of
the novel.

Two things destabilise Rowe's neat equation of prewar pastoral with
innocence and wartime city with transgression. First, the codeword that
triggers the spy plot in the first place – Rowe asking Mrs Bellairs to tell
him his future – actually breaks the law (Stewart 69). Later in the novel
Rowe is pressured into attending a séance led by that same fortune-
teller. Between 1735 and 1951, clairvoyant prediction and mediumship
could be prosecuted under the Witchcraft Act, and both were seen as
explicit threats to national security during the Second World War. The
medium Helen Duncan was the last woman to be prosecuted as a witch
in Britain, and she was incarcerated during the Second World War for
breaching national security by informing clients of the death of loved
ones before they received official notification of death from the government.[40] The second thing which destabilises the equation of prewar pastoral with innocence is the way that the fifth columnists themselves are
repeatedly associated with qualities of prewar England. Willi Hilfe uses
"antiquated" slang and forms a "Victorian family group" with his sister,
and Dr Forrester resembles a Victorian portrait (38–9, 115). Damon
DeCoste notes these Nazi sympathisers "are conspicuous in their being
palpably of another, earlier time" (435). This, too, undermines any easy
equation of the prewar period with innocence.

Rowe encounters his second simulation of prewar pastoral in a dream
in a public shelter. He dreams he is a child in a garden with his mother,
but the pastoral idyll transforms to a hallucinatory urban warscape:

> somebody was crying in the dark with terror. ... A policeman stood at
> his elbow and said in a woman's voice, "You had better join our lit-
> tle group," and urged him remorselessly towards a urinal where a rat
> bled to death in the slate trough. The music had stopped, the lights
> had gone, and he couldn't remember why he had come to this vile
> corner where even the ground whined when he pressed it as if it had
> learned the trick of suffering.
>
>   He said, "Please let me go away from here," and the policeman
> said, "Where do you want to go to, dear?" he said, "Home," and the
> policeman said, "This is home. There isn't anywhere else at all," and

whenever he tried to move his feet the earth whined back at him: he couldn't move an inch without causing pain. (65–6)

The nightmare comes true twice, the air-raid sirens mimicking the whimpering floor of his dream. When he wakes, the sirens are sounding the All-Clear, but "Nobody moved to go home: this was their home now" (66). In Rowe's final showdown with the spy Hilfe, the siren's sound "came from everywhere ... the floor of the urinal whined under his feet" (234). His nightmare mimics Blitz reality. But the seeds for the nightmare were laid in the *prewar* past: the guilt that drives the dream was caused by Rowe's pathological inability, even as a child, to witness the suffering of another. The rat bleeding in the trough condenses both a paralysed rat he slew in childhood and his pain-wracked wife he later murdered. Although Rowe himself draws emphatic distinctions between wartime city and prewar country, the nightmare belies the glib division. Rowe's wartime torments are rooted in pathologies which precede the war. As in Kavan, the novel complicates any neat binary of prewar rural idyll versus nightmarish wartime city.

Unexpected prisons: the Regal Hotel and a psychiatric hospital

Two additional places in Greene's novel invite scrutiny with respect to the home front's carceral spaces: the Regal Hotel and the psychiatric sanatorium, in each of which Rowe is confined. The hotel is at first presented as a triumph of modern design (99, 97) but it has a darker side. Rowe asks his guide " 'Do you unreel a thread of cotton?' " (98), implying the hotel is a labyrinth holding a minotaur at its heart. Further, the hotel is described as a place of death and interment: people "died here and the bodies were removed unobtrusively by the service lifts" (99) and the hotel rooms look "as if the inhabitants had been walled up" (100). Even the rooms of the living resemble walled graves.

The hotel is also characterised by the aural uncanny.[41] As Rowe walks through the halls, "A door in the passage was ajar and odd sounds came through it, as though some one were alternately whistling and sighing" (99) and the silence is more unnerving than the sounds:

This was a modern building; the silence was admirable and disquieting. Instead of bells ringing lights went on and off. One got the impression that all the time people were signaling news of great importance that couldn't wait. The silence, now that they were out of earshot of the whistle and the sigh, was like that of a stranded liner: the engines had stopped, and in the sinister silence you listened for the faint depressing sound of lapping water. (99)

Both Allied and Axis powers were menaced by submarines or "U-boats," and this silent edifice has resonances of a torpedoed ship. By February 1941 an average of 700,000 tons of British ships had been sunk each month (Calder, *People* 231–2).[42] As Rowe's night in the hotel progresses, the torpedoed boat analogy becomes even more apt for the spies have cut off all heating and light to their hotel room. "The world was sliding rapidly towards night: like a torpedoed liner heeling too far over, she would soon take her last dive into darkness" (107). The metaphor of the hotel as a sinking liner presents an architectural triumph of modernity through a bleak wartime lens. The hotel is a boat under attack; the city is a marine warfront.

   The second place in which Rowe is incarcerated is a psychiatric hospital. The spies' bomb at the hotel causes him to lose his memory, and during the subsequent months he is kept in a private psychiatric sanatorium run by Dr Forrester, a fifth columnist. Forrester decrees narcosis – "[P]lenty of sleep ... some very gentle bromides" (140) – and all the inmates are menaced by the euphemistic "sick bay," a locked wing for people under restraint. "Nobody cared to talk about the sick bay – grim things were assumed, a padded room, strait-jackets: you could only see the top windows from the garden, and they were barred. No man in the sanatorium was ignorant of how close he lived to that quiet wing" (129). As the novel progresses, it becomes clear that the sick bay is used to imprison and torture inmates who discover incriminating evidence against the doctor. Unlike Kavan's depictions of asylums, in Greene's version the asylum cruelties are not state-sanctioned but are due rather to the warped morality of his fifth columnists. Like Kavan's literary asylums the asylum is a place of seeming benevolence but actual horror. In both, asylums are less sites for restoring mental welfare than sites for stifling resistance.

   The novel's section titles imply the book describes a process of healing. Rowe moves from being "The Unhappy Man" to being the "The Whole Man," having reached greater knowledge of the world and a new romantic attachment. Analysis, however, reveals a more pessimistic narrative arc. Even at the end of the novel, Rowe still longs for air raids to destroy the city's buildings – "there was such a lot which had to be destroyed before peace came" (231) – and he finds himself confined in a new prison, that of eternal deceit. He and his new lover have to lie to each other forever. She is unaware he has remembered his murder of his wife, and is determined to protect him from that pain of that discovery, while he, in turn, is determined to conceal his returned memory, for he knows that would hurt her too. "They had to tread carefully for a life-time, never speak without thinking twice; they must watch each other like enemies because they loved each other so much" (236). Rowe is permanently webbed in a network of guilt, deception and loneliness.

In Greene's novel, Gothic trappings tend to bespeak threats to the state; in Kavan's, the Gothic bespeaks threats to the individual. For the narra-tor of Kavan's "Our City," the metropolis is a monstrous city of tentacles and bone-shearing metal; for Greene's Rowe, the city is a nightmare site of imprisonment and loneliness. In both, the wartime city is a carceral metropolis of strange signs, where outsiders suffer in isolation. The next chapter examines carceral spaces oriented towards production, asking how spaces of industry constructed otherness on the Second World War home front.

4
Gothic, Mechanised Ghosts: Wartime Industry in Inez Holden, Anne Ridler and Diana Murray Hill

This chapter examines texts which use the Gothic mode to depict the work done in Second World War factories. Government propaganda, film and workers' diaries present factory labour as community-building and personally enriching. By contrast, writing by Inez Holden, Anne Ridler and Diana Murray Hill constructs industry as a site of barbaric toil and isolation.

Since its inception, the Gothic has expressed class conflicts as well as intrapsychic ones. Industrialisation was crucial to the rise of the late eighteenth-century novels of Walpole, Radcliffe and others in that it gave rise to the growing class of the bourgeosie. This emerging middle class – particularly women – consumed Gothic novels voraciously, and critics have argued that their class anxieties underlie the novels' fantastic scenarios (Botting, *Gothic* 19; Moretti; Punter, *Terror* 2: 205, 215n36). In addition, industrialisation gave rise to new sense of compulsion: Lucien Goldmann suggests that under capitalism, regulation "impos[es] itself" on individuals "as the mechanical action of an outside force" (qtd. in Punter, *Terror* 1: 136). Link notes, following China Miéville, that twentieth-century Gothic, too, is "often fuelled by the anxiety that citizens are owned, controlled, and consumed by the structures of capitalist urban space" (521). Second World War industrial workplaces update these motifs of external coercion and class division. In the texts of this chapter, the Gothic mode enables commentary on the darker realities of industry during and directly after the war, depicting workplaces as fraught with violence both physical and psychological.

The second critical tradition invoked in this chapter is that of gender and the Gothic. When the Gothic novel emerged in the eighteenth century it was often written and consumed by women. In the early 1970s, Ellen Moers coined the term "female Gothic," defining it as Gothic writing *by* women, and arguing that such writing often depicts the horrors of childbirth, postnatal ambivalence or the struggle of a persecuted heroine (*Literary Women* 90). In Showalter's words, "the women's liberation movement of the late 1960s … [underpinned] the theorisation of the Female Gothic as a genre that expressed women's dark protests, fantasies, and fear" (*Sister's Choice* 127).[43] Moers's version of the female Gothic has been extensively critiqued for being essentialising, an accusation which gained even more force after Foucault's constructivism became pivotal to gender studies through the work of Butler (*Gender Trouble, Bodies that Matter*) and Eve Sedgwick (*Epistemology*). Critics influenced by these theorists recognise gender as a narrative construction, which is not to say that it is purely a matter of individual agency; it is inescapable and unconscious.[44] Alison Milbank and others demonstrated that an author's gender is no bar to engaging with "female" or "male" Gothic plots, and the 1990s saw several critics define female Gothic in terms of a characteristic plot rather than the gender of the author. Anne Williams, Claire Kahane and Eugenia DeLamotte, for example, suggest that female Gothic often features a quest for a lost mother and a flight from a diabolic father figure, ending with the heroine secure in a happy marriage.

In the 1970s and 1980s, Nancy Chodorow's work on the way traditional psychoanalysis effaces mothers inspired critics to revisit the way that female Gothic is often haunted by ghostly traces of a lost mother (Kahane 336; cf. DeLamotte; Miles, *Ann Radcliffe* 105–10). In the late-1980s/1990s criticism came under the influence of a different strand of feminist psychoanalysis: that of Hélène Cixous, Luce Irigaray and Julia Kristeva, poststructuralist feminists influenced by Jacques Lacan. Using their theory, critics analysed Gothic scenarios as metaphors for the ways that women are marginalised in a world that predicates language as masculine (Showalter, *Sister's Choice* 127; Bronfen, "Hysteria, Fantasy"; Jacobus 201; Sedgwick, *Coherence*). Although psychoanalysis has been used persuasively to analyse eighteenth-century Gothic as presenting family structures under patriarchy, it has sometimes led to dehistoricising texts, universalising the family as a nuclear oedipal unit and downplaying diverse material circumstances (A. Smith and D. Wallace, "Female Gothic"; Baldick and Mighall 227).

Miles warns against the term "female Gothic" "harden[ing] into a literary category" ("Female Gothic" 132). Faced with that risk, some of the richest deployments of female Gothic in the last two decades have taken historicist approaches. Kate Ferguson Ellis, for example, examines how Gothic was influenced by the social construction of domestic space in the late eighteenth century (*Contested Castle*) and Janet Todd (262), E. J. Clery (194n18), Ellen Moers (*Literary Women* 136) and Mary Poovey (323) have shown that women's anxieties over their fragile grasp of property underlie many Gothic scenarios, as I discuss in Chapter 5. Historicist criticism can analyse how the material circumstances of particular classes of women may be represented and interrogated in that period's Gothic forms.[45]

Despite their differences, all the aforegoing critical approaches to female Gothic tend to argue that a text's Gothic tropes and narrative forms permit nightmarish representations of the real experience of women, be that ambivalence towards birth or suffering at the hands of a cruel, unequal world. This chapter and the next explore how certain forms of gendered experience are described in the Gothic mode at this particular historical moment. Criticism of gender and the Gothic often focuses on depictions of women in domestic spaces, and I address this body of criticism in the next chapter. In this chapter I examine literary representations of subordinate work in wartime factories, themselves increasingly female spaces during the Second World War.

The texts of this chapter cannot be classified as female Gothic in the earliest definitions of the term. Although the writers are female, their novels do not demonstrate preoccupations with childbearing as Moers outlined, nor do they have the happy endings or other formal structures which critics have catalogued in theorising "Male" versus "Female" Gothic literary forms. These texts of wartime industry resist the traditional persecutory plot in three ways. First, the protagonists in these texts are tormented not by a particular diabolic villain but by impersonal authority, the machinery of government compulsion. Secondly, women are by no means the only marginalised figures: as I will show, noncombatant men occupied feminised positions during the war, and men marked as other by ethnicity, national identity, or mental illness were also represented in gender-ambiguous terms. Thirdly, the female protagonists in these texts are not innocent heroines. The concept of female Gothic first took shape in the late 1970s and 1980s, at a period when feminist criticism was often uncomfortable with texts that did not depict women as wholly positive; by contrast, more recent critical work recognises "women as being as capable of exploitation as men" (Horner and Zlosnik, "Skin Chairs" 99). Challenges to essentialist categories of gender have also triggered challenges to discourse of female innocence. Although Moers celebrated the "heroism" of female protagonists, texts classified as female Gothic tend to feature victimised heroines longing for rescue. Diane Long Hoeveler has argued that as such they enabled female readers to construct themselves as "professional victims" (xii), a disingenuous posture which belied women's own agency and complicity with power structures. Genz and Brabon call for the relationship between Gothic and feminism to be "re-imagine[d] ... in a way that does not take ... an essentialising positioning of women as innocent victims" (*PostFeminist Gothic* 7). The texts of this chapter recognise women as complicit with war violence. Like men, women could resist conscription by pleading conscientious objection, and although this course was rarely invoked and often unsuccessful, the fact the option existed shows that the government recognised war-factory work as implicated in violence.

Any claim that these texts feature the Gothic mode thus proceeds not from these texts' reproductive anxieties (which are negligible), nor from a particular "female Gothic" plot; rather, these texts show strands of the Gothic mode insofar as they depict a carceral reality of deadening alienation and insofar as they resist coherent narrative progression and a satisfactory *dénouement*. These texts do, however, use the Gothic mode to describe gendered inequities suffered at a particular period and place. The female (or feminised) protagonists of this chapter's texts experience claustrophobia, a sense of their options being limited due to their gender and the knowledge of being confined in a dangerous environment. These texts subvert a key national myth of the war period, namely, the notion of factories as sites of fellowship. By contrast, these fictions show failed communities, riven by prejudice and loneliness.

Women's wartime work

By 1939 women were not as housebound as in earlier decades but the complex responsibility of housekeeping was still women's work. As a result, in an era where even doing laundry meant a day of vigorous labour, most housewives could not work outside the home. The First World War had seen women enter many spheres of public working life including factories (Griffiths), but they were never conscripted. That changed in December 1941 when women were conscripted for civilian labour "for the first time in any civilised nation" (Calder, *People* 267). The first round of conscription specified only unmarried women aged twenty to thirty, but as war progressed it broadened until in July 1943 all women up to age 51 were registered, including married women whose husbands were not in the forces (Calder, *People* 268, 332).[46] Women worked in factories, the Auxiliary Territorial Service (ATS) (primarily transport), the Women's Auxiliary Air Force (WAAF), the

Women's Royal Naval Service (WRENS), the Land Army (agriculture) and numerous other roles, including spying and bearing arms in the Home Guard (Goodall, *Voices* 142). By mid-1943, 90 per cent of single women between ages of eighteen and forty were working as were many married women.[47] Mass-Observation noted in 1940 that many women "are now doing a man's job, sharing with men danger and hardship" ("Women and Morale" 1).

Feminist histories often depict women's work on the home front as enriching and liberating, permanently transforming women's lives for the better. Nella Last, for example, declares that her wartime work made her more independent, and muses, "I cannot see women settling [back] to trivial ways – women who have done worthwhile things" (510, 512). Fiction, too, features inspiring figures like the elderly protagonist of Edna Ferber's "Grandma Isn't Playing" (1943) who relishes factory work and the independence she gains. Close ties existed between the film industry and the Ministry of Information, the government propaganda body (Hartley 72), and films were even more consistently positive. The film *Millions Like Us* (1943), for example, was explicitly designed to encourage women to go to war factories. In the film, the women who work in the aeroplane factory overcome class divides, care for each other and feel satisfied by their labours. Similarly, the documentary *Night Shift* (1942) directed by Jack Chambers, shows women working in a tank-gun factory and finding it rewarding and comradely, and the influential propaganda film *Listen to Britain* (1942), directed by Humphrey Jennings and Stewart McAllister, depicts women working happily in a factory (Calder, *Myth* 239). Such energetic propaganda might suggest that the government was eager to see women permanently recognised as valued workers, but the government never intended to challenge sex discrimination in industry; a Treasury report noted, "it was not contemplated that the Government should run ahead of outside practice, and of course, sex discrimination is deeply embedded in industrial ... practice" (Barlow 67–8). Many elements of women's wartime work remained inequitable, particularly pay: women received on average half or less of the male wage (Riley 131).[48] In addition, much of the work was wearisome, basic and monotonous. Bryher laments that "What we wanted was ... the same right as men to work at interesting jobs. The First World War had opened a few doors but ... the Second slammed many of them shut" (120).

Furthermore, alternative narratives undermined that of heroic female labour. Documents praising women's work in industry often casts their success in domestic terms. Married women, for example, are hailed in government propaganda as "seem[ing] to carry over their household pride into their job" (Riley 124) and a 1943 propaganda pamphlet entitled "Women in Shipbuilding" declares:

> It is no exaggeration to say that the average woman takes to welding as readily as she takes to knitting ... both require a small, fairly complex manipulative movement which is repeated many times, combined with a kind of subconscious concentration at which women excel. (qtd. in Riley 127)

Advertisements propose similar equations. After women become bargees, for example, a Hoover vacuum cleaner advertisement declares "The Hand that Held the Hoover guides the Barge!" (Hoover 490). Such discourse tended to undercut women's working triumphs. As Gilbert and Gubar argue, "women who entered the labour force ... paradoxically faced a heightened rhetoric about women's proper place in the home" ("Charred Skirts" 214). Historians Penny Summerfield, Shelley Saywell, and Dorothy Sheridan argue that wartime propaganda actually did profound violence to women's interests, for "challenges to women's subordination were contained within an overarching nationalist rhetoric which positioned woman at the heart of the family in her idealised role of wife and mother" (Sheridan 3). Gill Plain observes that "traditional images of femininity remained throughout the war, contradicting and undermining the powerful figure of the female war worker" (27); advertisements and women's magazines frequently implied that women's chief desire was to be beautiful for men and to care for a house.[49] It was not just advertisements and women's magazines which depict women's feminine performance as integral to the war effort: the Ministry of Supply, too, chose to allocate some of Britain's scarce steel and rubber resources into manufacturing corsets (Hylton 211). Traditional ideas about each gender's rightful place were not erased by the need for wartime labour.[50]

A second discouraging echo of a Victorian framework of femininity is the infantalising language that accretes around women's factory labours, especially with respect to older women. Some managers inveighed against the inadequacies of "older women – over 31" (Summerfield 58–9), while others found such "older" women were best used for simple tasks: one (female) welfare officer declared, "A factory like ours always has a lot of more or less 'childish' jobs that would irk a lively youngster in five minutes, but which we find ideal for grannies" (Hylton 210) – the "grannies" in question being aged 35! Similarly, Denise Riley notes that older, married women were often depicted as "docile employees unbothered by repetitive tasks ... [who] were held to ... accept willingly, the traditional position of economic and prestige inferiority" (126). In this way, too, wartime discourse of femininity was still affected by nineteenth-century paradigms.

An additional way in which the Gothic meshes with wartime factory experience hinges on the conditions which characterised factory environments. Ernest Bevin made good working conditions a prerequisite for factories taking advantage of the Essential Work Order of March 1941 (Calder, *People* 235–6, 326) but decrees from the Ministry of Labour made many factories unpleasant for workers. Rooms handling munitions, for example, were obliged to have windows smaller than 3 square feet and at least 9 feet high from the ground (Mass Observation, *War Factory* 63) and the Home Office stipulated that factories should cover windows with paint or dark blinds in a "drastic" blackout (T. O'Brien, 220). Daylight was thus permanently scarce and the artificial light was often harsh. A character in J. B. Priestley's novel *Daylight on Saturday* muses that it is a "queer hard light, in which everybody looked as if they were suffering from some strange disease" (19). The simile of organic deterioration is apt, for munitions workers handled and inhaled toxic materials which damaged skin, hair and lungs. As demand increased some factory working conditions deteriorated to resemble the hell of nineteenth-century industry. Windows were often permanently sealed, blocking light and ventilation, sometimes with fatal consequences (Calder, *People* 328). Accommodation could be just as bleak, with munitions hostels resembling prisons (Goodall 173).

The carceral qualities of factory work were intensified by conscription. Since factory work was the least popular work, many women who delayed entering the workforce until conscripted found themselves directed to factories. The work could be monotonous and exhausting, as Kathleen Church Bliss recalls:

> The hours drag interminably, the clock never advances ... it seems to us that the hundreds of workers, though only separated from each other by a few feet, are each shut away in an impenetrable box of noise – and live their separate lives for 11 hours a day hardly able to communicate with each other. (Goodall 161)

By the end of 1940, many factories were working twenty four hour days, seven days a week (Calder, *People* 117). W. H. Thompson recalls, "To meet men and women who had worked on special rush jobs continuously for thirty-six hours was a commonplace experience" (118). So thoroughly were workers constrained by their punishing schedule that they often felt sealed off from the outside world (Mass Observation, *War Factory* 13). In addition to narrowing life to a small window of awareness, such hours made accidents inevitable, as I will shortly describe. Women not in hostels or billets faced added exhaustion from also doing strenuous housework (Riley 128).

Although it is impossible to generalise about home front labour, many workers experienced the "[c]aged quality of wartime" (Mackay 96). Priestley's novel describes the strangeness of an aircraft factory:

> There are no windows. The roofs are darkened. The factory inside is like a colossal low bright cave, lit with innumerable mercury-vapour lamps that produce a queer greenish-white mistiness of light. In there, three in the morning and three in the afternoon look just the same. ... You might be deep in a mountain or at the bottom of the sea ... all the budding, flowering and withering of the world, all have vanished. For this is a cave life. (2)

These unearthly, fantastical spaces inspire Inez Holden, Diana Murray Hill and Anne Ridler to deploy the Gothic mode, to unsettle dominant narratives of the jovial experience of wartime work.

"A hideous yellow gloom"

Holden was a socialite, journalist, worker, radical and paradox. During the 1930s she wrote comic novels, but after war began her writing became more serious. She worked in a wartime factory work herself and wrote two novels and several prose pieces inspired by her experience, as well as documentary scripts for the Ministry of Information. Her novel *Night Shift* (1941) depicts a fictional factory in London which makes camera parts for reconnaissance aeroplanes and bombers (20–1). Each of the novel's six chapters describes one night's war work at a factory, and on the final night, all in the factory die in a raid. Holden's second factory novel, *There's No Story There* (1944), is even bleaker: based outside an urban centre, this munitions factory is spared raids but is nonetheless wracked by injury, race hatred and murder. I will supplement my discussion of Holden's factory fiction with reference to two other writers. Hill's *Ladies May Now Leave Their Machines* (1944) also draws on the author's experience of work in a munitions factory, work so damaging to her health that she was eventually released on medical grounds

(Hartley 251). Ridler's play *Shadow Factory* (1946) describes a factory immediately post-war, in the years when the Ministry of Labour was still urging women to work in industry (Riley 154). The "shadow industry" consisted of factories run by private companies directed by state-run factories (Hornby 218), but in Ridler the "shadow" of the title becomes a metaphor for the malign environment. Each writer depicts wartime factory spaces as haunted by prejudices from earlier eras.

At first glance it may seem perverse to approach Holden's writing, in particular, through the Gothic. The Gothic is, after all, "not real-istic writing" (Punter, *Terror* 2: 119) and Holden has been hailed as a practitioner of documentary realism (Bluemel 109–10). Yet Holden and other writers of wartime industry respond well to scrutiny through a Gothic lens, on two grounds. First, as the war progressed experience became increasingly fantastical. In such conditions, realist imperatives could paradoxically require writers to venture into overwrought rep-resentation. As Botting notes, realism and the Gothic are not entirely incompatible modes (*Gothic* 12). Secondly, cold, grinding hopelessness and despair characterise these factories. Although both *Night Shift* and *No Story* have light-hearted moments, they are dominated by "violence, social dislocation, and psychological stress" (Bluemel 127) and *No Story*, in particular, makes "sad, cold reading" (K. O'Brien 488).

These factories are confining places. In Hill's novel, workers occupy a "network of cage and machines" (13–14) and the factory seems "vast and heartless" like a "State Penitentiary" (17). When the first-person narrator and her friend seek a transfer to another factory, they find any worker is trapped:

> surrounded by an iron ring of foremen, welfare officers, works doc-tor, management and labour exchange, and has just as much hope of escaping ... as convicts under a life sentence. The gates were shut on us, and here we were, well trapped. ... [M]unitions workers ... see the towers of the prison-house rising before them. (23)

She echoes Wordsworth's "shades of the prison-house" which close around a child ("Intimations" l. 67). Even the break room is "like a prison-cell" (80) and on Christmas day the narrator feels herself "watched like a convict in a concentration camp" (114). The munitions factory of Holden's *No Story* is similarly regulated The first words of the book command workers to submit to be searched for contraband, worker Mary Smith notices that she and the other women look like con-victs in their regulation clothes, and worker Linnet has grown so used to the attire that she barely notices how each worker has her name and clock number stamped on her garb (Holden, *No Story*, 179, 13). Some factories even echo prison architecture. In Ridler's play, the Director's panoptic position allows him to watch every worker:

> My office, you see, is the focal point;
> You get from here bird's-eye view
> Of the whole process. From this chair
> I can control the remotest part. (9)

One worker notes wryly, "Not bad to sit in a chair like God / And watch it all" (2). Punter notes that under industrialisation, "Even the sense of time acquired by living and working according to the seasons was being replaced by a different sense of time, the time of the machine and the time of the employer" (*Terror* 1: 193) and the clock indeed becomes a looming presence in Hill's novel, capitalised at each mention (21, 38, 48):

> The CLOCK became ... an ominous feature in our lives. That large square white dial hanging over the material store began to dominate our thoughts, so that we were for ever glancing up to see what it marked, and if we weren't looking at it, it was there, a white milky disc at the back of our brain. (Hill 48)

In Holden's *No Story*, the prison-like qualities are rendered more foreboding by the presence of a megalomaniacal authority figure, Inspector Jameson, who relishes seeing "a flicker of fear" in workers' eyes (134). One worker sees Jameson in Gothic terms:

> Inspector Jameson was looking down at some notes on his desk. The suit he wore was the same brown colour as the wood of the powerful bureau, so that Lofty had the impression that ... he had simply unlocked one of the drawers in the desk, taken out a couple of hands, and laid them down on the smooth brown surface of the bureau. (115)

For a hallucinatory moment it seems that Jameson stores dismembered limbs in his desk, an apt image for his malevolent control over workers.

The factories are carceral spaces, heterotopias in which normal rules are suspended. Like other heterotopias they feature heterochronies, in which – in this case – fragments of the past resurface.[51] Baldick suggests the Gothic "focuses upon a relatively enclosed space in which some antiquated barbaric code still prevails" (xv). As such, the Gothic can be defined as a literary mode of carceral heterochrony, in which a menacing past returns to threaten those confined in heterotopic space. In Holden's *Night Shift*, people are described as warped versions of peacetime realities, the supervisor's coat reminding the narrator of "the aprons Italian waiters wore in peace-time restaurant" (9) and the jugs for morning tea resembling those "used in Edwardian days for pouring hot water into bath tubs" (37–8). The factory supervisors on their bicycles seem "like strange creatures from another world. ... [G]oggles ... gave them the appearance of monstrous insects; two or three were round-helmeted ... and these last looked like Gothic ghosts come back to the world in a mechanised form" (21). The machines in Hill's novel are "antediluvian" (Hill 76) and "like an ancient steam-roller" (Hill 78). The past also returns in Lionel Rolt's story "Hawley Bank Foundry" (1948), in which murderous ghosts haunt a wartime factory situated on the remains of a nineteenth-century foundry. As I will show, this literature of Second World War industry depicts the return of the perils that afflicted nineteenth-century factories. In traditional Gothic fashion, the past arises again.

Nineteenth-century factories were notorious for physical injury. In the words of period activist J. R. Stephen, they coined gold "out of the blood and bones of the operatives" (Ward 183). The working class were more likely to work in factories and thus suffer the resulting injuries. Here, too, wartime conditions saw an unnerving resurgence of the previous century's perils. Air-raids were a new risk and factories were often targets: an attack on a Vickers-Armstrong aircraft factory, for example, saw ninety dead amid a scene of carnage. "[L]ittle of the roof remained; the steelwork was twisted and bloodstained; electric wires hung down like stalactites" (S. Freeman 20). The same fate befalls the factory of Holden's *Night Shift* at the end of the novel, but in *No Story*, the worst injuries are sustained not from Nazi attack, but from industrial accident. A girl assembling a detonator is blinded and later dies when her materials explode: "her face bleeds fast, blood runs down between her fingers over the loose sleeves of her white coat; she falls ... pulleys and rope smashed up, pieces of copper-coloured detonator and blood-splash" (*No Story* 78). Accidents could be caused by workers' inexperience – as Calder notes, novice workers "were all too prone to employ a hammer on components filled with explosives, or to use a stick of TNT as chalk" (*People* 326) – but accidents were also caused by long hours. In one case, Lord Beveridge, Minister for Aircraft production, ordered a factory to build a bomber in two days instead of the planned two months. The factory met his target, but in the process two workers were killed when they fell into the bomb bay – and were only discovered when their corpses fell out with the bombs over Germany (Calder, *People* 326–7). Spencer Freeman, entrusted by the government with the task of maintaining productivity, acknowledges "the volume of accidental fires in factories caused by overwork and fatigue inherent in the war situation" (jacket cover).[52] Accidents were also caused by malicious sabotage. In one case, male night shift workers deliberately adjusted a lathe to endanger and slow down a female day-shift user (Hylton 205). The wartime factory, then, shared some of the nineteenth century's physical dangers. As Stephen Shapiro notes, "No space is more haunted than the sphere of capitalist production ... no poltergeist more effective than the workplace thumping that is often literalised with disfiguring industrial accidents" (30).

These perils hover behind the metaphors of physical violence that dominate Holden's factory writing. Even stamping time-cards for the mid-shift meal is described in the language of physical attack – "One by one they dropped the cards into the clocking-in mouth, knocked in the knob, like a blow to the front teeth" (*Night Shift* 24) and "Silence guillotined down on the workers" as they enter the inspection huts (*No Story* 8). The night shift is in constant combat with the day shift, the latter "like the people of some distant totalitarian country whose methods we deplored and with whom we were always almost at war" (*Night Shift* 30–1). Inflicting physical violence is, of course, the factories' *raison d'être* in that they produce equipment to support military attack, and the factory of *Night Shift* is itself described in military terms: it has "battleship-grey walls" (40) and the narrator muses, "The air-raid destruction went on outside and the noise inside the workshop made me think of a ship which was always trying to leave port but never got under way" (36–7). When the workers go home the narrator notes, "the dispirited remarks we exchanged with each other were like whistled tunes taken up between tired soldiers on the march" (42–3). These working women are aware of their complicity in violence. One worker in *No Story* reflects that laughing while you work seems inappropriate when "'we're only making things to kill people. It don't seem right, do it?'" and another worker concurs: "'it would be all right [to enjoy yourself] if we were working here for something that was for all of us ... gramophones, perhaps, and food, clothes and musical instruments, furniture ... things you can use and things that you need, instead of things that just destroy themselves and everything around'" (*No Story*, 150).[53]

The violence within these factory spaces goes beyond physical injury and includes psychological damage. Karl Marx argues industrial labour alienates workers from the products of their labour, the natural world, their own sanity and other people (Marx 322–34; Punter, *Terror* 2: 197) and these factory texts contextualise those alienations for a particular time. First, many workers felt detached from the products of their labour, because they did not know what their fragment of the production line was producing (Hartley 74).[54] As a character says in *Night Shift*, "'that's the worst of industry, you do – oh, hundreds of the same thing, and you never know what they are for'" (47). Such obscurity inspired a popular song of the time that hails "the girl that makes the thing that drills the hole that holds the spring/That drives the rod that turns the knob that works the thingumejob" (Mass Observation, *People* 407). Holden's novels convey that mystery through intangible names for the labour. In *No Story* some work on "Time and Motion" (11) while others work on "smoke" (15). The work has the quality of arcane ritual: the women manufacturing detonators in *No Story* move with careful gestures, "strange and rather unreal" (74). The work could feel wholly abstract, Celia Fremlin reporting that her wartime factory work ironically felt completely detached from the war (471).

Secondly, industrial work sees workers alienated from the natural world (Marx 325; Punter, *Terror* 2: 197). The novels by Hill and Holden convey this form of alienation from real terrains by employing film and theatre metaphors. In Hill's *Ladies*, the factory seems "so theatrical that it might have been a huge cinema set or scenic studio" (18). Similarly, at the end of Holden's *Night Shift*, the factory burns to the ground in a scene of "pantomime unreality" (122) and onlookers seem like "a revue sketch crowd of actors carefully made up to seem absurd" (122). Such metaphors can be explained by the sense of unreality attendant upon sheer exhaustion, but Holden's film metaphors also indict the nature of the factory work itself. As workers gather to clock out in *Night Shift*, they "stood for a moment like a group waiting to be photographed" (24) and the nature of the photography is ominous: "on either side of us there was the wire netting; it gave the impression of a cinema set concentration camp. The light was dim and in this underground passage the round metal cases looked like heaped up skulls" (25). These workers seem to be inside a filmic illusion of a concentration camp. This metaphor implies the factory is a prison and place of torment.

A third damage sustained by industrial workers is alienation from the self, at its extreme resulting in madness (Punter, *Terror* 1: 197).

Constance Reaveley describes the maddening fatigue she experienced at factory work:

> When you are tired, which is most of the time, your thoughts repeat themselves as your machine repeats its process; you can't disengage yourself from them. You are imprisoned in your own imagination for hours on end, tied to some idea which has associated itself with the succession of the job. Nothing happens to break into the helpless cycle of these thoughts. (469)

Soon after beginning work the first-person narrator of Hill's novel feels her sanity fracture: "I used to get depressed to the point of feeling suicidal, and sometimes on returning from work would throw myself on my bed and go off into a kind of heavy torpor, from which I would get up feeling plumb crazy, with the room spinning round, not knowing who I was, or where or why" (22).

A fourth damage that Marx and Friedrich Engels identify in industrial workers is damage to their sense of human connections, for people become "monads," separated like atoms (Engels 48; cf. Marx 330). Factory communities in the Second World War were often fragile. The Ministry of Labour tried to present factories as sites of "jolly munition-worker camaraderie" (Hill 4) and Hartley notes that women's literature of the home front often responded to the war by producing a new "literature of commitment and citizenship" (15). Yet factory life stubbornly resisted such hopeful narratives, and Hartley acknowledges that "It was above all the factory which resisted the call to community in women's novels" (Hartley 81). The novels by both Hill and Holden do feature moments where workers support each other in affectionate camaraderie (Bluemel 126, 202n15). Often, however, these factory relationships dwindle into isolation or enmity. *No Story* features two women physically fighting, a supervisor murdered and a worker fantasising murder. In *Night Shift*, many of the workers feel lonely, including the male workers, and this loneliness can infuse even material objects in the space. The supervisor Patterson, for example, "picked up a hand reamer and stared at it in melancholy. He took a silver screw and seemed to get nothing but loneliness from it" (59–60). Similarly, in Hill's novel friendships fade, the three primary characters becoming detached from each other. Fellowship fails in these factories.

Class divisions remained significant in all spheres of wartime work (Summerfield 56). Holden's factory novels have been praised for their lack of class prejudice and commitment to the politics of the radical left

(Bluemel 104) and Holden herself occupied an ambiguous class position. On the one hand, in the late 1920s and early 1930s she socialised with "Bright Young Things," the glittering demographic whose privileged lives were satirised in Waugh's *Vile Bodies* (1930). On the other hand, she herself lacked financial security and always felt an outsider to that community. Bluemel notes that Holden herself traversed a "gradual movement from upper- to working-class identifications," coming to refer to workers as "we" not "they" in her war diaries (Bluemel 104, 107, 127, 200). Her factory writing, however, acknowledges discrepancies in the ways that middle-class and working-class workers experience factory work, noting that the working-class workers suffer "an unending night of never enough money – the horizon they see ahead is probably of the same dreary dust as the semi-quicksand they stand on now" ("Fellow Travellers" 121).

Literary representations of Second World War factories, then, invite comparisons with nineteenth-century catalogues of physical and psychological damage to factory workers. In addition, however, these wartime texts depict humiliations particular to women. The Second World War home front saw a prevalent belief that working women were sexually promiscuous (Calder, *People* 335), rumours so persistent that the government even investigated the number of pregnancies among unmarried women in the services (Hylton 142–3). In these fictional factories, too, women's work can be incongruously sexualised. When a male supervisor in *Night Shift* watches the women working at the machines, the female narrator is reminded of "some pier Peeping Tom, getting the story of 'what the butler saw' from a penny slot machine" (60) and when management ask one female worker to "co-operate" she thinks they mean "copulate" – " 'I thought that was the word for going with a feller' " (59). Women's labour is exoticised and acquires an imperial cast when the factory is compared to an oriental market: "An hour or two dripped by, this tedium of mechanical work, these slow-eyed girls with their bent heads, their thoughts in an inner haze made me feel as if I had been transported to an oriental bazaar" (109). In Hill's novel, certain kinds of labour are seen as an indication of lost virginity. When the unmarried narrator snaps equipment she is demoted to work on the "Burr Bench," sandpapering products made by others. The light work makes the Bench "known as the home of expectant mothers ... and when women left their machines for the Burr Bench, people nodded and watched" (33). Although the narrator is neither pregnant nor sexually active, she feels profound humiliation at the move: "To me it seemed the depths of degradation, and hot tears of shame rolled down my cheeks" (33–4).

The female workers' labour is also often described in terms of child-hood. Worker Mary Smith, for example, writes that the factory reminds her "how we used to play shops when we were kids, filling up little boxes and handing them backwards and forwards to each other'" (*No Story* 180) and it looks as though the women are using *papier-maché* toy boats (78). Julian watches women making detonators and their equip-ment makes him think of "a child's bead-counting frame" and they use a "kidstick" to measure. Julian muses, "[A]ll through these processes one comes up against words that carry you ... back to the nursery" (75). Elsewhere, factory work is compared to infant eating. The narrator of *Night Shift* sees "two of the girls sitting by the work bench near the big bath jugs were filing some brass bolts as disinterestedly as children lift-ing spoonful after spoonful of tasteless milk pudding to their mouths without the will to stop eating, to protest or even to sick up" (56). In *No Story*, the kitchen equipment is "so large that ... [it] seemed to dwarf down eaters and servers to the size of marionettes" (*No Story* 47). In Ridler's play even the literary form is childlike, iambic tetrameter giving the play a sinister nursery-rhyme quality. These female factory workers are framed by the language of childhood.

Yet women are not the only figures marginalised in these spaces. A non-fictional factory manager bewailed the types of labourers available in wartime in derogatory terms:

> Men over 60 and even over 70. Men taken from non-essential work. Women and girls from all sorts of jobs and from no job at all. Cripples, weak hearts, discharged servicemen, half-wits, criminals, all sorts of people so long as they can stand or even sit and turn a handle. These are our material. (Mass Observation, *People* 91)

As this manager's scorn suggests, male non-combatants held a com-plex gender position. The First World War had seen the Victorian ideal of the soldier as vigorous warrior challenged by the wrecked men who returned from the Front psychologically and physically maimed (Harris; Kavka 153). The medical category of "shell-shock" vexed tradi-tional medical wisdom that saw hysteria – in which emotional turmoil causes symbolic physical symptoms – as a fundamentally feminine illness.[55] World War II also saw a crisis in masculinity, exacerbated for noncombatant men since the home front was now an environment in which women were conscripted and militarised. Kristine Miller notes that such noncombatants occupied "embarrassingly passive wartime roles ... the gender dynamics on the home front caused some anxiety

for such men, many of whom describe wartime changes in gender relations as aberrations from the norm" ("The World" 138). Conscientious
objectors were yet another minority often excluded from the nation's
wartime comradeship. "Conchies" experienced harassment (Calder,
Myth 77) and some town councils forbade them from serving in fire
or ambulance services (Ziegler 119).[56] Only a few noncombatant men
were conscientious objectors, most noncombatants holding posts in
"reserved occupations" which they were forbidden to leave. Although
Kristine Miller suggests that various discourses of the time manage the
male noncombatant anxiety by stereotypically polarizing the genders as
active male and passive female ("The World" 138), three male characters
in Holden's factory novels blur that binary: Geoffrey Doran and Julian
in *No Story*, and the "unemployed man" in *Night Shift*.

A reclusive figure, Doran is an undercover participant-observer taking
notes for the early sociological organisation, Mass-Observation. He is
described in feminine terms as a corseted witch. One worker notes that
Doran would "be as lonely without his notebook as a witch without
her broomstick" (*No Story* 11) and another muses that "Geoffrey Doran
doesn't seem to take off his spiritual stays in company" (20). In addition, Doran talks oddly, ending sentences "on a sort of signaling note,
something like a typewriter bell at the end of a line" (20). At this period,
the typewriter was still a gendered technology, predominantly associated with female users (Thurschwell 87; Kittler 352; Shiach 116), so this
reference too, reinforces Doran as somehow feminised. Worker Julian
also occupies an ambiguous position. An ex-combatant invalided out of
the navy due to war trauma, he "had made the decision to let the State
take him over" (25). He is feminised to the extent that he sees himself as
wholly passive at this time when feminine was assumed to be more passive than masculine. His gender ambiguity is reinforced when he twice
falls into reverie over gender and makeup (15–16), materials charged
with libidinal significance for him in a cathexis marked with the ache of
an attachment to a lost mother (*No Story* 16). The "unemployed man" of
Night Shift has a similar passivity. He sits "quietly," "very seldom spoke,"
has "a kindly, gentle expression" (28) and is never named, inviting comparisons with the condition of women in a patronymic society (Gilbert
and Gubar, *Madwoman* 555). All three men occupy ambiguous positions, resisting the period's stereotypical constructions of masculinity.

Like noncombatant men, national others were seen as sub-opti-
mal workers and even potential threats. The Chief Security Officer of
Holden's *No Story* keeps Irish workers out of the office when plans for
a Royal visit are being drawn up, for fear they would try to injure the

King (*No Story* 87). It is a Jewish character, however, who suffers most. Holden's 1942 *Night Shift* featured a Jewish foreman (27) and no anti-Semitism, but as the war progresses and Holden's fiction grows bleaker, her factories are depicted as containing small pockets of virulent hatred of Jews. In *No Story*, the Jewish worker Gluckstein suffers in his consciousness of this hatred, tormented by "the persecutions which were always in his thoughts. It spread through him like a fever" (128). Though born, raised and identifying as English, he realises as a child that he and his family are excluded from the horizontal comradeship that allegedly characterises a nation at war. His brother dies fighting for Britain in World War One (127, 130) and a few weeks later Gluckstein was sheltering with his father in an air-raid. They see a woman weeping. "Gluckstein's father tried to console her ... but she shouted back at him 'This war is terrible! Both my sons have been sent home wounded; but you wouldn't understand that, being a foreigner.' After the raid was over, Gluckstein had walked home with his father in silence" (130). The woman cannot imagine that the Gluckstein family may share her nationality and have made even more severe sacrifices. Experiences like this teach Gluckstein that he is irrevocably other, and this knowledge haunts him: "all the time the horror was there, like a leopard waiting in a dark wood, suddenly it would leap out and bare its teeth" (129).

At the factory, Gluckstein is again read as foreign, a reading he refutes: "'A foreigner!' said Gluckstein. 'I'm not a foreigner; I'm English'" (127). The same misreading occurs for Jewish women. When Julian watches a woman making detonators, he is struck by a difficulty in reading her national identity from her physiognomy: "'she doesn't look English with those eyes slanting down at the corners – don't suppose she's a foreigner, though. I know what it is, she's Jewish'" (76). This is the woman later killed by the exploding detonator. As in the case of Gluckstein's brother, Jewish blood-sacrifice is not always readily legible in the nation's narratives of its communal struggle.

Gluckstein lives in terror of cruelty from co-workers. The vast majority of his coworkers are not fascist, and indeed several fought fascism in the Spanish Civil War. Yet anti-Semitism is written even into casual slang; when Gluckstein buys cigarettes and gives a florin instead of a crown by accident, the serving-woman asks "in her good-natured way," "'You trying to Jew me down or what?'" (*No Story* 133). That such a verb can be uttered by someone "good-natured" is a bleak testament to the extent to which anti-Semitism is embedded in the language of the time. Gluckstein's anguish reaches a peak near the end of the novel when a co-worker Phyllis Jenkins writes her initials in the road as a message to her friend.

Gluckstein is appalled when he sees the initials, for "It was the same mark he had seen in the East End years earlier. It was chalked in white on the road. 'P.J.' – Perish Judah" (*No Story* 136). "P.J." was a Nazi greeting, cruel graffiti and a popular slogan at the Nordic League and other pro-Nazi groups (Thurlow 81). As in my previous chapter, we see a marginalised person obliged to decipher menacing signs for his own safety.

Gluckstein's dreads are not fulfilled in the course of the novel, but his fears are not groundless. His co-worker Lofty longs to murder him.

> The Jew Gluckstein was strong … he walked about on the group with strong quick steps. … Gluckstein would get himself a foreman's job before long. There was nothing to stop him, although there were plenty of men far more fitted to be foremen than Gluckstein, the stepped-up sheeny! … Lofty spat on the ground. (119)

Lofty dwells with hatred on the Jew's body and as the novel progresses his fantasies become increasingly vicious. He stamps on insects, telling himself " 'That's Gluckstein!' " The violence of this fantasy and the equation of a Jew with vermin are even more disturbing given the horrors of contemporaneous events on the Continent. Late 1941 and early 1942 saw the first Death Camps constructed. Treblinka, Sobibor, Auschwitz-Birkenau and others were factories specifically designed for mass murder, the Nazi "Final Solution" (Wasserstein 121–2).

Deadly spaces and disintegrating narrative

The Gothic mode involves more than particular tropes; it is also characterised by particular narrative structures. Eighteenth-century Gothic typically features happy endings in which the spectral menace is tamed and propriety restored, and these wartime factory texts do not match that structure. Yet many texts acclaimed as twentieth-century Gothic feature grim endings with uncertain closures (Punter, *Terror* 2: 207) and Holden's *No Story* and Hill's *Ladies* follow a similar despairing spiral. In this, the novels are at odds with diarists of wartime factory work, who tend to redeem the drudgery within a framework of national worth. These novels offer no such consolation.

Hill's factory novel is dominated by what Hartley has called a "downward trajectory" (83) in which working skill, friendships and even sanity disintegrate. The first person narrator, "Di," is released from the factory on medical grounds, her health having "broke[n] down so definitely" (128). Lil moves to work at another factory and her fiancé is killed in war. Gwen continues to work at the factory and moves into lodgings with her married lover, but her life deteriorates rapidly from a combination of the draining work at the factory and the experience of being a social outcast (for fraternising with a married man) until she begins to go mad: "'I feel I shall go crazy, wherever I look after leaving the place I see nothing but machines and hear nothing but that noise'" (Hill 128). She accompanies her letter with a copy of the fortune-telling magazine *Prediction*, "with 'I think I am going crazy' scribbled over it" (129). As Hartley notes, the novel:

> closes on an unusually low note. The three women we have been following all leave the factory and go their separate ways, weary, ill and depressed. "Release from the machines" is all that can be hoped for, and there is no interest in what lies ahead. The book depicts the factory as ... resistant to humour, glamour or higher meaning. (84)

Holden's *Night Shift*, too, dwindles to a close. The factory burns down in a raid, and the onlookers are desultory and directionless: "All these watching people had the cardboard look of people who are too tired to be either awake or asleep" (123). These closures echo the inconclusive endings that characterise some forms of horror narrative. Salomon notes that "the final note is always, in one way or another, a dying fall ... we move if at all only toward anticlimax" (93, 98).

In addition, the very form of the narrative itself is jerky and halting; just as the factories are sites of violence, these novels of factory life feature violence against narrative form. Haggerty says of the traditional Gothic that "Story lines are ruptured, fragmented, misplaced, even forgotten" (*Gothic Fiction* 20) and the same is true of these wartime texts. The very title of *No Story* bespeaks the lack of narrative coherence possible in the place, and the novel ends with a letter in which a worker presents the factory life as resisting narrative progress: it is "'jagged and uneven, not straightforward like a storybook'" (185). *No Story* comprises "a disjointed series of casualties and disappointments ... tiredness and factory rhythms crush the narrative impetus" (Hartley 83). As Salomon has said of horror, events accumulate in a chaotic, random way: plots of "and then" replace plots of "because," implying the world lacks causality or logical progress (96–7). In these industrial contexts, people are subordinated to an externally-imposed repetition with no development possible. These factory texts yoke the passage of time to an imperative to repeat without change. This sense of a mechanical fatality characterises another Gothic narrative – Freud's theory of the death drive. Freud reached this theory through observing the "compulsion to repeat" (14: 360–1). He saw this compulsion as ultimately self-destructive since, if taken to its logical conclusion, it would fundamentally aim to return to the earliest state of all: the oblivion before life. As such, he calls this drive to repeat the "death drive." These wartime factories are indeed sites of compulsive repetition which throw the mind back to earlier states – in *Night Shift*, for example, the worker Feather falls into a dream-like trance reliving memories of childhood, and in *No Story* one worker describes the deadly daze induced by monotonous repetition, "slow paralysis ... an active kind of poison, a malady that drags you ... into a deep morass where treacled-up time ticks slowly over you" (22).[57]

The novels' movement towards disintegration is shared by the workers themselves. In the novels by Holden and Hill, the factory equipment awakens longings for death in the workers. In *Night Shift*, worker Mabs craves self-destruction: "she leant toward the machinery as if inciting it to murder. There had been a night when her hair got caught in one of the wheels. She had been dragged closer to the machine at great speed" (75). The narrator observes, "Death was with her already, but still she wished for death. She did not know that she wanted to be killed Perhaps she was a murderee" (66). Mabs laments missing the air raid that destroys the factory: "'I wish I bin there, I wish I bin there to-night with the others'" (124). In *No Story*, Julian feels a similar death-wish. He wishes he had died in battle and is jealous of those who did (19, 16). The factory equipment triggers suicidal fantasies in him: as he looks at explosives, "his death-wish overwhelmed him again" (19) and when he carries gunpowder, he daydreams of dropping the material and dying in an explosion (73). Finally, in Hill's *Ladies*, some workers deteriorate into madness and a longing for suicide (22).

The factory environments of these novels are inimical to life. The factory buildings of *No Story* are a "city of the dead" and the trucks resemble a "long line of military coffins" moving like a cortège (13, 163, 163). When the narrator of Hill's novel first enters the workshop she finds it

> bathed in a hideous yellow gloom ... the effect on the unsuspecting who walk into it for the first time is that they are walking straight into a tomb.
>
>   Everything at once seems to go lower: your vitality sinks so suddenly. ... Even the roof seems lower. Under it people's faces look mauve and pasty like corpses.
>
>   ... The first feeling was that nobody could possibly live in such a light. (18–19)

When working she often feels "more dead than alive" (28) and the break room holds small niches like "coffin-like cupboards." "On nights, the rest room resembled a morgue, with a lot of bodies laid out, apparently lifeless, in heaps along the benches and chairs" (80). She compares some parts of the factory to "a dark abysmal ... black void reminiscent of an Edgar Wallace film" (91). These deathly spaces render workers spectral. In Ridler's play, when one character sees workers labouring behind a sheet, she murmurs, "They look like ghosts" (2) and in Hill's novel, workers become "unseen hands" (Hill 90) and "shadowy figures, leading a kind of half-life in the unfamiliar shades and silence of the dimly-lit [work]shop" (21). Workers are reduced to phantoms.

In the "hideous yellow gloom" of these fictional factories, stories falter and fail. Against the dominant official discourse of factories as places of fellowship and class-levelling, the texts in this chapter present the wartime factory spaces as spaces of marginalisation and dark cravings for death. The Blitz was an impetus to industrialisation, but as war progressed the production pressures gave some factory spaces disturbing echoes of inhumane nineteenth-century industry, the shadows of earlier practice resurfacing as Gothic, mechanised ghosts. The next chapter examines wartime Gothic that offers similar challenges to the Blitz myth's dominant rhetorics of home.

5
Elizabeth Bowen's Uncanny Houses

> "This did not look like home; but it looked like something – possibly a story."
>
> (Bowen, *Heat of the Day* 47)

From the first days of war, the Gothic was enacted in home front houses. The blackout transformed even daylight interiors into dark, claustrophobic chambers, and mass evacuations made the city strangely silent. When raids began in 1940, Blitz destruction made houses seem fragile, with three and a half million homes destroyed in London alone (A. Taylor 502): parts of London were reduced to "long vistas, chiselled by destruction" (M. Anderson 24). The Gothic trope of live burial became literal for those trapped in rubble, an experience so traumatic that people who remained aware during the experience were more likely to die than those knocked unconscious (Haslewood 21). Yet the texts of this chapter employ not only Gothic tropes but also Gothic modes of writing, febrile narrative voices that sense uncanny presences in domestic spaces and challenge linear conceptions of time.

Benedict Anderson argues that feeling part of a nation requires having a sense of stories unfolding simultaneously alongside one's own, a sense forged by newspapers and realist novels which construct narratives of simultaneous living (*Imagined* 33–5). The nation is a unified collective moving through time, "a solid community moving steadily down (or up) history" (26). The texts of this chapter challenge such linear progress. Time is frozen, distorted or interrupted by the past. These disturbing interiors contradict the dominant home front rhetoric which constructs the domestic sphere as a place of triumphant collective labour.

Homes and nation

Ever since the first nation-states emerged in the eighteenth century, homes have played a powerful role in Western national imaginations. Richard Cook notes that terms like "home-rule" and "home front" indicate "that rhetoric of nation and nationalism is motivated by a need to locate a limited physical space of origin and social sovereignty" (1055). Furthermore, while nations' stories of their pasts are often staged in public spaces – battlefields, places of government – their stories of their present are often imaginatively staged in private domestic interiors, a natural consequence of the cornerstone of national identity being the sense of ordinary people living alongside each other. One of the most powerful metaphors for a nation is that of the familial home, the structures of public authority mapped onto the home's (usually patriarchal) figure of authority. By analogy, the father's naturalised authority lends credence to the authorities heading the nation-state.[58]

Home is also an apt metaphor for nation in that both are predicated on invisible labours and marginalisations. Iris Marion Young, following Luce Irigaray and Bonnie Honig, defines a longing for home as "the effort to retreat into a solid unified identity at the expense of those projected and excluded as Other" ("House" 158). Gendered labour, in particular, underpins the idealisation of home in the national imaginary. Since the late eighteenth century, home has been increasingly imagined as a private sphere distinct from public space, the public sphere gendered male and the private female (Ferguson Ellis, *Contested Castle* ix; Mathews 2075–6). The misleading binary of public and private spheres obscures the extent to which both are mutually constituted (Blunt and Dowling 18, 21). Homes are social spaces, regulated by convention and law. Through the lens of this deceptive binary, women's obedient dwelling within the home and elision from public spaces could be read as dutiful labour necessary for the stability of the nation.[59] On the Second World War home front, government discourse made the link between domestic labour and serving the nation explicit.

Wartime's disturbing domestic interiors invite comparison with the confined spaces of late eighteenth-century Gothic tradition, often read as nightmarish symbols of women's experience in the domestic sphere. Kate Ferguson Ellis notes that "The vast, imprisoning spaces that appear so regularly in the Gothic as castles, monasteries and actual prisons can be read as metaphors for women's lives under patriarchy" ("Can You Forgive Her?" 258). Vulnerable and terrorised, the heroines of eighteenth-century Gothic do not experience the domestic interior as a sanctuary, and twentieth-century Gothic continues to feature women immured in prison-like houses (Wisker 104). This chapter examines how these Gothic conventions mesh with literature of the British home front in World War II. Gendered readings are not the only analytic response invited by these texts, however: in addition to testifying to gender inequity, these texts explore how the wartime domestic imaginary was transformed by complex national identifications, psychological strain and changes to domestic labour. Like the factories of the previous chapter, the ensuing homes are carceral heterotopias characterised by hallucinatory presences and bizarre temporalities. I introduce the dominant national narratives of home as a site for war-work, and then examine how Bowen's writing unsettles that narrative of home as a stage for confident human action.

Constructing the home front

The interwar period saw domestic imagery become increasingly central to English national identity. Alison Light notes the interwar years saw the emergence of a "domestic" Englishness, "the picture of the 'little man,' the suburban husband pottering in his herbaceous borders" (8). Although such domesticated national imagery incurred scorn from literary elites, it became increasingly central to prose representations of the nation in newsprint and literature. Not class-neutral discourse, the home depicted is usually the middle-class home of the expanding suburbs. Home was thus already especially sensitised when the Second World War began. Chapter 2 discussed how the blackout transformed the city streets, but it also changed the stories people wove about their home interiors. Brittain records that, "During the dark, interminable evenings, many English families, tired of traveling through the cold blackness to clubs and restaurants, come to know their homes as they have never known them before" (*England* 29) and a December 1940 jazz tune laments, "There's no place like home, / But we see too much of it now" (Mass-Observation, *War Begins* 195). Since moving through the blacked-out city was a perilous challenge, people spent more time at home.[60] In addition, homes were the site of two rituals that supported the imagined community in war. Benedict Anderson argues that an imagined community is bolstered by members of a nation imagining that some of their daily routines are shared by others they will never meet (*Imagined* 22). On the Second World War home front, listening to the wireless and doing housework became shared rituals that constructed the home as itself a terrain for battle.[61] Radio enabled wartime government exhortations to enter homes with unprecedented ease. By 1939 wireless was increasingly affordable, three-quarters of British homes owning a licence (Havers viii) and not exclusively the wealthy or middle-class (Woon 24). The government recognised that radio gave direct access to a multitude of listeners, and official broadcasts abounded including political speeches, clarifications of rations, and exhortations to support the nation's war effort.[62] This new emphasis on radio as the source for up-to-date news on war events made the home the space where many formed a sense of their place in the struggle. Radio advertisers exploited this conjunction, as in a Philips wireless advertisement which declared, "THE LION HAS EARS. The nation stands to; alert, watching ... listening. At every outpost of Empire, at every fireside at home, modern radio enables listening ears to follow the events of a world at war" (Philips Wireless 3). A regal leonine silhouette implies that the listener is a British Lion, but the location for this imperial posturing is the ordinary British home. Listening to the radio becomes a martial act, repeated around countless firesides in the knowledge of thousands doing the same.

The radio's symbolic significance was intensified by the fact that the wartime radio service subsumed all regions into one nationwide Home Service. Regional radio programming did not resume until July 1945. There were admittedly some fracture-lines in this uniformity. Wireless ownership was less in Wales, Scotland and Northern Ireland, and although the BBC news team remained in London for the duration of the war the BBC switched to using the Scottish and Northern wavelengths to increase the service's resilience if London transmitters were destroyed in raids. Nonetheless, London kept a grip on broadcast content and form, and even the five-minute signal heralding announcements was a recording of Bow Bells (Havers vii, 8). The wireless, then, contributed to forging imagined community for a nation at war under the direction of the English capital.

Housework, too, became a highly-charged ritual, for the heroic housewife was a key figure in the martial home. Although World War II saw women conscripted to work outside their homes, home remained a gendered sphere (Kristine Miller, "Even a Shelter" 140). Although in 1939 women were not as housebound as they were in earlier decades, the complex responsibility of housekeeping was still shouldered by the majority of women. The interwar years had seen many changes to domestic forms, live-in maidservants replaced by "daily helps" who did not sleep on the premises and mortgages making it possible for more people to buy their homes (Light 9–10, 225), but even new labour-saving appliances could not defeat the leaden litany of domestic practice. As servants became more scarce, middle-class women took on more housework, and Jan Struther's semi-fictional Mrs Miniver gloomily observes, "Every morning you wake to a kind of list which begins: *Sink-plug. Ruffle-tape. X-hooks. Glue.* ... Your horizon contracts, your mind's-eye is focused upon a small circle of exasperating detail. Sterility sets in; the hatches of your mind are battened down" (Struther 93). Mollie Panter-Downes's story "Year of Decision" describes how life can "contract ... to a strip of floor between stove and sink" (158). Noncombatant men, too, had to struggle with domestic labour. The protagonist of Panter-Downes's story imagines his son asking him what he did during the war, and having to reply, "Stood at the sink, my boy, and got the sticky cereal unglued from your spoon" (163). His day is dominated by washing dishes and struggling with the boiler, which glares at him "like a cold, malevolent black goblin" (163). Recent scholarship of home-making has noted the creative dimension to the work (e.g. bell hooks; Blunt and Dowling 5, 20, 47), but wartime literature rarely celebrates domestic work as positive.

The blackout was only the beginning of a series of government injunctions transforming domestic space. After German U-Boats began attacking the cargo ships importing food to Britain, radio campaigns exhorted listeners to conserve resources (Gardiner 120). Rationing began in January 1940, the "Dig for Victory!" campaign enjoined householders to grow their own vegetables in gardens or allotments, the Ministry of Food broadcast thrifty uses of provisions and flavor substitutes and posters and radio broadcasts urged householders to recycle paper, collect pig swill, not waste food, and perform numerous domestic practices to resist the siege. One listener noted that the wireless changed "from an agreeable companion to an official bully" (Havers 24). The "Home Front" radio broadcast series began at the end of 1939, and the "Kitchen Front" series began in June 1940 and attracted 5.5 million listeners at its peak. By the end of 1945 nearly 1,200 broadcasts had concerned food (Havers 21, 22, 28). These broadcasts targeted housewives. One Ministry of Food pamphlet, for example, imagined "Medals for Housewives. The British Housewife is helping make a second front – the Kitchen Front – against Hitler," and Ministry of Food advertisements encouraged women, "*You've got a fighting job on hand too. ... Food is your munition of war*" (Minns 110, 115, emphasis in original). An advert by the Ministry of Information ventriloquises this heroine:

What do I do ... if my job is that of housewife and mother? I remember that this is a war-job too! – and I try to do it even better than usual. I shop with special care. ... I try to keep myself and my house trim and cheerful and I take special pains with my cooking, because I know this keeps my men's spirits up. ... [I]n this way, though I may not be winning medals, I am certainly helping to win the war! ("What do I do" 3)

Such government exhortations explicitly construct home space as a war arena. Kristine Miller notes, "Public policies such as household ration- ing and the blackout charged the home with political energy" ("Even a Shelter" 142), but they did more than this: they imbued the trappings of domestic interiors with military associations. This process is made vivid in a 1942 Board of Trade announcement posted by shopkeepers explaining to customers that luxuries are now rare because the factories that produce them are producing war-time alternatives:

> CORSETS become Parachutes and Chinstraps;
> LACE CURTAINS become Sand-fly netting;
> CARPETS become Webbing Equipment,
> TOILET PREPARATIONS become Anti-Gas Ointments; ...
> MATTRESSES become Life Jackets;
> SAUCEPANS become Steel Helmets;
> COMBS become Eyeshields. (Minns 33)

Viewed through this list of fantastical substitutions the ordinary home becomes a nightmarish stage for war preparation. At once familiar and strange, the list exemplifies Freud's definition of the *unheimlich,* "that class of the frightening which leads back to what is known of old and long familiar" (14: 340).

When air raids saw the home front become a literal front, the housewife's heroism became even more celebrated: as the female poet F. Tennyson Jesse writes in 1940, "Here there are broken homes, burnt homes, / But hearts undefeated to meet each day" (293). Despite such heroic representations, however, women on the British home front had not entirely escaped the vulnerable position of women in eighteenth- century female Gothic. Bowen's fiction undermines two strands of the dominant national discourse of home. First, it challenges the idea of home as a stage for martial triumph, instead presenting it as a site of uncanny life hostile to the inhabitants. Secondly, her work challenges the nation's narrative of simultaneous lives moving forward together in time: instead, time is elastic, frozen or reversible.

Nation and the domestic uncanny

Uncertainty about life dominates much discussion of the uncanny. Ernst Jentsch argued that the defining feature of the uncanny is uncertainty between life or lifelessness, "the natural tendency of man to infer ... that things in the external world are also animate" (13). He illustrates his point by imagining a diabolically animated domestic interior: animism inspires a child to "populate his environment with demons" and to "speak in all seriousness to a chair, to their spoon, to an old rag" (13). In his 1919 reply, Freud echoes Jentsch's interest in the ambiguous vitality of "uncanny" objects but rejects Jentsch's analysis on the grounds that not all intellectual uncertainty is accompanied by the sense of horror which characterises the uncanny. Lexicographical analysis persuades Freud that the *unheimlich* (uncanny, disturbing) cannot be defined as a straightforward opposite of the *heimisch* (cosy, home-like) – instead, they are twin aspects of a single thing. "*[H]eimlich* is a word the meaning of which develops in the direction of ambivalence, until it finally coincides with its opposite, *unheimlich. Unheimlich* is in some way or other a subspecies of *heimlich*" (14: 347). Anthony Vidler observes that for Freud, "'unhomeliness' was more than a simple sense of not belonging; it was the fundamental propensity of the familiar to turn on its owners, suddenly to become defamiliarised, derealised, as if in a dream" (7).

Freud argues the uncanny can have two origins: a return of repressed material (repressed for being incomprehensible or too threatening to admit into consciousness) or the return of "surmounted" material (old beliefs from early childhood which are unnerving when they return, since they imply the psyche is regressing into an earlier stage of development). The uncanny is "everything ... that ought to have remained secret and hidden but has come to light" (14: 345). Core to both the triggers Freud identifies is the image of a human consciousness being usurped by more powerful forces. I suggest that the uncanny can thus be defined as a crisis of narrative, in that it is fundamentally about feeling in the grip of a narrative governed by an alien intelligence outside one's own conscious control – even if, as Freud argued, that alien intelligence is one's own unconscious desire. Freud himself experienced this very effect when wandering through an Italian town.

> I found myself in a quarter of whose character I could not long remain in doubt. Nothing but painted women were to be seen at the windows of the small houses, and I hastened to leave the narrow

street at the next turning. But after having wandered about for a time without enquiring my way, I suddenly found myself back in the same street, where my presence was now beginning to excite attention. I hurried away once more, only to arrive by another *detour* at the same place yet a third time. Now, however, a feeling overcame me which I can only describe as uncanny, and I was glad enough to find myself back at the piazza I had left a short while before, without any further voyages of discovery. Other situations ... result in the same feeling of helplessness and of uncanniness. (14: 359)

The uncanny involves feeling helpless in the grip of a narrative we cannot recognise or shape. We sense a malevolent design behind events/an encounter/an object, but we are shut off from knowing that meaning.[63]

Since Freud himself tends to explain the uncanny as emerging from the repressed material of the individual subject, critics tend to read the uncanny as symptomatic of an individual's personal repressions. Yet Freud never defines repression as purely a matter of an individual's interior world. He argues, after all, that the self-censoring superego is in part an internalisation of the interdictions of caregivers, and as such repression is partly a function of that which a particular community deems unthinkable. In addition, Freud formulated his concept of the uncanny in the aftermath of World War I, when shell-shock, war neuroses, and collective bereavement had taken him into dark meditations on humankind's tendency towards despair and complex psychological self-injury. Vidler suggests that Freud's theorisation of the unhomely is "particularly appropriate to a moment when, as Freud notes in 1915, the entire 'homeland' of Europe, cradle and apparently secure house of western civilisation, was in the process of barbaric regression" (7). The uncanny, in other words, may be useful in describing a society, not just a psyche.

Freud illustrates his argument by analysing E. T. A. Hoffman's short story "The Sandman" (1817) and identifies castration anxiety as the root of the horror underpinning the uncanny tale. This interpretation has been persuasively debunked by psychoanalytic feminist critics (Chisholm 427–9), but Freud's description of castration anxiety triggering the uncanny may still be useful if we follow Lacan in broadening the concept of castration anxiety to encompass the dread felt at the prospect of *any* profound threat to the joyful sense of bodily integrity and individual power which accompanies primary narcissism. Jacques Lacan speaks of the "mirror stage" in which an infant sees a reflection for the first time and is flooded with epiphanic glee at the image of the intact and seemingly powerful body. This illusion of wholeness remains with the subject and Lacan coins the term the "imaginary" to describe the fantastical, narcissistic realm in which it holds sway. In Lacan's model, the uncanny threatens the imaginary by showing cracks in the illusion of wholeness. As Botting notes, for Lacan the uncanny "marks the decomposition of the fantasy underpinning imaginary subjective integrity" ("Gothic Production" 34). Lacan's definition of the uncanny as threatening the illusion of wholeness is thus also of value to theorists of nation, for a nation, too, can have an imaginary, in the sense of a deceptive image of itself as single, whole and powerful – and this imaginary, too, can decompose. Bhabha argues that such "decomposition" of a fantasy has a specifically national valence in much discourse of the home, suggesting that uncanny phenomena mark moments when private world of experience is torn by the inequities of its time: "the intimate recesses of the domestic space become sites for history's most intricate invasions. ... The unhomely moment relates the traumatic ambivalences of a personal, psychic history to the wider disjunctions of political existence" ("The World" 445, 448). As such, the uncanny marks moments where inequities around gender, nation and class break into serene domestic tableaux. Bowen's wartime fiction depicts such decomposition of national fantasy.

"Strange growths": uncanny life in Bowen's interiors

Furniture and the objects of middle-class domestic interiors are of perennial interest for Bowen. Critics have analyzed the significance of her interiors (Chessman; J. Rose; Inglesby; Ellman, *Shadow* 128–175), but what has not yet been done is to put Bowen's interiors in dialogue with the proliferating wartime discourses of home. While others emphasise the way in which Bowen's household objects have some kinship with the humans who use them, my reading emphasises the alien qualities of domestic artifacts.

Bowen's work often suggests that household objects are cherished repositories of memory which embody human emotions and intentions. Bowen's novel *The Death of the Heart* (1938), for example, implies a symbolic equation between a household's furniture and its histories; the family's housekeeper notes that "'Furniture like we've got is too much for some that would not have the past"' (Bowen, *Death* 81). Ellman argues that furniture in Bowen's writing bears continuity from past into present and future: "furniture ... embodies narrative in solid form, impacted onto metal, fabric, wood, and stone" (*Shadow* 143).[64] Bowen herself says as much in her 1942 memoir *Bowen's Court*, a history of her family's hereditary house in Ireland and an early example of what is now called house biography (Blunt and Dowling 37). Bowen suggests that the dead accumulate in the rooms they used: "With each death, the air of the place had thickened: it had been added to. The dead do not need to visit Bowen's Court rooms – as I said, we had no ghosts in that house – because they already permeated them" (451). In much of Bowen's fiction, this accretive life-force is a benevolent repository of memory and generational continuity, and damage to it is a dreadful thing. Bowen herself articulated such a view in her description of the pathos of those bombed out of their homes: "People whose homes had been blown up went to infinite lengths to assemble bits of themselves – broken ornaments, old shoes, torn scraps of the curtains that had hung in a room – from the wreckage" (*Mulberry* 97). In this reading, a bombed home is not a site of heroic martial defiance; rather, it is a site of tragedy.

The female protagonists of Bowen's wartime fiction, however, do not necessarily see their own home interiors as benevolent, beloved places. They tend to be custodians rather than beneficiaries of domestic order, required to maintain it rather than savour it. This obligation is also true of women more widely at the time, since wartime narratives of women's triumphant domestic agency are undermined by wartime legal definitions of home. Female conscription evoked an outcry that such enforcement would cause homes to fall into disarray, on the assumption that homes are tended by women on behalf of men. One (male) ARP Warden, for example, warns, "If married women are called up home life will vanish and it will be very hard to revive it after the war. ... Men ... will come back to cold, untidy houses with no meal ready" (Hylton 208; cf. Calder, *People* 333). With such objections in mind, the Ministry of Labour differentiated between "mobile" and "immobile" women, the former tied to household management and unable to move or take up additional duties and the latter available for wartime labour. In determining a woman's mobility, however, very particular criteria were deployed. A woman could only plead responsibility for a home if it were inhabited by her husband or by her parents, or was near her husband (e.g. his barracks). Home was defined "not ... in relation to the wife herself but only to the husband" (Summerfield 48).

Many critics have noted that property is a key preoccupation in eighteenth-century Gothic written by women, for "Fear is an appropriate response in a world where women have property or at least the opportunity of transmitting it, but where they have little power to control it" (Todd 262; cf. E. J. Clery 194n18; Moers, *Literary Women* 136;

Poovey 323). Although the women of the Second World War were not as vulnerable to oppression as the heroines of eighteenth-century Gothic, their relationship to domestic interiors remains ambiguous. This ambiguity is clear in Bowen's novel *The Heat of the Day* (1949) which describes the experience of two women in wartime: Stella Rodney, an upper-middle-class divorcée, and Louie, a working-class soldier's wife. The novel is dominated by Stella's romance with Robert Kelway, who turns out to be a spy for the Nazi regime. The novel can be described as a catalogue of ways in which people respond to particular interiors.

At first glance, wireless and newspapers seem to function in home interiors in ways paradigmatically Andersonian. They inspire Louie to identify as part of a collective:

> Dark and rare were the days when she failed to find on the inside page of her paper an address to or else account of herself. Was she not a worker, a soldier's lonely wife, a war orphan, a pedestrian, a Londoner, a home- and animal-lover, a thinking democrat, a movie-goer, a woman of Britain, a letter-writer, a fuel-saver, and a house-wife? (152)

Louie also wants to listen to the wireless (147). Stella, on the other hand, supports the war and even works for the government, but is not committed to imaginatively waging the war in her own home. She spurns the wireless: while her cousin Francis in Ireland keeps the radio beside his chair, for "it had pleased him to have the war at his elbow," she is pleased to find the radio battery dead (168). Stella recognises that domestic interiors are sites of war – "The grin and scream of battles, mechanised advances excoriating flesh and country, tearing through nerves and tearing up trees, were indoor-plotted" (142) – but she does not identify with that interior struggle, and does not enact rituals within the space to confirm her membership of an imagined community. She is not even fond of her homes and embraces the war as an opportunity to become free of them: instead, she takes a London flat furnished, "having given up the last of her own houses and stored her furniture when the war began" (23). She has not personalised the décor and the only possessions of her own in the flat are her son's pyjamas and photographs of her son and lover. Stella experiences the rooms as distant from her personally, always at least "one ... remove from reality" (24).

By contrast with such female ambivalence, almost all of the men we encounter in *The Heat of the Day* are eager for domestic stability. Even as a child, Stella's son Roderick is fascinated by domestic objects, "collections of any kind in cabinets, a haunted room, a model railway ... a desk with a secret drawer" (60–1). As an adult, he is disconcerted when his mother puts all her possessions in storage and is anxious that she may have discarded his pyjamas, the only thing of his remaining in the space (49). Later, he is distressed to realise that she does not have a regular place in the sitting room for someone to put a tray:

> He sighed. In this flat, rooms had no names; there being only two, whichever you were not in was "the other room." Somewhere between these chairs and tables must run the spoor of habit, could one but pick it up. He could not envisage his mother so completely alone as one would be without any customs. Fred and his other friends were all for the authoritarianism of home life; the last thing they wished was Liberty Hall. (51–2)

Similarly, Stella's would-be lover Harrison is preoccupied with acquiring and maintaining a home. A British counter-intelligence agent who tries to blackmail Stella into having an affair with him, Harrison claims (accurately) that her lover Robert is a Nazi agent. In many ways, however, Harrison's aim is less to have sexual access to Stella than to have access to her home. He loves being in her flat, revering the ornaments and furniture. "'Pretty,' he said softly, 'All your things are so pretty. ... Even this ash tray'" (27). He himself explains his blackmail in terms of his desire to have a home – "'Is it so odd I should want a place of my own?'" (34) – and feels bliss when sitting in her armchair: "'You know, this is very nice. I so often think of this place, if you won't mind my saying so, now I feel quite at home'" (128). Stella, by contrast, fancies that Harrison's presence contaminates the interior: "the papers, letters, among which she had rested her elbow, listening to him, seemed to be contaminated; she shrank, even, from phrases in purple type on which, in the course of the listening, her eyes had from time to time lit. ... She wanted to burn the lot" (57–58). Harrison leaves threatening traces within the home and the interior even becomes physically damaging – playing with the curtain cord leaves a "red spiral weal" on Stella's finger (23).

Elsewhere, too, traces of male authority awaken malevolent agency within the home's ordinary objects. The menacing otherness often seems shaped by past inequities of gender roles, class roles, and national positions in a way reminiscent of Clery's analysis of the function of the supernatural in eighteenth-century Gothic, in which "The supernatural ... arrives to announce and correct a lapse in the rightful possession of property" (71). Ghosts tend to return to correct an error in property lineage, often siding with the vulnerable heroine whose rights have been usurped. Similarly, the strange presences within these Second World War interiors seem to be on the side of propriety and tradition, but they are not benign for women. Louie's soldier husband Tom, for example, leaves an eerie impact on the home he has left to fight. Meeting his gaze in his photograph makes Louie feel annihilated:

> She avoided it. She had seen ever so many times where it said how a photograph comforts you; but the reverse was true. ... His going off on his own initiative to the studio had been one among the last of his farewell acts – consequently, what the camera had recorded had been the face of a man already gone ... the eyes looking straight, measuringly, unexpectantly at nothing. To attempt to enter or intercept that look at no one was to become no one. (159)

Though Louie "piously" (159) dusts it daily, she tries not to meet his obliterating regard. Less easy to elude is the relentless gaze of Tom's customary chair: it "stared at her. ... It directed something at her whichever way she pushed, pulled, or turned it, in whatever direction she turned herself" (146). The empty chair is an accusatory presence, and Louie is more half-hearted custodian than inhabitant of this home. It is confining territory: "For her part, as things were now, she was glad to get out of it every morning: she neglected the rooms – front and back ... leaving the bed slatternly" (17).

Male authority has a similar ghostly manifestation in Bowen's short story "The Demon Lover" (1945) in which an empty London house is haunted by a ghost from the previous war. The middle-aged protagonist, Mrs Drover, is living outside London with her family during the Blitz but returns to London to collect a few things from her closed home. The silent city is uncanny: "In her once familiar street, as in any unused channel, an unfamiliar queerness had silted up" (661). The emptiness is personified – "Dead air came out to meet her as she went in" – and the house has suffered violence, with a "bruise" in the wallpaper and "claw-marks" on the floor (661). When she enters her abandoned house she finds a letter from her dead First World War *fiancé*, accusing her of betrayal for marrying another and threatening a tryst this very day. As she reads the letter she becomes uncomfortable with her back "exposed to the empty room. ... The hollowness of the house this evening cancelled years on years of voices, habits and steps" (664). The ghost returns in the silence and steals her away for some dread fate.

However, the uncanny phenomena in Bowen's interiors do not always map neatly onto traces of male authority. Equally often, the presences seem wholly inhuman. Reading objects as sympathetically animated by human feeling is fundamentally Romantic and wartime Britain saw a resurgence of such animism, often revolving around the notion of a *genus loci* or spirit of place. Such presences have long been features of British romanticism in the tradition of Wordsworth's intuitions of an exalted "one life" running through all things ("Tintern Abbey," ll. 95–103) or (less nobly) Samuel Taylor Coleridge's disparaging notion of "fancy" in which we animate another object with qualities we have ourselves (Wu 525). In these transfigured states, the animated entity is experienced as harmoniously in accord with the perceiver's own emotions. To date, much criticism of Bowen has discerned the same equation at work in Bowen's literary animism (e.g. Ellman, *Shadow*; Bennett and Royle). Inglesby notes that "[O]nly a handful of Bowen's critics have come close to separating ... [her animate objects] ... from their presumed roles as mirrors of character" (312). However, Bowen's most disturbing wartime texts do not fit neatly into the romantic reading, their life instead being radically alien, unknowable and menacing.

In this, Bowen is typical of other interwar female writers. Light notes that female interwar writers often represent domestic objects as acquiring a kind of life.

> In many of these novels home takes on almost an independent character, often a negative one, and becomes a protagonist often warring with the heroine and intruding on her hopes and dreams. ... Frequently the woman at home feels herself to be a kind of sorcerer's apprentice desperately fighting to keep control of the things which make up a home. (137–8)

Similarly, the presences that infuse Bowen's household objects in wartime are not always experienced as an objective correlative of the spectator's conscious emotions, but can instead be threateningly other, opaque and powerful. Such are the cursed human hair of "The Happy Autumn Fields" and the clock of "The Inherited Clock," both of which, as I will show, do violence to the very structure of time. Jacqueline Rose suggests Bowen's objects swallow the perceptual faculties of the perceivers in the manner of Wilfred Bion's "bizarre objects" (36–40), a characteristic of persecutory schizophrenia in which the subject's very apparatus of perception is imaginatively projected into an inanimate object which is then experienced as menacing (Bion 36–9).

Ellman concurs: "in Bowen, consciousness escapes into the object, leaving human beings as vacant as the landscapes that threaten to devour them" (*Shadow* 7). These rapacious living objects, in other words, obtain their life through the disintegration of the human mind that beholds them. Rose and Ellman's readings are persuasive, but Bowen's complex national identity offers an alternative entry point to explicating these radically alien presences.

"Dark ate the outlines of the house": Bowen's national position

The London interiors of Bowen's wartime fiction are continually in dialogue with a very different place, the Anglo-Irish "Big House" of her own ancestry. Gender, class and national affiliation are mutually constitutive rather than self-contained categories, and in Bowen these categories intersect in intricate ways. Bowen's family settled in Ireland in 1653 (Davenport 28). She was raised in a nation in which the categories of class, nation and religion were arranged around two binaries: the upper-middle class Protestant Anglo-Irish Ascendancy to whom the British crown had given hereditary authority, and the less privileged Catholic Irish.[65] The Protestant Ascendancy in Ireland occupied an ambiguous position and their Big Houses, too, were hybrid. "Imposed on seized land, built in the rulers' ruling tradition, the house is, all the same, of the local rock" (*Bowen's Court* 31). In some of Bowen's writing, the Irish land itself has power which resists colonial control. Such is the experience of Stella's son Roderick when he enters the Big House he unexpectedly inherits. He senses strange life both within and outside:

> Something more than silence there had been to be heard. ... Dark ate the outlines of the house. ... The air had been night itself, re-imprinted by every one of his movements upon his face and hands. ... The place had concentrated upon Roderick its being. ... He was left possessed, oppressed, and in awe. ... [It] woke in him, for the first time, the concept and fearful idea of death, his. (*Heat* 311–12)

This territory simultaneously comforts and disturbs the British soldier, encapsulating Anglo-Irish ambivalence towards Irish land as paradoxical threat and solace.

Bowen herself experienced the twin pulls of imperial and local. *Bowen's Court* defends the landed gentry (455), but she speaks with pain of "The scandalous and infinitely regrettable Union" (*Mulberry* 144) and acknowledges that the Bowens' wealth and property was rooted in "inherent wrong" (*Bowen's Court* 453). Bowen's allegiances were even more complex than those of most Anglo-Ireland for her childhood also challenged the binaries urban/rural and Ireland/England. Her early childhood was spent alternating between Dublin and Bowen's Court, and at the age of six Bowen moved with her mother to England (Glendinning 22). During the War Bowen served as an Air Raid Warden in London and as a British spy in Ireland. Claire Wills notes that "It is a well-established contention by now that Bowen's concern with duplicity, betrayal, and double identity reflects her own sense of torn allegiances" (139).

The ambiguous position of the Anglo-Irish is echoed in the discourse that circulates around their houses.[66] They were designed in the eighteenth century to be triumphant markers of England's control of the country through the Protestant Ascendancy but as the nineteenth and twentieth centuries progressed, the imperial fantasy of the Big Houses dwindled alongside the empire that spawned them. Elegaic language gathers around the Houses; as John Hewitt writes, "The house will fall; / it is the nature of stone to fall and lie" (71). In the twentieth century, this poignant quality of the Houses gains a new significance when they become symbols of "the drama of modern man's (and woman's) isolation" (Lubbers 17). Instead of being cornerstones of fellowship, the big houses are emblems of isolation. Moynahan observes, "the Irish big house is about as convincing a symbol of community as the House of Usher" (83–4). Such Gothic intertexts gather around discussions of Anglo-Irish identity. Sheridan Le Fanu and Bram Stoker, Bowen's fellow Anglo-Irish writers of Gothic, have been analysed for the way in which their Anglo-Irish circumstances inflect their use of the Gothic mode (e.g. Ingelbien) and Bowen herself concurs with that assessment. She argues that the Gothic of le Fanu's *Uncle Silas* was shaped by his own Anglo-Irish experience: "The hermetic solitude and the autocracy of the great country house, the demonic power of the family myth, fatalism, feudalism and the 'ascendancy' outlook are accepted facts of life from the race of hybrids from which Le Fanu sprang" (*Mulberry*, 101). Bowen's depiction of the Anglo-Irish Big House develops the traditional Gothic trope of the sentient building (Miéville): it always seems alive, with a "hypnotic stare" (*Mulberry* 26). Speaking of her own family's Big House, she notes wryly, "A Bowen in the first place, made Bowen's Court. Since then, with a rather alarming sureness, Bowen's Court has made all the succeeding Bowens" (*Bowen's Court* 32).

How, then, does the Anglo-Irish "Big House" connect with Bowen's wartime London interiors? London was core to and constitutive of Anglo-Irish identity. An Anglo-Irish child growing up in Ireland, Bowen was "infested ... imaginatively" by London (*Mulberry* 85): "Nobody ever told me about London, or explained to me what or why it was – I was assumed, I suppose, to have been born knowing" (*Mulberry* 85–86). As in any colonial relationship, the connection was reciprocal, and a discourse of "Irishness" bolstered England's sense of itself as imperial power. Strikingly, however, Bowen's wartime fiction represents time in ways subversive of England's imperial narrative.

"The infected zone": time and the uncanny

Carol Jacobs notes that realist narrative typically makes a call to a specific structure of time, "a temporality that has a before and after, in which sequence and progression are taken for granted" (4). Such linear progression of time underpins Benedict Anderson's theory of the imaginative work of community. Texts in the Gothic mode often challenge such linearity, Bhabha suggesting that the defining characteristic of uncanny moments is a bizarre temporality, the private and public spheres meeting in the home in a "border existence" characterised by "a stillness of time" ("The World" 451). Time in Bowen's fictional wartime interiors is unpredictable. Wartime London becomes occupied by pre-war Ireland in ways which unsettle the linear temporalities which underpin Benedict Anderson's imagined communities.

When Stella Rodney travels to the Anglo-Irish Mount Morris, she feels that the Big House is strangely outside time:

> as she stood looking down the length of a room at a fire distantly burning inside white marble, [this hour] seemed to be outside time – an eternal luminousness of dusk in which nothing but the fire's flutter and the clock's ticking out there in the hall were to be heard. Or, in her fatigue she could have imagined this was another time, rather than another country, that she had come to. (*Heat* 163)

By traveling to this house of the Irish Protestant Ascendancy Stella feels she remains in London, travelling in time rather than place in a sleight of hand which dramatises the truth that a colonial centre is always constituted by its colonised peripheries. In addition, London's wartime fires echo the conflagrations that scarred Ireland in the 1920s and 1930s as a direct result of England's imperial yoke. Moynahan notes,

"A London of houses on fire from incendiary bombs and streets torn apart by high explosives was also a reliving of her late teens and early twenties, when country houses and whole towns in Ireland were raided and burnt out by the Black and Tans, Sinn Fein, and the IRA" (74). Bowen says as much herself: "For Ireland, between 1918 and 1939, 'peace' contracted into a shorter space than people in England realise. ... Flames were making people run through the night when, in their beds in the peaceful darkness of England, people dreamed that war would not occur again" (*Bowen's Court* 436–7). Hewitt writes of the Big Houses expiring in "noise and flame" to be replaced by flourishing rosebay willowherb (71) and the same transformation happened at the heart of the City of London. In this sense, Ireland's past becomes London's wartime present.

The disintegration of linear temporal progression is hauntingly expressed in Bowen's story "Summer Night" (1941), set in an Anglo-Irish Big House. In this story, the protagonist Aunt Fran treasures personal mementoes which have become empty talismans:

> From these objects the original virtue had by now almost evaporated These gifts' givers ... were by now faint as their photographs: she no longer knew, now, where anyone was. All the more, her nature clung to these objects that moved with her slowly towards the dark. (598–9)

These objects no longer evoke memories, for the past once embodied in these objects has been annihilated. They and their owner now inhabit an eternal and menacing present:

> The blood of the world is poisoned, feels Aunt Fran ... even the heroes shed black blood ... [W]ho shall stem the black tide coming in? ... The shadow rises up the cathedral tower, up the side of the pure hill. There is not even the past: our memories share with us the infected zone; not a memory does not lead up to this. Each moment is everywhere, it holds the war in its crystal; there is no elsewhere, no other place. (599)

The idea that time is linear and memory is cumulative is challenged by a dreadful present, an "infected zone" where objects no longer trigger memories. The zone sees linear time challenged in two ways: objects are leached of their history and past merges horribly with present. The onset of war saw many writers produce nostalgic autobiography depicting the past as idyllic refuge (Hewison 102–5) but Bowen sees the past in more negative terms, less creatively productive than the present: "there it stands, there it lies, mounting, extending, never complete" ("Cult of Nostalgia"). In the "infected zone" of her wartime fiction, the past contaminates the present.

Time is often frozen in Bowen's wartime interiors. In the blackout, for example, Stella's flat lacks "apprehension of time": "a mysterious flutter, like that of a fire burning, which used to emanate from the minutes seemed to be at a stop" (*Heat* 56). Even the décor of Stella's London flat is static: "the flat, redecorated in the last year of peace, still marked the point at which fashion in this matter had stood still" (24). In further violence to linear time, objects are emptied of their past instead of being embodiments of memory, as in the "infected zone" of the Anglo-Irish house. When Stella sits in her flat with her son Roderick, they feel as though they are suspended in emptiness even though they are surrounded by domestic objects. "Though this particular sofa backed on a wall and stood on a carpet, it was without environment; it might have been some derelict piece of furniture exposed on a pavement after an air raid or washed up by a flood on some unknown shore" (55). The novel identifies the cause of this emptying as wartime's emotional strain:

> from hesitating to feel came the moment when you no longer could. ... By every day, every night, existence was being further drained. ... Their trouble, had it been theirs only, could have been written off as minor – the romantic dismay of two natures romantically akin. But it was more than that; it was a sign, in them, of the impoverishment of the world. There was not much left for either of them to say, and in this room in which they sat nothing spoke, either. (55–6)

Here the strain of wartime is inimical to the capacity to invest the environment with personal meaning.

Bowen's wartime representations of strange time are linked to the decay of particular imperial fantasies. The short story "Mysterious Kôr" (1944) imagines moonlit, blacked-out London as a lifeless city named after the Kôr of H. Rider Haggard's *She*, "a completely forsaken city, as high as cliffs and as white as bones" (*Stories* 729). Time functions strangely in this necropolis: Kôr has "no history" (729) and time does not pass there in the normal way, the changing of minutes shown only by coloured gases changing colour; in Kôr there is no other sort of time" (731). This static, ancient city represents the decay of an imperial dream in three ways. First, the very name of the city represents the impossibility of further colonial adventures. The protagonist Pepita finds the name in Andrew Lang's poem about *She*, written in 1923:

> "That [poem] was written some time ago, at that time when they thought they had got everything taped, because the whole world has been explored, even the middle of Africa. Every thing and place had been found and marked on some map. ... [T]hat was why he wrote the poem. 'The world is disenchanted,' it goes on." (730)

Secondly, the moon-bleached metropolis is an implacable reminder that all empires ultimately fail. "London looked the moon's capital – shallow, cratered, extinct" (728). Kôr is a marmoreal commemoration of lost imperial majesty. Finally, Pepita's fantasy of Kôr soothes her in that it offers an escape from the knowledge of those suffering in the present war. She asks, "'How can anyone think about people if they've got any heart? I don't know how other girls manage: I always think about Kôr'" (*Stories* 730). Pepita's fantasy of a time-frozen city unmasks three fracture points in national narrative: the defeat of imperial adventure, the inevitability of the British Empire's extinction and the emotional agony – rather than majesty – of war.

Trauma theory is helpful in explicating these challenges to linear temporality. Although Freud primarily discusses the uncanny in terms of repression, Bhabha suggests that uncanny phenomena have the logic of traumatic return rather than the return of the repressed ("The World" 448). The processes differ in that while repressed material returns disguised in dreams, parapraxes and bodily symptoms, traumatic experience returns without disguise, in dreams and flashbacks (Caruth, "Trauma" 5). Air raids (both Allied and German) were often traumatic, combining overwhelming violence with profound grief, and Bowen describes home front experience in the language of trauma, where imagination cannot encompass experience:

> [these stories] are disjected snapshots – snapshots taken from close up, too close up, in the middle of the *mêlée* of a battle. You cannot *render*, you can only embrace – if it means embracing to suffocation point – something vast that is happening right on top of you. (*Mulberry* 99, emphasis in original)

Robert Jay Lifton notes that the experience of trauma survivors often features "the death imprint," "indelible images ... of grotesque ... forms of death" accompanied by a strange representation of time, "something close to the end of the world, and end of time" (*Future* 236). These wartime interiors in which linear time disintegrates can be read as mimicking traumatic collapse of narrative. In the infected zone of the wartime home front, temporal progress is fragile.

In another form of the infected zone, the past returns to usurp the present. In Bowen's short story "The Happy Autumn Fields" the protagonist Mary visits her bombed house to retrieve possessions. While looking through the rooms, she unearths a box of yellowing, nineteenth-century photographs, diaries and a lock of human hair. They function as cursed objects. Holding them, Mary falls asleep and dreams that she is a Victorian girl called Sarah. When Mary wakes she has become profoundly dissociated from her own body, and still identifies as Sarah:

> she all but afforded a smile at the grotesquerie of being saddled with Mary's body and lover ... she looked ... [at her own body] ... [T]he irrelevant body of Mary, weighted down to the bed, wore a short black modern dress, flaked with plaster. The toes of the black suede shoes by their sickly whiteness showed Mary must have climbed over fallen ceilings; dirt engraved the fate-lines in Mary's palms. (*Stories* 677)

In this indirect interior discourse Mary uses the third person about her own body, psychotically estranged from her own flesh. This particular broken house is an infected zone where present is usurped by past.

The disturbing erasure of the difference between present, past and future finds another form in a non-fiction diary kept by ambulance worker I. S. Haslewood during the London Blitz. She describes her work on a stretcher crew alongside events in her personal life, including furnishing a new flat. Her descriptions of decorating her home and choosing household objects are juxtaposed with descriptions of sorting through the household wreckage of others, entangled with their corpses (19). The juxtaposition is uncanny: while some entries tell the story of creating a home, other entries tell of homes destroyed

Bowen's wartime fiction depicts an additional way in which time becomes strange. Although women were invited to become active outside the home, part of their war work was passive: they had to wait. Plain notes that "men return to women and the home they represent, in the expectation of finding them fundamentally unchanged by the passage of time. This expectation of stasis is ... reinscribed across the potentially liberating and disruptive record of women's wartime experience" (x). This expectation of stasis undermines official discourse depicting women as heroic agents. Bowen's story "The Inherited Clock" (1945) dramatises the damage that prolonged waiting does to heart and mind. Passive waiting can be toxic labour, making a home into a space of heterochronous horror. The cruelest entity in these domestic spaces can be time, personified as a ravenous entity.

In Bowen's story, wealthy Cousin Rosanna has named two young heirs, Clara and her cousin Paul. Clara, now middle-aged, has spent her life in a state of suspense, waiting for the money which will make it possible for her to marry. Clara's suffering was not accidental: Rosanna had to wait for years in the same way and she deliberately selects young heirs in the hope they will suffer likewise. As Clara's co-heir Paul notes dryly, "'The younger the heirs you name, the longer they have to wait, and the more the waiting can do to them'" (*Stories* 637). The damage that waiting can do is rendered through a skeleton clock which terrifies Clara, a clock "threatening to a degree its oddness could not explain":

> The clock was without a face, its twelve numerals being welded on to just a visible wire ring. As she watched, the minute hand against its background of nothing made one, then another, spectral advance. ... [S]he could anticipate feeling her sanity being demolished, by one degree more, as every sixtieth second brought round this unheard click. (628-9)

The clock is alive; its components have a "sensible quiver" (628). It obsesses Clara in childhood and curses her in adulthood. After Rosanna dies and Clara finally inherits the wealth that means she can now marry, the clock seems to blight her hope:

> no kind of exultation was possible. The newly-arrived clock, chopping off each second to fall and perish, recalled how many seconds had gone to make up her years, how many of these had been either null or bitter, how many had been void before the void claimed them [?]. She had been subject to waiting as to an illness; the tissues of her being had been consumed by it. Was it impossible that the past should be able to injure the future irreparably? ... [S]he made herself face the clock; she looked through into the nothing behind its hands. (631)

Waiting has done violence to her. Clara flees the ticking clock and walks into the blacked-out city, and experiences further violence to time. As

Lawrence Phillips suggests, Bowen's wartime writing depicts "the war-time city counting down time like a monstrous antique clock" (18).

> Clara, walking at high speed into the solid darkness, was surprised all over her body to feel no impact: she seemed to pass like a ghost through an endless wall. No segment of moon peered at her, no stars guided Brought to a halt for breath, she began to spy with her torch at the things around her – a post-box, a corner with no railing, the white plate of a street-name. Nothing told her anything ... (632)

Objects become meaningless and she forgets her own story. When she enters a warden's post to seek directions and they ask her where she wishes to go, she temporarily cannot remember where she lives. The wartime present again becomes an infected zone, where cumulative memories fade and linear narratives falter.

Female cruelty in the domestic interior

Although this chapter has focused on ways in which women can suffer within wartime houses, women, too, can poison domestic interiors. Bowen's writing confronts us with the possibility of maternal cruelty. Robert's mother Mrs Kelway terrorises her family, particularly her husband and son. Their home Holme Dene is "a man-eating house," "one of a monstrous hatch-out over southern England of the 1900s. Conceived to please and appease middle-class ladies, it had been bought by a man whose only hope was [such appeasement]" (*Heat* 257). Mrs Kelway's power stems from her profound self-containment and indifference to all others: "she had all she needed: the self-contained mystery of herself" (109). Stella finds Mrs Kelway's regard so annihilating that on meeting her, she has to press her own thumbs to reassure herself she is still alive (114) and Robert says his mother makes him feel "that I don't exist – that I not only am not but never have been'" (117). Mrs Kelway's authority is described in terms military, magical and sacred. She occupies a "strategic" position, from which "she commanded all three windows" (108); "it was the indoors she selected, she consecrated ... this was a bewitched wood" (108–110). Like the men who leave imperious, ghostly traces in the homes of Louie and Stella, Mrs Kelway's silence is a demanding presence. The first thing that makes Stella aware of Mrs Kelway's entrance is her commanding silence that makes Stella turn quickly as if called (108). Under Mrs Kelway's sway, the empty rooms at the top of the house are "flock-packed with matter – repressions, doubts, fears, subterfuges, and fibs" (256) and her grandchildren's rooms are frightening. "Extinct, at this night hour Stygian as an abandoned mine-working, those reaches of passage would show in daylight ghost-pale faded patches no shadow crossed. ... [S]ervants fled Holme Dene, superstitiously, long before darkness fell" (258). Mrs Kelway's tyranny makes the household a place of permanent constraint. In this environment Robert's father is reduced to a submissive shadow and Robert himself feels driven to treachery, explaining his treason as an attempt to fight back against his mother's emasculation of his father (272–3). Women are not necessarily innocent of cruelty in household interiors.

In addition to maternal cruelty, domestic interiors can feature class cruelty, either deliberate or unwitting. Bowen's female protagonists are, like her, almost always upper-middle class, and on the occasions they are not, they sometimes ventriloquise working-class women as reverent to middle-class femininity, eager to see middle-class women maintain decorum and the privileges of their position. Louie, for example, feels awe towards Stella (*Heat* 247–8). Similarly reverent is the housekeeper of Bowen's short story, "Oh, Madam ..." (1941), a transcript of the housekeeper's conversation with a wealthy wife with the latter's replies omitted. The family have gone to live outside London during the Blitz and the wife has come into town to examine bomb damage to their London house. As the dialogue progresses the reader becomes aware that the elderly housekeeper has made unconscionable sacrifices in order to maintain this home over the years, a home to which the family themselves are only casually attached. We discover that the housekeeper does not even know if her own *family* survived the raid, but is nonetheless eager to prioritise making her employer's home habitable again. "'I daresay I am funny in ways, madam, but it's been quite my life here, really it has'" (*Stories* 581). Ultimately, such writing alerts us to the unpalatable fact that the doll's-house exposure of a Blitzed home not only reveals destructive traditions of men exploiting women, but also that of wealthier women exploiting those of the working-class.[67]

Overall, then, Bowen's wartime interiors are sites of suffering and temporal confusion. In a 1948 essay, Bowen describes the mental change that she imagines would herald death: "This is our apprehension – the white, too quiet morning on which we wake to find we have lost the power to live. Absolutely unmeaning, furniture round the bedroom would, that morning, meet the waking eye" ("Lost Art" 2). At that moment of waking, one discovers that one's domestic interior has become meaningless, the objects no longer "speaking" objects, no longer embodying one's personal past. This transformation characterises the uncanny domestic interiors of wartime, undermining mainstream discourse of the home as arena for confident human agency. While imagined community is predicated on a sense of simultaneous living, these texts present the home as a place of heterochronous horror, locked in its own unreachable time.

The texts of this chapter depict domestic interiors collapsing into threatening chaos. In "Summer Night," a character discovers that in each room, "human order seemed to have lapsed – discovered by sudden light, the chairs and tables seemed set round for a mouse's party on a gigantic scale" (*Stories* 596) and in the short story "In the Square" (1945) the drawing room has become a "dead room," rendered lifeless and strange by dust and disorder (610). These wartime homes are not refuges, sites of grace and order, but sites rendered strange by grief, psychological strain and decades of inequity. The last words of this chapter go to the indirect discourse of the sad young widow of Bowen's short story "I Hear You Say So" (1945) who wanders a house at night sleepless with grief. The words of Keats's "Ode to a Nightingale" come to her, prompting her to think of walking amid a field of flowers. She glances down at the carpet in search of some kind of pattern, harmony and order and her effort is soundly defeated:

> Disjected lines of poetry, invocations, came flooding into her mind. *I cannot see what flowers are at my feet.* She looked down at the carpet, wondering if a secret were in its pattern. Naturally, it was too dark to see. (*Stories* 757)

6

"The Rubbish Pile and the Grave": Nation and the Abject in John Piper, Graham Sutherland and Mervyn Peake

This last chapter deals with last things. While the preceding chapters examine the city's shops, streets, workplaces and homes, this focuses on morgues, cemeteries and graves. I argue that literary depictions of the corpse subvert the neat memorialising performed by the British nation-state. First, I will discuss how the dead were built into a narrative of British national heroism, and then I will examine how the wartime writing of John Piper, Graham Sutherland and Mervyn Peake does not distance and tame corpses into a straightforward story of national triumph. Unlike the work discussed in my previous chapters, these moments of abjection do not merely subvert the dominant narrative by offering an alternative story, but rather mark points of fracture where narrative falters altogether.

National narratives of the dead

Bluntly, nations do well out of war death. Ever since the modern nation-state emerged, the language of mourning has underpinned nations' narratives of themselves. Renan suggests that heroic deaths are valuable for the nation because they enable national narrative of "endeavours, sacrifice, and devotion ... the social capital upon which one bases a national idea" (19). Benedict Anderson echoes Renan:

> There are no pre-nation [collective] cenotaphs. ... It is above all these readings of these deaths as political, and their serial alignment ... that structure the national narrative. ... [T]his narrative ... makes each death not an end, but a foreshadowing of each succeeding death, in a long movement toward a resplendent living present. ("Narrating" 659)

A soldier's willing death is sacred for a nation, the bodily sacrifice benefiting the horizontal commonality of the nation-state. Benedict Anderson notes that since the nation as a construct came into being during a time when the old religious modes of thought were fading away, national consciousness took on many of those religious qualities. This religious valence is clear in the reverence accorded to war cenotaphs and Tombs of Unknown Warriors (*Imagined* 9).

Cenotaphs – literally "empty tombs" – have been erected for millennia for private individuals when a beloved corpse could not be retrieved The nation-state, however, saw variations on cenotaphs in which they mark the death of thousands specifically for a national aim. World War I saw a flood of such commemorations. The most famous in Britain are the Cenotaph at Whitehall, London (designed by Sir Edwin Lutyens, erected in temporary form in 1919 and made permanent a year later), and the Tomb of the Unknown Warrior at Westminster Abbey, in which an unknown British soldier was interred at a funeral on Armistice Day November 1920. The public outpouring of grief that accompanied these monuments dwarfs the response to Princess Diana's death in 1997. The Unknown Warrior was brought from France to Dover and then via slow train to London. Thousands of silent mourners lined the track and filled every station on the route. When it reached London's Victoria Station the day before the funeral, crowds tried to clamber past the barricades and climb onto the train, and the following day silent crowds lined the route of the cortège. Both monuments inspired the language of worship. The *Manchester Guardian* said the cenotaph was surrounded by "a light ... like a light on an altar," another newspaper reported "moments of silence where the dead seemed very near, when one almost heard the passage of countless wings," and the *Daily Mail* said "you could scarcely see the Cenotaph for the aura, the halo, the throbbing air that encompassed it" and that mothers' tears had "consecrated" the monument (Hanson 401, 418–19). The Tomb of the Unknown Warrior evoked even more reverence as both war memorial and a literal grave for one anonymous warrior.

Such memorials recuperate war deaths into a narrative of national glory. Lutyens tried to design the Cenotaph to be anational (Hanson 415), but Prime Minister Lloyd George desired the memorial to be "a national shrine, not only for the British Isles, but also for the whole Empire" (qtd. in Hanson 462).The public heard that the Unknown Warrior "died that [the British ruler's] kingdom might endure," and that he died "for the people of the British Empire." The temporary slab declared he fell "FOR KING AND COUNTRY," and the permanent marble slab says he died "for King and Country, for loved ones, home and Empire" (qtd. in Hanson 457, 431, 474, 479). As such, Philippe Ariès argues that the Cenotaph and Tomb of the Unknown Warrior were "an expression of patriotism" (74–5) but this overstates it, since the massive public participation was motivated more by personal grief than by abstract patriotism, the Unknown Warrior taken metonymically – and sometimes literally – to be a family's lost son/father/husband. Nonetheless, the organisers deliberately constructed the ceremonies of the Cenotaph and Unknown Warrior to frame the deaths in terms of a national narrative of glorious death.

By the time the Second World War began in 1939, Armistice Day rituals revering the Cenotaph and Tomb were firmly established, including wearing poppies and observing a public silence (Hanson 483). Their impact intensified even more when the ceremonies began to be broadcast live on radio after 1928 (Cannadine 225; Drake-Carnel 108). Combatants who fell in the Second World War were built into these existing structures of memoralisation, the names of recent fallen appended to existing memorial sculptures and Armistice Day renamed to Remembrance Day to commemorate those fallen in all British wars. Second World War civilian deaths were recuperated into the same national narrative, Churchill declaring in 1940 that "This is a war of the Unknown Warriors. ... The whole of the warring nations are engaged, not only soldiers, but the entire population" (233).

I suggest that such national narratives of glorious death are enabled by a ventriloquised corpse. This trope of the speaking dead remains widespread in the discourse of nations, even featuring in Barack Obama's 2009 presidential inaugural address in which he declares that the "heroes who lie in Arlington [National Cemetery] whisper through the ages" (Garamone). In the imagination of the living, the dead declare that their sacrifice was willing and worthwhile. Nowhere did the Second World War home front encounter the speaking dead more clearly than in the "Letter from an Unknown Airman" in which officer Vivian Rosewarne, writing to his mother, describes his joyful sacrifice for the country:

> History resounds with illustrious names who have given all; yet their sacrifice has resulted in the British Empire where there is a measure of peace, justice and freedom for all, and where a higher standard of civilisation has evolved, and is still evolving, than anywhere else. ... I count myself lucky and honoured to be the right age and fully trained to throw my full weight into the scale. (307–8)

His superior officer, obliged to read all mail, was struck by its fervour, and asked Rosewarne's mother permission to publish it. The letter was reprinted anonymously in *The Times* and then as a pamphlet, reprinted three times to meet demand. It became a film titled *An Airman's Letter to His Mother,* directed by Michael Powell, in which Rosewarne's letter was narrated by John Gielgud. Public enthusiasm for the text was enormous.

What is effaced by such celebrations of the heroic dead, however, is the reality of the body itself. Mark Whalan notes that cenotaphs conceal racial identification, age and the body's other markers, and in the lacunae that result it tends to be assumed that the warrior in question is part of the dominant majority. In the case of the British Unknown Warrior efforts were made to ensure that only a truly unidentifiable body would be chosen, so that all families whose dead were never found could imagine that the tomb held their own. As such, the *Times* could declare that:

> The Unknown Warrior whose body was to be buried may have been born to high position or to low; he may have been a sailor, a soldier or an airman; an Englishman, a Scotsman, a Welshman, an Irishman, a man of the Dominions, a Sikh, a Gurka. No one knows. But he was one who gave his life for the people of the British Empire. (qtd. in Hanson 431)

However, behind the scenes there were actually multiple restrictions on the body selected. The corpse was required to date from the early part of the conflict in 1914 which meant that the Unknown Warrior would be a volunteer recruit rather than a conscripted recruit of the war's later years or a member of a Commonwealth army (Hanson 431–3). In addition, the possibility that he might be Jewish was curtly dismissed by the Dean of Westminster when several people expressed concern at the explicitly Christian content of the commemorative inscription (Hanson 480). Only certain bodies qualify for a particular nation's narratives of heroism.

The present chapter examines a second corollary to eliding the corpse. The cenotaph hides not only the identity of the soldier, but also the radical silence of the dead. This dimension of the human encounter with death is expressed powerfully in D. H. Lawrence's short story "The Odour of Chrysanthemums" (1909) in which the story's protagonist is struck by the self-containment of her husband's corpse. "[H]ow utterly inviolable he lay in himself. ... [She] embraced the body of her husband, with cheek and lips. She seemed to be listening, inquiring, trying to get some connection. But she could not. She was driven away. He was impregnable" (86). Here, the character recognises that a corpse is radically silent and cannot be recruited to the stories of the living. Rather than uttering messages of willing sacrifice and the value of their death, the war dead – like all dead – literally do not speak.[68] The silence of the corpse poses particular challenges to narrative.

Julia Kristeva defines the abject as that which annihilates the subject's mental ordering of the world and boundaries between self and non-self, "what disturbs identity, system, order. What does not respect borders, positions, rules" (4). She argues that the human's first experience of abjection occurs as an infant, in terror of the power of the overwhelming maternal body, a "stifling" power that can "pulverise" the child. In desperation, the infant differentiates itself from the maternal body by repudiating it in ambivalent revulsion (10). Critics have used Kristeva's theory of abjection to describe how a community associates some members with visceral disgust (McClintock 71–2; Iris Marion Young, "Abjection"; Butler, *Reader* 106–7; Miles, "Abjection"). While Kristeva describes the individual as constituting his or her identity by imaginatively expelling the abject, these critics imagine communities defining themselves and establishing their boundaries by imaginatively expelling the abject. This use of abjection has been fruitfully deployed in Gothic studies with regard to nation, Miles, for example, examining how eighteenth-century narratives of British nationhood abject threatening others, notably Catholics ("Abjection"). My previous chapters do similar work, examining how wartime representations of British national fellowship rely on exclusions. There is a risk, however, that such applications of the abject can elide the horror of the category. The abject elicits not only contempt, but also nausea and dread. Kristeva herself takes the corpse as paradigmatic of the abject in that it evokes such horror:

> refuse and corpses *show me* what I permanently thrust aside in order to live. ... [T]he corpse, the most sickening of wastes, is a border that has encroached upon everything. ... In that compelling, insolent thing in the morgue's full sunlight ... I behold the breaking down of a world that has erased its borders. ... The corpse, seen without God and outside of science, is the utmost of abjection. It is death infecting life. (3–4, emphasis in original)

Kristeva declares that unless the beholder is supported by the redemptive mental framework of religion or the detached discourse of medicine the corpse shatters the explanatory structures of the beholder's world. The corpse's "compelling, insolent" silence destabilises all story.

The threat which actual corpses posed to the nation's narratives can be gauged by the care with which officialdom sought to conceal them. Booth has coined the term "corpselessness" to denote the British government's erasure of the dead in World War I, in which "corpses would not be shipped home for burial and that photographs of corpses would not be circulated" (11). The Second World War saw the same edicts, even official War Artists barred from representing dead human figures. Images of broken buildings, seemingly faithful documentation of the scenes, have been relentlessly exposed to the gaze of contemporaries and historians. Yet despite these pictures' seeming transparency, they in fact do work of concealment. As Winston Ramsey notes, "There are endless 'sanitised' photographs of wrecked buildings and one can easily forget that these are invariably taken some hours later after the casualties have been taken to the mortuary" (2: 237). Rarely does one see photographs of the corpses removed from these ruins, for pictures of bombing incidents were always checked by censors. Yet the materiality of corpses on the home front was hard to erase.

City of the dead

Historians have long noted that the first cities were necropoli. Lewis Mumford observes:

> Mid the uneasy wanderings of Paleolithic man, the dead were the first to have a permanent dwelling: a cavern, a mound marked by a cairn, a collective barrow. ... The city of the dead antedates the city of the living. In one sense, indeed, the city of the dead is the forerunner, almost the core, of every living city. (14–15)

Wartime London produced a new twist on the necropolis. David Cannadine argues that the deaths of the Second World War had less impact on the British popular imagination because the total fatalities were lower even when civilian deaths were combined with combatant deaths (232–3). However, what Cannadine's assessment omits is the impact of the 60,000 British civilian dead on the home front. As he notes elsewhere (235) there is a difference between witnessing war and only grieving for those who are in it, and the home front featured significant civilian encounters with war dead.

London was in no way a Dresden, a Belsen or an Auschwitz. Out of London's millions, between September 1940 and May 1941, 41,987 people were killed in bombing. Yet though rescue services worked quickly to remove fatalities, corpses were sometimes heaped up in streets. Sylvia Townsend Warner's short story "Noah's Ark" features a character casually mentioning "how the corpses were heaped up where the old coffee-stall used to be" (85). Revolting events occurred all around Britain: one young woman, for example, was brought out alive after being buried for 106 hours holding a dead baby (Calder, *People* 202), and one pedestrian was struck by dismembered limbs 150 yards away from an explosion (Ramsey 1: 80). Equally ghastly anecdotes are furnished by the people who worked with the dead. Artists trained in anatomy, for example, were useful morgue assistants, and Frances Faviell recalls such work:

> We had to somehow form a body for burial ... there were so many pieces missing. ... The stench was the worst thing about it – that, and having to realise that these frightful pieces of flesh had once been living, breathing people. ... I think that this task dispelled for me the idea that human life is valuable. (115)

Rescuers collected baskets of unidentified flesh, and one warden committed suicide because he could no longer bear to disentangle broken bodies from ruins (S. Jones 19). The diary of ambulance driver I. S. Haslewood aims to resist "whitewashing ... the results of modern warfare" (i) and she describes her first sight of mass dead occurred when a public shelter collapsed killing 70 people. "The scene was of death and devastation. Huge slabs of concrete trapped poor mangled bodies. ... Poor twisted bodies – blackened and begrimed from the blast and dirty. Bits of bodies lay in puddles of water, blood and filth" (4) amid which the rescue men "disintegrated [sic] bodies from the debris" (5). She coins the verb to convey the horror of unsticking wet human tissue from rubble. The results of underground explosions were particularly grotesque. When two tube trains were bombed at Sloane Square tube station, Haslewood recalls:

> the utter carnage of the disaster beggared description. ... Most of the poor bodies had been stripped of their clothing from the blast. Two stark and mutilated bodies of young girls hung high up in the twisted steel girders – trapped by their feet hanging downwards. The men could not get them released for days and had to work under this ghastly spectacle. (42)

The hundreds of thousands of fatalities which the government expected never materialised (Ziegler 11) but it was necessary to commandeer swimming baths as mortuaries in several cases (Ramsey 2: 242) and some areas used mass graves (Harrison 185–6). The city's olfactory geography was also testament to the presence of the dead.[69] Greene recalls "the sweet smell of corruption" which endured for days (*Escape* 83, 88) and Doris Leslie's novel *House in the Dust* (1942) describes the stench of hidden corpses in craters (8). The stink of death is itself abject and invasive, a penetrating odour that is hard for humans to endure. No matter how swiftly the rescue services worked, people were increasingly conscious of the dead.

Rather than building the voice of the ventriloquised corpse into nation-bolstering narratives, the texts I will examine next acknowledge the silence of the dead. It is no accident that this chapter examines not novels nor short stories but rather poetry and prose fragments, for when the corpse is recognised as material fact – when its silence and opacity are recognised – it cannot sustain story.

"Murdered Bodies": anthropomorphic ruins in neo-Romantic art criticism

Art criticism can itself be national mythmaking. At first, wartime art history constructed a narrative of centuries of continuity within British art, describing home front painting as continuous with the Romantic landscapes of the early nineteenth century. As the war progressed, however, art criticism gradually moved away from a romantic preoccupation with national landscape towards an equation between broken building and a broken body, a conventional Gothic trope (Warwick, "Lost Cities" 79).

As in the First World War, the Second World War saw the British government create an Official War Artists' Scheme, administered by the Ministry of Information. The brief of the WAAC was recording the war (Stansky and Abrahams 17) and it defined recording in two ways: topographical drawings that represented damage realistically and fine art that created imaginative visions inspired by that damage. At bombed Coventry Cathedral, for example, Randolph Schwabe was sketching the devastation topographically while John Piper was creating visionary images (Yorke, *Spirit* 94). Praising the recording capability of fine art, Kenneth Clark says of the best artists of the previous War, "These men not only painted good pictures, but did leave a record of the war which the camera could not have given. There are certain things in life so serious that only a poet can tell the truth about them" ("Artist in Wartime" 810).

The particular truth which the WAAC prized was the fundamentally Romantic idea that our landscapes are ourselves.

Clark, leader of the War Artists' Advisory Committee, argued that a particular visionary mode was especially appropriate for representations of the wartime home front: "the best hope for a continuation of landscape painting consist[s] ... in an extension of the pathetic fallacy, and the use of landscape as a focus for our own emotions" (*Landscape* 241). The "pathetic fallacy" is the imaginative work of equating external landscapes with interior emotional states. John Ruskin coined the term in the nineteenth century to describe a characteristic device of Romantic writing. Many British wartime artists explicitly embraced this vision. Graham Sutherland, for example, declares: "the painter must learn to recognise himself ... in the landscape and the landscape in himself" (Pritchett *et al.*, 658). Landscape and particularly buildings were readily anthropomorphised.

Adopting Romantic tropes was partly a deliberate act of national myth-marking. Regaining a lost tradition of English landscape painting was the cherished ambition of several home front artists, a group which art history has labelled the British "neo-Romantics."[70] The most widely-recognised of these are Paul Nash, Piper, Sutherland and Henry Moore (1898–1986). Many of these artists were also prolific writers. Piper, for example, wrote art history, popular guidebooks, and articles for the *Cornhill Magazine, Architectural Review Horizon* and the *Spectator* as well as radio broadcasts (Jenkins 24, 38). Outside fine art circles, too, neo-Romantic tropes and forms saturated visual production of the period. David Mellor catalogues its influence in everything from stage design to advertisements (*Paradise*). Piper and Sutherland, in particular, saw themselves as working within the same tradition as the English landscape artists of the early nineteenth-century.[71] In his pamphlet *British Romantic Artists* (1942), Piper contends that all British art since the Romantics has been an unbroken extension of that Romantic tradition and Sutherland makes a similar argument, approvingly quoting Jean Cocteau's dictum that "[T]he more a poet sings in his genealogical tree, the more his singing is in tune" (Sutherland, "A Trend" 11). As well as providing a narrative of national continuity, neo-Romanticism lent itself well to the ideological work of wartime in other ways. In part, Romantic enthusiasm for landscapes was a response to a sense of a threatened land. Piper recalls, "By 1938 the looming war ... made the whole pattern and structure of thousands of English sites more precious as they became more likely to disappear" (Ingrams 22).[72]

Ruins, a favourite trope in neo-Romantic work, were readily recuperable into national story. A magnificent structure in partial ruin can display remnants of monumental grandeur and as such can be a metonym for a noble past and an enduring history. The sense of a unified spirit of place which characterises Romanticism could be woven readily into narratives of the nation's antiquity (Yorke, *Spirit* 25, Harrod 20, Mellor, *Paradise* 16). British authorities used such art for national ends in multiple ways. Among other things, artists designed murals for the communal "British restaurants" for people who had been bombed out or could not self-cater due to shift work, and Piper designed vast moonlit ruins for such restaurant murals (Jenkins 37).

In addition to making a viewer think of a nation triumphantly spanning centuries, a partially intact building could connote an exemplary life lived to maturity. In an essay titled "Pleasing Decay," Piper contends: "men made buildings, as God made men, to be beautiful in age as well as in youth ... a good designer will have half an eye on the visual future of his work, remembering that some people will see it as an aged warrior or matron" (85). Similarly, the epigraph to Rose Macaulay's nonfiction book *The Pleasure of Ruins,* written immediately after World War II, imagines ruins as benevolent, "sentient" living monuments. Such soothing conceits, however, depend on the anthropomorphised ruins being weathered only partially and gradually by the passage of time. Yorke notes that neo-Romantics relished ruins as long as "Nature had already begun to claim them back" (*Spirit* 20-1). For ruins to be inspiring, the violence of the ruining itself must be distanced in time. As a result, when Piper describes painting home front bomb sites, he tries to recuperate the ruins into a soothing narrative of damage wrought gently through time and water rather than sudden fire, describing "Walls flaked and pitted, as if they had been under water for a hundred years" (qtd. in Yorke, *Spirit* 88). Similarly, Macaulay's extensive catalogue of ruins lists only those tamed by time and distance, mentioning not a single Second World War ruin despite being written in the immediate aftermath of the war. Macaulay reveals why in her afterword: "New ruins have not yet acquired the weathered patina of age. ... [N]ew ruins are for a time stark and bare ... blackened and torn, they smell of fire and mortality" (453). She mourns these anthropomorphised ruins, for "like murdered bodies, their wounds gaped and bled" (454). The body destroyed in violence disrupts the comforting metaphor of a nation's monumental majesty spanning the ages.

The slain human body is particularly significant for three neo-Romantics in particular, Sutherland, Michael Ayrton and Keith Vaughan. Like Piper, Sutherland was both artist and writer, working as War Artist, writer, broadcaster, and munitions gauge maker (Stansky and Abrahams 54). Like the other neo-Romantics, both his writing and art are preoccupied with a sense of the inanimate as alive (Berthoud 82). His diverse wartime work encompassed bombed Swansea, Cornish tin mines, and coal-mining in Wales, but his most disturbing war work is his Blitz *Devastation* sequence, tortured nocturnes of wrecked streets. He becomes preoccupied with mortality while drawing this sequence:

> even a mattress that had been blown out of a house into the middle of the street looked more like a body than a mattress. From butcher's [sic] shops which had been hit the meat spewed on the road, and I remember feeling quite sick when seeing this for the first time because I thought that here was a body which hadn't been picked up. ("Images" 19)

In this death-sensitised necropolis even mattresses and meat resemble corpses. A funereal quality dominates Sutherland's drawings. He always used black deftly in his work, thick black lines typically bisecting vivid colours, but in the prolific *Devastation* sequences, Sutherland's pictures are no longer merely bisected with darkness but are also relentlessly bounded by it, in tomb-like enclosures.

Sutherland's wartime oeuvre arguably ends with his Belsen-inspired studies for Northampton Cathedral's *Crucifixion* (1946) (Illustration 1).

1 Graham Sutherland, *Study for the Northampton Crucifixion* (1946), oil on board. © Tate Gallery. Photograph copyright © Tate, London 2008.

This crucified Christ was influenced by photographs from *K-Z* (*Konzentrationslager*), a booklet issued by the United States Office of War Information in June 1945 with the aim of raising German awareness of the atrocities. Sutherland recalls:

> It was a kind of funeral book. In it were the most terrible photographs of Belsen, Auschwitz and Buchenwald. These photographs were to have a great effect on me, I saw them just before I received a commission to paint a Crucifixion – in them many of the tortured bodies looked like figures deposed from crosses. ("Images" 153).

After reading this text, Sutherland came to believe that the crucifixion could finally be approached anew ("Images" 153). As he told the Church council, he wished Christ's agony to sum up "the agony and suffering of the war" (Berthoud 128). Sutherland tries to be positive, arguing that although amid war's horrors "one can only 'mutter in darkness – spirit sore,'" an artist always "has in one's hand the instruments of transformation and redemption" ("Thoughts on Painting" 378). Yet the work is not one of unequivocal hope: critics described *Crucifixion* as harrowing, and Sutherland himself wrote that it denoted "the continuing beastliness and cruelty of mankind, amounting at times to madness" ("Images," 153). Mellor says of it that "the certain promise of the Resurrection, might have been cancelled out by the unremitting grey horror of the body" (*Paradise* 75).

Like Sutherland, some of Keith Vaughan's art and writing can be fit into a redemptive frameworks. Some depicts figures ascending into the heavens triumphant. However, the bulk of his work is a profoundly haunting meditation on the fragility of the body. Mellor notes that Vaughan's work is influenced by his exposure to broken bodies in his wartime work in the Army Medical Corps, and notes that Vaughan's wartime diaries rehearse a continual "lament ... a threnody for the bodies of young men about to die" (*Paradise* 26). Michael Ayrton's art and writing, too, are preoccupied with the fragility of human flesh. In his art and writing, "Skulls gape, foetal and malignant dwarves sneer, poison vials are spilled. Throughout, a misshapen, Romantic Gothicising is extended into a black extravagance, an excess of bones and worms" (Mellor, *Paradise* 67). Paradoxically, there was a keen appetite for such horrors on the home front in wartime, an appetite leading to poetry collections like Phoebe Pool's *Poems of Death* (1945) which meditates on mortality in lurid terms and is illustrated by Ayrton. Indeed, even living figures painted by the neo-Romantics often had a petrified, marmoreal quality, largely due to widespread adoption of Henry Moore's innovation of using "wax resist," mixing wax crayon with colour wash to give "a weathered, mottled texture as if the flesh had already been turned into carved stone" (Yorke, *Spirit* 128).

In a May 1941 review of official War Art, Piper contends that the latest war pictures "show signs that [artists] are going to create something out of the war instead of merely keeping a tradition alive through it" ("New War Pictures" 50):

> It is not camouflage nor uniforms, nor the clean lines of a gun, nor even heroic profiles, that make good subjects for war pictures; it is death and destruction, and the agony that stays about the rubbish pile and the grave ... a wall falling like a short man; the broken carcase of a lift-shaft; machinery dangling its severed limbs in the bare well of a mantle-factory. (50)

In this apologia for war art, Piper argues that the best war art depicts buildings as though they are broken human bodies. Piper's shift in focus was echoed by several other neo-Romantics, Mellor arguing that as the war progressed, neo-Romanticism became increasingly preoccupied by the ruined human form:

> the stresses and re-structurings of British society during the Second World War imposed new strictures on the human body; a tender body that was bombed, conscripted and exposed to an incremental technological violence and degradation. ... By the mid 1940s both body and land were expelled from the national fantasy of Britain-as-Eden, expelled and displaced into a blitzed ruin. (*Paradise* 16)

While the early 1940s saw neo-Romantics create uplifting dreams in which where anthropomorphised buildings reflect heroic and mature human life, by the end of the war some had drifted towards grotesque renderings of the human body in pain, death and decay. Some of the most sustained explorations of the latter occur in the writing of Mervyn Peake (1911–68). Like Piper and Sutherland, Peake is an artist and writer whose work challenges the glib equation of ruin with monument and who unsettles dominant national stories in the process.

Mervyn Peake's wartime writing

Peake is best known for his Gormenghast novels *Titus Groan* (1946), *Gormenghast* (1950) and *Titus Alone* (1959, rev. 1970), often mis-labelled a trilogy.[73] Like the neo-Romantics discussed above, he imbues the inanimate with life. Yet he does not share neo-Romantic reverence for a uniquely English tradition (Peake had Welsh ancestry) and he was ambivalent about romantic trappings.[74] In particular, Peake complicates the neo-Romantic trope of the regal anthropomorphised edifice, offering instead a Gothic vision of a flayed, agonised body.[75]

From 1941 to 1943 Peake was a conscripted soldier serving in various roles, including as an anti-aircraft gunner near the Thames (Winnington, *Alchemies* 131). Submitting to military discipline was inimical to his personality and he describes his suffering in his poem "Fort Darland" (*Poems* 80–1; cf. Gilmore 32). He had a nervous breakdown in 1942 and was invalided out in 1943 (Winnington, *Alchemies* 154; Gardiner-Scott, "Memory" 26). Yet despite such hardships, the Second World War was a highly creative period for Peake. He wrote a substantial portion of *Titus Groan* while serving as a soldier and convalescing from the ensuing nervous breakdown, and the war years saw him write the poems collected in *Shapes and Sounds* (1941) and *The Glassblowers* (1950). *The Rhyme of the Flying Bomb* (1962) was written soon after the war. Peake was also prolific artistically, commissioned by the WAAC to draw war workers and independently creating a harrowing "Portfolio of the Artist Hitler" for propaganda purposes (not ultimately used). In addition, after the war entered its final stages, Peake travelled to the devastated Continent with journalist Tom Pocock, on assignment for London-based *Leader* magazine to record the suffering of prisoners-of-war, Displaced Persons, and the inmates of Bergen-Belsen (Gilmore 53).

Most Peake criticism concentrates on the Titus books rather than his poetry and I wish to amend the critical balance by examining the poetry he wrote during and soon after the war, particularly that collected in *Shapes and Sounds*.[76] Peake's poetry is sometimes dismissed as overly influenced by the flamboyant "New Apocalypse" movement led by Henry Treece and J. F. Hendry between 1938 and 1943. The New Apocalyptics sought to transform the consciousness of individual readers through lurid verse festooned with "skulls, swords, mystic missals, lanterns and chalices" (Hewison 127) and period critic John Lehmann parodies the style when he scorns the new Apocalypse as "a sickly fungoid growth on decaying jam" ("Armoured" 168). Ronald Binns argues that Peake's anthology *Shapes and Sounds* is influenced to its detriment by the New Apocalypse, contending that "His style is indulgent and archaic, full of references to angels, centaurs, skulls, battlements, coffins, doom, hemlock," and concluding that the poems of *Shapes and Sounds* are "war imagined from a distance, not war experienced" (23).

This chapter questions that reading, arguing that some of Peake's lyric verse grapples with some of the most difficult aspects of war without falling into the glib narrative of the Blitz mythology.

In addition to focusing on Peake's poetry rather than his prose, I also take a different approach from that dominating Peake criticism to date. Much work has fruitfully sought to "locate" Gormenghast in the sense of mapping the disturbing castle onto Peake's own experiences such as growing up in China, serving as a soldier and, in particular, witnessing Belsen-Bergen after liberation.[77] Such studies confirm that in a barbaric world, dark fantasy can have realist force. What has not yet been done, however, is to examine how Peake's writing relates to the discourses of nation dominant at the time. Adam Roberts opens the way to such analysis, noting that the Titus books are "accounts of the catastrophe in traditional Englishness occasioned by the war ... the decay of an *idea* of England: the collapse of a particular fantasy of the realm" (par. 4). Peake was not a Pacifist; he was committed to the war effort, and frustrated that he was at first denied from using his artistic talents in the service of it (Moorcock, "Achievement" 81; Winnington, *Alchemies* 121; Neill, "Peake" 30). Nonetheless, his verse depicts mass bombardment as barbaric – "the scythe of an ape at play" (*Poems* 180) – and unsettles the nation's more simplistic stories of triumphant conflict. Peake's work undermines the way that the corpse was used in British national discourse in two ways. First, he undermines the national agenda of the neo-Romantics by anthropomorphising buildings into death rather than into heroic monumentality. Secondly, his work resists some of the most troubling ways in which the liberation of Belsen-Bergen was assimilated into British home front narratives.

The silent dead

Like the neo-Romantics, Peake depicts buildings as sentient. Castle Gormenghast is an anthropomorphised edifice where every stone throbs with projected human emotion (Le Cam). Although Gormenghast is a site of loneliness and profound interpersonal dysfunction (Ciambezi), the building itself is benevolent. In draft notes for a theatrical adaptation, the Castle explains, "I am ... the component exhalations of the shell and the interstices, from my battered spine of stone to the vaults," and it speaks gently to baby Titus, urging him to sleep (Manuscripts 7.iii). The tenderness of this edifice invites comparison with Peake's poem "London, 1941" which depicts devastated London as a mother.

Maternal personification is a staple of London writing (cf. Moorcock, *Mother London*) and much wartime writing uses the convention. Bottome's *London Pride* (1941), for example, depicts the voice of

Big Ben as "the voice of London, speaking to her children" (10) and the siren sounds as though "Mother Earth herself had become afraid for her threatened children and was giving them a final warning" (47). Similarly, Margery Lawrence apostrophises London as a triumphant, protective Mother in her poem "Londoner's Song" (73). Peake, however, unsettles the maternal trope, anthropomorphising London as mother only to render her as dead or dying:

> Half-masonry, half pain; her head
> From which the plaster breaks away
> Like flesh from the rough bone, is turned
> Upon a neck of stones (*Poems* 89)

Hers is a liminal body, flayed, breasts burned, ribs exposed and skin cold. Yet two details show this shattered figure is still in some way alive: she is in physical agony, and she struggles to protect her children. The ravaged body is maternal: "Her breasts are crumbling brick where the black ivy / Had clung like as fantastic child for succour" (*Poems* 88), but while other texts cheerfully anthropomorphise London as a survivor, declaring "London can take it!" (M. Smith 83–4), this mother cannot save her children. She stands amid the stillness, silence and obscurity of the Burkean sublime: "All else is stillness save the dancing splinters / And the slow inter-wreathing of the smoke" *(Poems* 89). The corpse-like buildings of Peake's poem "The Shapes (London)," too, are linked with the death of a mother. The empty ruin is a "vacant womb," and the speaker asks:

> What of the skin that once enclosed all this?
> Oh it will fall to darkness, to cold darkness
> For it is ichabod and Life had fallen
> Down into darkness ... (*Poems* 84)

The Biblical name "Ichabod" means "the glory has departed" and the name is inextricably entangled with the image of a dead mother, for Ichabod is given his name when his mother dies in childbirth.

These ruined edifices are corpses rather than living figures:

> What are these shapes that stare where once strong houses
> Rose with their sounding halls and rooms of breath?
> No, not their skeletons for those have fallen
> Dragging to earth
> The coloured muscles from a thousand walls.
> ...

> The rubble that is rotting in the rain
> Exhales the breath of Warsaw and Pompeii,
> Guernica, Troy and Coventry – all cities,
> And every breathing building that died burning. (*Poems* 83–4)

The dead buildings are not unique to any one nation's story but rather stand metonymically for all ruined cities. Peake anthropomorphises the edifices in order to evoke the disintegration of the body after death. As such, this personification defies the usual narrative of ruins as markers of the triumphant resilience of the nation. Instead of monumental ruin, Peake describes squalid wreckage, "rubble that is rotting in the rain" – rotting like its organic corollary.

Like the neo-Romantics discussed earlier, Peake personifies edifices, but there is melancholy in the vision. London is a loving entity, yet cannot protect her children. The inability of people to protect and even to fully connect with those they love is a perennial preoccupation in Peake's verse, and is particularly poignant when it depicts the inability of parents to commune with children. "Because Last Night My Child" is a haunting meditation on the insurmountable distance between all human minds:

> he clung to me, his small wet mouth, his heartbeat
> Were close to me
> But he was not mine.
> A wilderness of flying leaves and bids
> Lay in between. (*Poems* 131)

Even when bodies are close, minds are far apart. The gulf between living and dying is even vaster and more unbridgeable, as the following 1941 lyric shows:

> Is there no thread to bind us – I and he
> Who is dying now, this instant as I write
> …
> Is there no power to link us – I and she
> Across whose body the loud roof is falling?
> Or the child, whose blackening skin
> Blossoms with hideous roses in the smoke?
> …

There is no other link. Only this sliding
Second we share: this desperate edge of now. (*Poems* 103)

In contrast to the horizontal bonds of imagined community, this lyric
depicts the impossibility of connection in the face of death.

Peake's verse acknowledges the stark silence of the corpse. In "The
Shapes (London)," personified houses stand like soldiers. "Rank after
rank their wounded faces stare" (*Poems* 83). Yet unlike the dead ventriloquised into a story of national triumph, these dead soldiers do not
speak, but stand in "silent profile" (*Poems* 83). *The Rhyme of the Flying
Bomb*, too, features silent dead:

> "Can you tell me the nearest First Aid Post"
> The sailor said to the man,
> But the lounging figure made no reply
> For the back of his head was gone. (*Poems* 182)

Rhyme describes a deranged sailor, maddened by war's horrors, roaming London during a raid and finding a newborn baby alive in a gutter.
He carries the child through burning streets, taking shelter in a church
which is destroyed by a V1 doodlebug. Before they die, the baby mani-
fests supernatural powers. It flies and speaks, and claims to have been
reincarnated through all the ages. He encourages the sailor to accept
death, but the sailor is not comforted:

> "... I am not ready to die, O child,
> I am not ready to die
> Dear Christ, if my hands and my eyes were gone
> I would not be ready to die." (*Poems* 194)

The sailor does not die willingly. Here and elsewhere, Peake acknowledges the horror of violent death. His poem "If I Would Stay What Men
Call Sane" declares "Now, now, the bomb strikes, and flung limbs are
strewn / Severed and fresh since this short poem started / In (who cares
what poor country)" (*Poems* 123). In such poems, Peake implies that the
brutal materiality of death is something that cannot be glibly recuperated into narratives of national endurance.

"A ghastly hive of horror": British depiction of the holocaust

The sheer quantity of the home front dead, however, never equalled
those of the Nazi concentration camps or the cities bombed by the

148 Urban Gothic of the Second World War

Allies. I will briefly discuss how these faraway deaths were built into Britain's home front narratives of its own wartime labours.

British Bomber Command pursued a policy of "obliteration bombing" of Nazi territory. Brittain argues that "on Germany alone, up to the end of October, 1943, we had already inflicted more than twenty-four times the amount of suffering that we had endured" (*One Voice* 114). In the firebombing of Dresden at least 35,000 people died and the searing conflagration melted human flesh (Mickey Z; F. Taylor 417; Biddle 254–7; Rotter 137). As for Berlin, British war artist Mary Kessell described the destruction: "Berlin smells of death. Incredible, like a million-year-old ruin ... pale figures creeping ... Pools of water, pale in moonlight, and white ruins like great teeth bared. Oh, unforgettable smell of thousands of dead" (600–1). The devastation of Hiroshima and Nagasaki was even more comprehensive, with combined death tolls of more than 240,000 if those who died from radiation are included (P. Norris 38). Kavan noted grimly, "Atom Bomb opens new era in world destruction, entire city vaporised in black rain" (*Sleep* 179–180). Although those in Britain only gradually learned of the horror of radiation, Lifton describes the despair which followed the attack, "a sense of ultimate annihilation – of cities, nations, the world" (*Death* 14). In Marge Piercy's *Gone to Soldiers* (1987) the reports of atomic bomb explosions make one character muse, "'I feel as if I looked out through a vast eye and saw the future of the world in a plain of ashes, of sand turned to glass, flesh vaporised, time itself burned up'" (688). These metaphors suggest that the very substratum of narrative – linear time – is destroyed in the calamity. Such Allied attacks did not fit neatly into narratives of national heroism and splendid struggle. That simple story was again challenged by the silence of the dead.

Yet the most notorious mass killing of World War II was the Holocaust, the first genocide in history to slaughter millions through factory technologies. The majority were Jews, although the camps also included gay men, lesbians, activists, people with mental or physical disabilities and others whom the Nazis defined as impurities in the Reich. Numbers are difficult to estimate since camp commandants destroyed records in the final days of war, but critical consensus agrees that at least six million people were killed. Words struggle to convey the scale of the horror. Martha Gellhorn describes the heartbreak of Dachau:

the bodies were dumped like garbage, rotting in the sun, yellow and nothing but bones, bones grown huge because there was no flesh to cover them, hideous, terrible, agonising bones. ... Nothing about war was ever as insanely wicked as these starved and outraged, naked, nameless dead. (597–8)

Similarly, eyewitness Ronald Monson writes hauntingly of the sight of the dead:

> The indignity of death above ground – the bared teeth, the revealed frame that should be sacred, and once was sacred to some loved one, the piled bodies in their ghastly greyness, the pitiable little thing with claws instead of a hand that was a baby, still within the protective grasp of an emaciated bone that was once a mother's arm. (qtd. in Caven 232)

Gellhorn and Monson are rightly sensitive to the way that such exposure violates the dignity of the dead, a violation all the more deplorable that it echoes the violations the victims suffered when alive. But although these writers emphasise the humanity of the dead, that dimension was elided in much home front media coverage. Shockingly, some commentators were even inclined to see the degradation of the survivors as signs that they had always been subhuman (Seaton, "BBC" 76–7). Media representations of Belsen-Bergen, liberated by British troops, were especially problematic. I will now briefly examine how these media representations contributed to the Gothic of home front experience.

Until a British government delegation personally confirmed the truth of the reports, most British media did not foreground the claims of atrocities (Seaton, "Broadcasting" 139). The reasons for this failure are complex. First, fake atrocity propaganda used in the First World War had rendered the public so suspicious of atrocity stories that during the Second World War the Ministry of Information decreed that atrocity stories should rarely be used (P. Taylor 221). In an infamous memorandum, the Ministry advised media producers that "horror stuff ... must be used very sparingly and must deal always with treatment of indisputably innocent people. Not with violent opponents. And not with Jews" (TNA PRO INF 1/251; qtd. in Caven 229). This memo illustrates the second reason why Holocaust material was not much emphasised in the media until liberation: anti-Semitism existing even at the upper levels of British organisations (Seaton, "BBC" 66). Paradoxically, a third reason for the muted media response to reports of atrocity was that some people of progressive politics feared that singling out the Jews as a persecuted category would perpetuate Nazi doctrine (Kushner, "Memory" 187–8). The BBC and other media organisations were heterogeneous, multiple reasons combining to cause muted coverage of camp atrocities.

A further flaw in home front media coverage was the way that little of it conveyed Bergen-Belsen's complex role in the Nazi system (Kushner, "Memory"; Lattek; Breitman; Cesarani; Caven). In the war years before 1943 it served as a camp for Soviet prisoners of war and after 1943 it became an "exchange" camp for privileged Jews whom Himmler planned to ransom to the Allies to fund the Nazi war effort. The Soviet army's successful march on the eastern Death camps like Auschwitz-Birkenau triggered a radical change in Belsen after January 1944. Jewish prisoners consigned to death were increasingly transported to Belsen instead of the purpose-built Death camps, and over-population caused Belsen's living conditions to deteriorate dramatically. In December 1944 conditions plummeted when Josef Krämer, ex-commandant of Auschwitz, became camp commandant of Belsen and reformulated the camp on brutal lines. 1945 saw Belsen's population soar when Nazis from the eastern camps compelled prisoners on forced death marches to Belsen, away from the advancing Russians. Belsen-Bergen was designed to hold 4,000 but now held 40,000. Thousands starved.

When British forces entered Belsen-Bergen in April 1945 at least 10,000 dead lay unburied, and approximately 14,000 more people died after liberation.[78] The days and weeks after liberation were filmed by the Army Film and Photography Unit (AFPU) and by professionals (including Alfred Hitchcock). The mass dead dominate all these records. So numerous were the dead and so slow the burial process that bulldozers were used to push heaped dead into the mass graves.[79] These and other images have been critiqued for dehumanising the victims into an anonymous heap (e.g. Kushner, "Memory" 186–7; Haggith 91). AFPU cameramen recorded some inmates' names but media coverage usually dropped them (Caven 224). The *Daily Mail* supplement *Lest We Forget*, for example, a collection of holocaust photographs published in summer 1945, erases the personal stories of the dead, making them mere illustrations of the cruelty of a regime defeated by British heroes (Kushner *et al.*, "Approaching Belsen" 5).

Sheer numbers and the need to prioritise succouring the survivors made it difficult to gather individual histories, but even so the dead and the survivors were too often described in the anonymous plural, their personal histories rarely noted even when shared with the rescuers. Such elisions obscured the fact that the majority of the camp's prisoners were Jewish even though 67 per cent of the 60,000 people liberated at Belsen were Jewish (Caven 209; Haggith 93; Reilly 77; Kushner, *Holocaust* 213). Similarly, the few people who were singled out for individual history were often uncharacteristic of the many in the camps.

For example, Leonard Cottrell's BBC radio play *The Man from Belsen* (1946) describes the experiences of Harold Le Druillenec, one of the few British citizens liberated at Belsen, and similar Britain-centrism shaped the way the media reported the photograph of Belsen survivor Louis Bonerger. The photographer's sheet records he is an "Englishman ... born in London ... Belgian parents but claims British nationality, was a spy for Britain and parachuted into Germany in 1941, but was caught," but a British newspaper caption describes him only as "a starving Londoner," eliding his continental connections (Caven 224).

In addition, British home front media representations of the liberation of the camp often featured a triumphalist slant. A BBC Assistant Director of the BBC European Service, for example, decreed, "The European Service must give the fullest possible attention today to the concentration camps. ... Establish the war guilt. ... Show that this was the justification for the war" (BBC Written Archives Centre E2/131/22). That narrative is disingenuous because destroying the camps and rescuing persecuted Jews was by no means a primary war goal; BBC news controllers themselves noted that Britain had "turn[ed] ... a blind eye to Buchenwald and Dachau and the Jewish pogroms" (qtd. in Bardgett 134). Nonetheless, after liberation the camps were presented as something which Britons explicitly strived to defeat. George Murray, writing in the Daily Mail's *Lest We Forget* supplement, presents the story of the holocaust within a framework of a triumphalist British narrative, a "reminder to the British people of the menace they have beaten" (4). Patrick Gordon Walker produced a thoughtful radio report on Belsen (Bardgett 134), but even this is framed in national terms: it opens with camp inmates playing the British national anthem *God Save the King* and closes with children from the camps singing *The English: Long May They Live in Glory* (Gordon Walker 137, 141). After the last hut had been burned down the British flag was ceremoniously raised on Belsen's grounds. Given that the suffering at the camps was so profound, such use of the camps to bolster narratives of British triumph has been critiqued as ethically suspect (Kushner *et al.* 31, 17, 26; "Memory" 191).

In 1944, London saw light-hearted depictions of the camps, one waxwork exhibition purporting to depict "Horrors of the Nazi concentration camps ... tortures, flogging, crucifixion, gas chambers ... children's amusement section no extra charge" (Ziegler 309). Such cavalier representations ebbed after April 1945 when newsreels of the camps were screened in Britain. Ziegler records that, "Crowds queued for hours, watched in shocked silence, left without applauding or even passing casual remarks" (309). Panter-Downes believed that such film had finally brought home "to the slow, good-natured, skeptical British what, as various liberal journals have tartly pointed out, the pens of their correspondents have been unsuccessfully trying to bring home to them since as far back as 1933" ("Photography" 590). Yet British home front media representations of the camps, including this footage, continued to fail to note the particularity of each camp, victim and survivor, merging the camps and the suffering into an icon emptied of real lives. This is the work of myth as Barthes describes it, evacuating an emblem of its complexity. The ensuing icon can readily be built into simplified narratives of nation.

Home front media also elided differences between camps. The relentless media attention on Belsen made it possible for people to ignore the purpose-built death factory of of Auschwitz-Birkenau, which was strangely downplayed in histories of the holocaust in the years after the war (Kushner, "Memory" 188). In addition, media reports regularly confused Belsen-Bergen with Eastern camps to the extent that even broadcasters themselves described their horror at gas chambers at Belsen-Bergen, which did not exist. Belsen's appall-ing deaths were achieved through starvation (Kushner, "Memory" 188–9). These details matter because such errors play into the hands of holocaust deniers, and because victims and survivors deserve to have their particular experiences recognised. Each camp was part of a wider system for administering death, a lethal network that should itself be anatomised.

Peake's visit to Belsen influenced his depiction of the death fac-tory in *Titus Alone*, "a ghastly hive of horror: a hive whose honey was the grey and ultimate slime of the pit" (*Gormenghast* 905). He also produced poetry and sketches. He recognised, however, that the ethics of creating artistic representations from suffering are fraught. Theodor Adorno famously declares that, "to write poetry after Auschwitz is barbaric" (qtd. in Gubar 4), and Peake grapples with a similar idea in his poem "The Consumptive, Belsen 1945."[80] The poem describes a young woman dying of tuberculosis contracted in the camp. As the speaker of the poem watches her, he is tempted to create a painting of her suffering: "my schooled eyes see / The ghost of a great painting, line and hue / In this doomed girl of tallow" (*Poems* 133). The speaker of the poem describes resisting that tempta-tion, but Peake himself in fact created two works of art in response to her suffering: the poem itself and the haunting sketch *Dying Girl in Blanket* (Illustration 2). Both Peake and his son Sebastian felt shame

2 Mervyn Peake, *Dying Girl in Blanket* (1945), charcoal; rpt. in Sebastian Peake *et al.* (133). Reproduced by kind permission of the Peake Estate. © Mervyn Peake.

at his transforming such agony into art (Winnington, *Alchemies* 179; Pocock 146; S. Peake 211–12), but nonetheless, I suggest that Peake's work in fact resists some of the ethical flaws in British discourse of the camp liberation.

First, Peake's work, especially his poetry, foregrounds the challenge of adequate emotional response in the face of horror, a key issue for those in Britain consuming these images. Peake's verse emphasises the need to not grow numb to sights of suffering. In "The Consumptive," Peake laments that:

> Her agony slides through me: I am glass
> That grief can find no grip ...
> ... O God,
> That grief so glibly slides! (*Poems* 134)

Similarly, his lyric "What Is It Muffles the Ascending Moment?" written in response to Blitz war deaths years before he visited Belsen-Bergen, asks how a person can become strangely numb to the agony of another:

> What is it clouds the anguish of crushed limbs?
> Through darkened glass I watch the mimes of death
> ...
> What is it holds the senses back from knowing?
> And the eyes from perceiving?
> And the dazed brain from grieving?
> That drugs my heart, and stays the tear from flowing? (*Poems* 95–6)

Such a response is paradigmatic of trauma as discussed in Chapter 2, an experience so emotionally overwhelming it could not be fully absorbed at the moment of the experience itself. The lyric's litany of questions are all the more forceful when one considers that Peake's poetry normally presents vision as an astoundingly powerful sense, which can "gather tempests to the tiny lens" (*Poems* 56) and "Mint gold ... ceaselessly between the lids" (*Poems* 22). Yet vision fails in this Blitz lyric, for the speaker's eyes are like "darkened glass," "webbed against the omnipresent day" (*Poems* 95). An increasing numbness to horror afflicted many people in Britain viewing the pictures of camps' suffering, and Peake notes the ethical necessity of keeping horror sharp when aware of another's agony.

Peake was also sensitive to the camp survivors' need for simple dignities. In his lyric "Victims," he describes poignantly how the camps' inmates died without any of the kindness that one might hope for in death: "They had no quiet and smoothed sheets of death. ... There was no hush of love" (*Poems* 137). In such moments, Peake's work is sensitive to the humiliation that some survivors experienced in the wake of liberation. Josef Rosensaft, himself a survivor, says that the liberators "had forgotten that we were not brought up in Belsen, Auschwitz and other concentration camps, but had, once upon a time, a home, and a background and motherly love and kindness; that before the calamity we, too, had our schools and universities and Yeshivot" (qtd. in Steinert 74). Some said they felt that the liberators tended to think of them as always having been in some way subhuman in order to have been able to be degraded to such a level. Peake's verse resists such dehumanising. In addition, although the dying girl remains anonymous, he does not take the usual route of depicting the dying in multitudes of heaped bodies. The girl of the poem retains two forms of (admittedly diluted) agency. In the portrait, she returns our gaze, and in the poem, she is paradoxically eloquent. "Those coughs were her last words ... through them was made articulate / Earth's desolation on the alien bed" (*Poems* 134). Rather than the poet or the artist, it is this dying girl who can "make articulate" the horror of "Earth's desolation." Finally, Peake does not blur the dying girl's suffering into a background for a narrative of national triumph.

In conclusion, Peake's war poetry can be read as a catalogue of necessary violence done to the deceptive simplicities of narrative form. Indeed, his poem "Victims" presents story as itself cruel: "In twisting flames their twisting bodies blackened, / For History, that witless chronicler / Continued writing his long manuscript" (*Poems* 137). In the poem "As Battle Closes In My Body Stoops" the speaker is an exultant devourer of the dead: "Lolling on senseless massacre I lie / Capacious while the innumerable dead / From battlefields and cities rise to me" (*Poems* 170). Here mass deaths are not recuperated into a triumphant story of a nation's struggles. Peake's writing implies that rather than build war deaths into narrative, we should recognise that violence destroys human stories. Thus torn paper flutters through the skeletal corpse-buildings of "The Shapes (London)," "torn papers that, bespattered, / Flutter their hollow wings" (*Poems* 84). The violence Peake's wartime work does to narrative form is laudable: he offers no consolation by ventriloquising the fallen as glorious dead. As such, Peake's work is an antidote to the simplistic tropes that saturate home front representations of death.

A regular refrain throughout wartime writing was the hope that after the war London could be regenerated and that Britain as a whole could be transformed into a better society. Such hopes were substantially realised in a range of initiatives, including the 1942 Beveridge Report (which created the modern welfare state), urban planning initiatives (such as Patrick Abercrombie's Greater London Plan) and the 1951 Festival of Britain, which ran from May to November 1951 and was designed to be a forward-looking celebration of Britain's cultural and economic strengths. However, even these hopeful narratives of national progress are veined through with more troubling tropes of dismemberment and bodily injury. One poster which ostensibly celebrated new houses built on Blitz wreckage, for example, holds reminders of the suffering that accompanied the clearances of the older buildings (Illustration 3).

The image recalls the myth of Excalibur, the enchanted sword presented to King Arthur by a graceful arm rising from a lake. English national mythology is marshalled to look forward to a proud national

3   Poster advertisement for Lansbury Council Estate, "New Homes Rise from London's Ruins." The Museum of London, image accession number 95.249. © Museum of London.

future. Yet there is a darker way in which this image speaks a truth of the war. The juxtaposition of flesh and ruined house makes viewers aware of the human bodies dismembered in these clearances. The wreckage at the base of the poster and the disembodied arms remind us of the reality of those corpses, in a grim challenge to the Arthurian intertext. As Peake says, this London is "half masonry, half pain"; human agony and death are written into the very fabric of the wartime and post-war city.

Afterword: The Politics of Lamentation

The texts of this book exemplify subjective fracture and anguish – indeed, the "Gothic mode" can be defined as having those formal qualities. As such, they are of not only historical interest but also of profound contemporary value, in that they present alternative ways to respond to collective agony. Recent studies of nation and memory propose a new ethics of mourning in which normative mourning – working through grief, accepting loss, and ultimately finding solace – is increasingly seen as ethically suspect. Ultimately, this book suggests that Gothic literary forms are valuable in that they do *not* neatly subsume loss and death into a narrative of healing and survival.

Resistant mourning

Freud published his definition of normative mourning in 1917 in the shadow of the First World War's unprecedented combat fatalities. He differentiates between two responses to loss: normative mourning and pathological melancholia. In Freud's model, the act of becoming attached to an object involves object cathexis, i.e. investing emotional and physical energy (libido) in one's mental representation of that object (Laplanche and Pontalis 62–5). A beloved object will have a "thousand links" to the ego and mourning requires dissolving each link in painful *Trauerarbeit*, grief work (Freud, 11: 265–6, 253). In normative mourning a person gradually reaches acceptance of the loss. Yet such acceptance is not always possible. In Freud's version of melancholia, the griever does not repress the knowledge of their loss but does repress the full realisation of their pain and what that person meant to them. Such mourners avoid the process of painful acceptance by instead unconsciously internalising the lost object, keeping the beloved alive in themselves by taking on their personality attributes. Freud argues that, "by taking flight into the ego love escapes extinction" (11: 250, 267). Melancholics' rage at the lost object for abandoning them is then unconsciously channelled into self-torment and suicidal despair.

Acceptance of loss, then, is fundamental to Freud's definition of healthy mourning, and it is this acceptance which has inspired many to argue that there are ethical problems with normative mourning. The challenges normative mourning poses to progressive politics are two-fold. First, mourners' acceptance can allow the state to avoid recognizing the suffering ensuing from war. Grief can be profoundly disruptive to a society's ruling bodies. Rae notes there is a sense that the accept-ance in normative mourning "amounts to a forgetting of, or an abdica-tion of responsibility for, what has been lost, and that this amnesia has been too often demanded and paid in the interests of serving the *status quo*" (18). Nicole Loraux, for example, describes how ancient Athens set legal prohibitions on passionate displays of grief by bereaved moth-ers. Secondly, rituals of collective normative mourning often elide the deaths of the marginalised. In this regard, Butler notes many cultures imply a distinction between "grievable" and "ungrievable" lives, the latter unrepresented in nations' discourse of mourning (*Precarious* 36). As a result of these two problems, some critics pose a third alternative: resistant mourning, which rejects both the acceptance of normative mourning and the unconscious denial of pathological melancholy.[81]

"Resistant" mourning discerns political value in incomplete mourn-ing and ongoing emotional pain, denying neither the painful loss nor the circumstances that caused it. Such grief arguably has political force. Butler notes:

> What grief displays ... is the thrall in which our relations with others hold us, in ways that we cannot always recount or explain, in ways that complicate the self-conscious account of ourselves as autono-mous and in control. I might try to tell a story ... about what I am feel-ing, but it would have to be a story in which the very "I" who seeks to tell the story is called into question by its relation to the [dead] Other. ... My narrative falters, as it must. (*Precarious* 22–3, 30)

In other words, grief complicates any presumption of the self as intact and autonomous. It draws the eye out to the limits of the self, where we connect with others, and as such, it can be argued that grief can ultimately enable a fuller sense of community. Butler, for example, sug-gests something can be gained from grieving, "from remaining exposed to its unbearability and not endeavouring to seek a resolution for grief through violence" (*Precarious* 30). Champions of resistant mourning contend that there is ethical merit in *not* moving on from horrors, that there may be political value in not being healed.

Another influential opponent of normative mourning is Jacques Derrida, who advocates a third way rejecting both the closure of normative mourning and the rhetoric of the dead living on in the living. The latter construction has been formalised in psychoanalytic discourse with the concepts of identification, introjection and incorporation.[82] Derrida (following Jacques Lacan and Maria Torok) differentiates between healthy introjection and delusional incorporation, defining introjection as a psychologically healthy gradual bringing of memory of the lost object into the self, in a "slow, laborious, mediated, [and] effective" process, and contrasting it with incorporation, which he defines as a delusional, devouring mode, "fantasmic, unmediated, instantaneous, magical, sometimes hallucinatory" (Derrida, *"Fors"* xvii). Andrea Liss defines incorporation is "the self's almost obscene desire to overwhelm the [dead] other" (24), to incorporate the dead into the narratives of the living.[83] Derrida rejects both introjection and incorporation as unethical, arguing that both deny the insurmountable absence of the other. Instead, Derrida advocates an "aborted" interiorisation which combines an internalising of the other with recognition of the impossibility that any internalisation can be mimetic. This aborted interiorisation is "at the same time a respect for the other as other, a sort of tender rejection, a movement of renunciation which leaves the other alone, outside, over there, in his death, outside of us" (*Mémoires* 35). Like Butler, Derrida discerns the possibility of such grieving leading to a new, more ethical intuition of community with those who suffer. Derrida argues that an awareness of the dead is crucial for progressive politics:

> No justice ... seems possible or thinkable without the principle of some responsibility , beyond all living present, within that which disjoins the living present, before the ghosts of those who are not yet born or who are already dead, be they victims of wars, political or other kinds of violence, nationalist, racist, colonialist, sexist, or other kinds of exterminations, victims of capitalist imperialism or any of the forms of totalitarianism. (*Spectres* xix)

Such dead should be held within us, argues Derrida, in a way that never rounds off their loss into tame acceptance.

Literary texts frequently inhabit that contemplative position, tarrying with the pain. Indeed, the very literary forms of modernism arguably enshrine such a posture (Booth; Forter 44; Dalzielle; Summers-Bremner; Hellen). Rae argues that in literary modernism:

> the famously "split," sometimes manifold, modernist subject, speaking indirectly and ironically through objective correlatives and multiple personae, becomes a figure ... whose losses cannot be assimilated to the *status quo*. ... When set against the background of discourses of public mourning that reinforce injustice ... these strategies do not seem irresponsible retreats into privacy and madness, but rather conscientious objections. (38)

A similar argument can be proposed for the Gothic. Some forms of resistant mourning have been criticised for eliding the agonising affect of the position (Forter 242) but the texts explored in this book resist that temptation, choosing instead to dwell with painful affect.

"Crying with phantom tongue": poetry that resists consolation

Peake's poem "The Craters" focuses on the pain of loss and resists conventional consolations.[84] It opens with the craters of the bombed city being seen as an objective correlative for the anguish of the war-bereaved: "the city crater is the mocking / Shadow of that zoneless chasm their breasts / Are empty with" (*Poems* 91). Peake's poem captures the sensation of an internal void correlating with the loss of a beloved, as does the accompanying illustration in his anthology *Shapes and Sounds* (Illustration 4).

The empty breast is a metaphor for an interior world impoverished by loss, inviting us to draw a link to the psychoanalytic theory of introjection and incorporation. Yet this wound is arguably closer to the ambiguous third state lauded in different ways by Butler and Derrida. Both use metaphors of strange speech to describe the ambiguous way in which mourners can imagine holding the dead within themselves. Derrida urges us to imagine "an apostrophe to an absent, deceased, or voiceless entity, which ... confers upon it [the lost entity] the power of speech" (*Mémoires* 35) yet he emphasises that this is always "mere ventriloquism" (Rae 17). The dead person remains, as Derrida says, "over there, in his death, outside of us" (*Mémoires* 35). Similarly, Butler argues that when grieving "I might try to tell a story ... about what I am

4 Mervyn Peake, illustration from *Shapes and Sounds*. Reproduced by kind permission of the Peake Estate. © Mervyn Peake.

feeling, but it would have to be a story in which the very 'I' who seeks to tell the story is called into question by its relation to the [dead] Other, a relation that ... clutter[s] my speech with signs of its undoing" (Butler, *Precarious* 23).

The bereaved of Peake's poem are filled with such eerie voices. They contain a "world of ... emptiness,"

> ... that yawns and opens
> Into a firmament beneath their ribs
> That knows no planets, but a few dead stars
> That wander desolately through the darkness,
> Crying with phantom tongue of what is heard,
> Of where they live and what their cold names are.

(Poems 91)

The poem exemplifies "respect for the other as other, a sort of tender rejection, a movement of renunciation which leaves the other alone, outside, over there, in his death, outside of us" (*Mémoires* 35). The voices within the mourner cry with "phantom tongue" and drift rootless through darkness, even their names now "cold." So vast is the distance between dead and living that even the internal representation of the dead is scarred by strangeness. As such, the poem arguably recalls the ambiguous state advocated by Derrida and Butler, in which the dead are not internalised to bolster the mourner's story of the self but are internalised in ways that unsettle and wound the living.

The depiction of grief in the poem also deftly undermines the key neo-Romantic trope of pathetic fallacy, for the speaker of the poem rejects the consolation of seeing the world outside himself as an echo of his own inner state. At first Peake's poem seems to make a similar move when the bomb crater parallells the "chasm" within the bereaved, but as the poem proceeds we encounter the radical failure of the outside world to provide a soothing echo of the speaker's suffering. The craters are merely "Huge figments of their wounds" which mock the grievers (*Poems* 91). Agonising though the state of grief is, however, the speaker has no longing for closure and the healing of time, and scorns time as "unfaithful" because it dilutes the pain of the loss.

A poem that so deftly evokes the pain of mourning underscores the need to be cautious in advocating mourning as a political strategy. Yet there is an unpalatable truth to the first sharp agony of the mourner and perhaps some collective wounds should not be healed too easily. The literary texts of this book similarly resist tidy closures. Narratives which efface the agony of war should be questioned; like these texts, perhaps we should tarry with the pain.

Notes

1 Introduction: The Urban Gothic of the British Home Front

1. The closest material consists of articles about Elizabeth Bowen, but even in her case, the wartime work has been relatively under-explored in terms of the Gothic tradition. Julia Briggs mentions Bowen's wartime writing briefly in her article on "The Ghost Story" (130) and Bowen's pre-war ghost stories have been examined as Gothic, particularly her short story "The Shadowy Third": see David Punter ("Hungry Ghosts") and Diana Wallace ("Uncanny Stories"). Bowen was Anglo-Irish, and as such has a complex relationship to national identity; this dimension of her work has been explored through a Gothic lens in articles by Nicholas Royle and Julian Moynahan.
2. Cultural geography differentiates between "place" and "space." Humanist geographers like Yi-Fu Tuan associate place with security and space with freedom and threat (Cresswell 8) but the binary of space and place falls into the same traps as all binaries: one pole tends to be valorised and liminal positions between the two are effaced. I use "space" because I distrust the nostalgia that has often accreted around "place," and because – as my discussion of post-imperial geographies will show – even clearly demarcated places are sites of incorrigibly intersecting mobilities (Chapter 2). In this I follow the cultural geographers who contend that place is constituted by reiterative practice (Thrift; Pred) and is open and hybrid (Massey).
3. George Chesney's *The Battle of Dorking: Reminiscences of a Volunteer* (1871) was one of the earliest of these invasion fictions, and as the century advanced a large market for the genre emerged William Le Queux was the most prolific writer in the genre, his most famous book being *The Invasion of 1910, With a Full Account of the Siege of London* (1906).
4. When writing *War in the Air* Wells was wholeheartedly opposed to war but he eventually became persuaded of its occasional justification and wrote propaganda for the First World War. In 1913 he wrote a book for children describing rules for using toy soldiers in tabletop war games (Aldiss, "Introduction" to *War of the Worlds* xxviii). Wells's ongoing ambivalence to war is encapsulated in the slogan he crafted for the First World War: "the war to end war" (Winter, "Nightmare" xxiv).
5. Like all vampire mythology, *Return of the Vampire* invites comparison with Freud's description of repressed desires which "are not dead in our sense of the word but only like the shades in the Odyssey, which awoke to some sort of life as soon as they had tasted blood" (4: 348). The taboo desires most often repressed are destructiveness and sexual desire and *Return of the Vampire* features both, for the bombing frees something that had been left buried for years, something violent and sexually predatorial. As I show in Chapter 3, however, it can be more fruitful to approach the film through sociohistorical analysis of home front xenophobia.

6. For discussions of First World War Gothic, see Terry Philips and Martin Tropp.

7. Car headlights were initially covered with cardboard but as pedestrian deaths mounted headlights were partially concealed with a metal grid (Gardiner 79).

8. For discussion of the sensory geography of wartime London see Adey (par. 8) and Wasson.

9. Conscription was reintroduced in May 1939 under the Military Training Act (Gardiner 53).

10. John Piper produced a book entitled *British Romantic Artists*, Michael Ayrton wrote a Collins booklet about British drawing, David Low wrote about British cartoons, H. J. Paris wrote about English water-colours, John Russell wrote about British portraits, Cecil Beaton wrote about British photography and Major Guy Paget wrote about English sporting prints (Yorke, *Spirit* 88).

11. For details of IRA attacks in England from January 1939 onwards, see Calder (*Myth* 65–6) and Kee (101–3, 241–2, 283–4). Sinn Fein published pro-German pamphlets early in the war and there were isolated strands sympathetic to fascism in both Eire and Northern Ireland (Fisk 28, 50, 425–37, 50, 379, 437, 460–2) but many people in Northern Ireland enlisted voluntarily to support the Allies or served in support capacities (Calder, *Myth* 65–6).

12. British fascism has a complex genealogy with some strands inspired more by Mussolini than Hitler, and British fascist ideologies grafted onto existing traditions of British conservative thought in varying ways. Many British fascist groups disagreed with each other, not least in the way they imagined a Jewish "threat." For more on anti-Semitism in British culture and literature during the 1930s and 1940s see Phyllis Lassner (Chapters 6–7), Bryan Cheyette, Andrea Loewenstein, Tony Kushner (*Holocaust*), Richard Thurlow (66–9), Jon Stratton (132), Colin Holmes, Kenneth Lunn, John Morell, Gisela Lebzelter ("Henry Hamilton"; *Political Anti-Semitism*) and Stuart Hylton (88–96). Anti-fascist movements rose to defy anti-Semitism, particularly among organised labour (Thurlow 101–2), famously clashing at the Battle of Cable Street of 4 October 1936.

13. From mid-November 1940 the *Luftwaffe* attacked other industrial cities around Britain, including Cardiff, Bristol, Swansea, Plymouth, Clydesdale, and most thorough of all, Coventry. That midlands city was the base for many aircraft factories, and on the night of 14 November 1940 it was devastated by a massed attack of 449 bombers. 554 people were killed, 865 were seriously injured and 100 acres of the city centre were flattened. In 1942, the "Baedeker" raids began in retaliation for Allied bombing of the north German town of Lübeck in March. The retaliatory "Baedeker" raids, named after the popular series of German guide-books, targeted towns like Bath, York and Canterbury (Jenkins 35).

14. Peake, speaking of the bombing of Mannheim and Wiesbaden, notes: "Terrible as the bombing of London was, it is absolutely nothing – nothing compared with this unutterable desolation. Imagine Chelsea in fragments with not one single house with any more than a few weird shaped walls where it once stood, and you will get an idea in miniature of what Mannheim and Wiesbaden are like" (Gilmore 52–3). Middlebrook and Everitt record Dresden's damage: "In the firestorm at Dresden, caused by British incendiary attack on 13 February 1945, which was followed by USA Air Force daylight assault next day, more

than 40,000 people probably died, and perhaps more than 50,000" (663–4). By contrast, T. H. O'Brien notes that "Over the entire war, according to British official figures, 29,890 died during enemy action in London, two-thirds of them in 1940–41. Slightly more died elsewhere in Britain: 30,705" (677).

2 Nightmare City: Gothic *Flânerie* and Wartime Spectacle in Henry Green and Roy Fuller

15. Benjamin argues that *flânerie* ceased to be possible as the nineteenth century progressed (Tester 14–15). Nonetheless, *flânerie* is still invoked as an influential trope even in the twenty-first century, and was a precursor of late twentieth-century psychogeography. For postmodern successors to *flânerie* see Jenks and Mazlish.

16. The city itself is regularly feminised in nineteenth century writing and since. The narrator of *Paris Spleen*'s "Epilogue," for example, compares the city to that of a prostitute (108). Anne McClintock suggests, "If the woman's body is the child's first space for knowledge and self-discovery, later the city, as the first space of modern self-knowledge was mapped as a feminine space. Once feminised, the city was more easily represented and made docile for male knowledge and power" (82).

17. Ration books were designed and printed at the end of the 1938 Munich Crisis ("War Doesn't Change" 16–17). Food rationing began officially on 8 January 1940 but was already operating unofficially in many places after November 1939 (Gardiner 120).

18. Interwar psychoanalysis had already punctured any sentimental belief that children lack ferocity; see Melanie Klein.

19. For analysis of how new lighting was integrated with commodity display, see Bowlby (*Just Looking*), Rosalind Williams, Michael Miller and Hrant Pasdermadjan.

20. Similarly, when the word appears elsewhere in the novel it is often in a context of vision and danger. For example, the novel describes First World War soldiers blinded by mustard gas as "caught" by blindness (21).

21. Conventional bulbs were sometimes replaced with violet bulbs to reduce the risk of accidentally breaching the blackout.

22. The empire/emporium contrast is proposed in a sociology MA dissertation by I. Roderick (Shields 74).

23. With transport methods and petrol scarce, the Auxiliary Fire Service commandeered 7,500 of London's 15,000 taxis (Ziegler 47).

3 Carceral City, Cryptic Signs: Wartime Fiction by Anna Kavan and Graham Greene

24. The victims of eighteenth-century Gothic are often female, a heterosexual frisson animating the relationship between captor and captive.

25. For discussion of crime in wartime, see Steve Jones, Harold Smith (86–97), Calder (*People* 337), Ziegler (229–32), Hylton (186–202), Mackay (127–8). For wartime prison life see Steve Jones (71–8).

26. For discussion of the legal categories of "alien" and "stateless alien" (denationalised by their country of citizenship), see Fraser (2–28, 65).
27. London's Imperial War Museum holds examples of such documents (e.g. the Papers of Miss Tea Lewinski).
28. The first (equally fictitious) fifth column was invented in the Spanish Civil War, when a General claimed that he had four columns of troops and a secret fifth column of supporters embedded in his opponent's territory (Calder, *Myth* 111). For debunking of the British fifth column, see Wasserstein (82).
29. For Churchill's role in internment see Peter and Leni Gillman, Wasserstein (87) and Lafitte (xiii–xiv).
30. For Second World War refugee experience on the British home front see Lafitte's 1940 exposé of the camps. Histories incorporating testimony from internees include Fred Uhlman, Connery Chappell, Gilman and Gillman, Yvonne Kapp and Margaret Mynatt, Miriam Kochan (*Britain's Internees; Prisoners*), Hilda Ogbe, Ziegler (23, 75, 93–8, 176, 279, 320), Hylton (1–35), David Cesarani and Tony Kushner, Calder (*People* 129–33), Steve Jones (71–78) and Richard Dove.
31. For one example among thousands, see the papers of Mr Otto Pond at the Imperial War Museum. Mr Pond escaped from Dachau and was interned when he reached Britain.
32. After learning of this anti-Semitism the British government did seek to improve treatment of deported internees (Wasserstein 88–90).
33. For government papers on shell-shock see Freeman and Berrios. For an introduction to the cultural history of shell-shock see Showalter (*Female Malady*), Robert Hemmings, Jay Winter ("Shell-Shock"), Ted Bogacz, Martin Stone, Chris Feudtner, Richard Slobodin, Alan Young and Pat Barker. In the Second World War, shell-shock tended to go by the term "battle fatigue" (K. Jones, *History* 235).
34. For details on the Act, see Kathleen Jones (*History; Asylums*). Conditions improved between the Wars (K. Jones, *Asylums* 134), although the Act's efficacy has been questioned and many of the torments identified by Lomax were found in the same hospital in the 1970s (Hopton).
35. A desire to correct the flaws in British psychiatric treatment was a key part of the proposals for reform that culminated in the 1942 Beveridge Report, underpinning the formation of the National Health Service in 1948 (K. Jones, *History* 272–5; Cherry 208; Lowe; Barham).
36. The language of "case" permeates Kavan criticism, as in the title of Callard's biography, *The Case of Anna Kavan*. Most critics approach Kavan's writing autobiographically (Reed 45; Aldiss, Introduction to *Ice*; Zambreno; Callard, "Bitter Pilgrimage"; E. Young; Stuhlmann). Kavan herself did not explain her work that way, saying "I've often started autobiographical things, but never finished them" (qtd. in Garrity, "Nocturnal," 274n6, 253).
37. Others used sleep therapy before Klaesi, but his was the first technique to become widely adopted. For discussion of sleep as psychiatric cure, see Shorter (200–9), Windholz and Witherspoon, Palmer and Braceland, F. E. James, Joanna Moncrieff and Andrew Scull.

38. For more on the vagaries of tribunals, see Wasserstein (77–8). The government sought to remedy oversights (Hylton 3) but in any case the internment laws of 1940 saw category distinctions blur.
39. For sound itself becoming a threatening entity in wartime London, see Wasson (90–4).
40. Clairvoyance trials also invoked the Vagrancy Act of 1824. See Malcolm Gaskill for a cultural history of legal regulation on psychic activity during the Second World War, and Victoria Stewart for discussion of the ways in which Greene's medium is represented in accordance with negative gender stereotypes of female mediums as unnatural women.
41. For detailed discussion of the uncanny, see Chapter 5.
42. For history of the U-Boat siege, see Calder (*People* 231–2, 286–7).

4 Gothic, Mechanised Ghosts: Wartime Industry in Inez Holden, Anne Ridler and Diana Murray Hill

43. Although now discredited as essentialist, Moers's original definition of female Gothic is still valued for its role in the emergence of Gothic Studies as a discipline. Feminist criticism was itself influenced by Gothic tropes, notably that of the male villain threatening the heroine's property (Fitzgerald 15).
44. Social constructivist gender studies unites well with Gothic studies in that both value unstable systems with fluctuating boundaries. See Haggerty (*Queer Gothic*), Judith Halberstam, Andrew Smith and William Hughes, Stéphanie Genz, Genz and Brabon, Claudia Johnson, Botting ("*Dracula*") and Mair Rigby.
45. For a review of the development of female Gothic in criticism, see Julian Fleenor's edited collection, the 1994 special issue of *Women's Writing* exploring women's writing in the Gothic tradition edited by Robert Miles and the 2009 collection edited by Andrew Smith and Diana Wallace.
46. For the legal apparatus underpinning female conscription see Riley and Summerfield (34–37). Neither the 1941 Registration for Employment Order or the 1942 Control of Engagement Order conscripted women with children under the age of fourteen (Riley 123).
47. Women's experience of wartime work varied by age, class and region. See Saywell, Mass-Observation (*War Factory*; *People in Production*), Amabel Williams-Ellis, Summerfield, and Riley.
48. For discussion of women's pay see Riley (125–6), Mackay (130), Hylton (208) and Calder (*People* 403).
49. For discussion of gender in Allied wartime advertising see Honey, Gilbert and Gubar ("Charred Skirts" 214, 440n11), Calder (*People* 377) and Hylton (210–11).
50. Mixed messages were exacerbated by the fact that the government's ministries were not homogenous. While the Ministry of Labour encouraged women to work, the Ministry of Health warned that children's psychological health would be damaged if mothers worked (Riley 110–49). The Ministry of Health's views won out after soldiers were demobilised and over a million British women ceased work in the year after the war (Gilbert and

Gubar, "Charred Skirts" 214). For discussion of women's demobilisation see Summerfield, Riley, Calder (*People* 73, 235–6) and Hylton (207–8).

51. For Foucault's theory of heterotopia, see Chapter 3.

52. Despite war factories' drawbacks, one must acknowledge the dramatic increase of welfare staff in factories, including medical officers and counsellors (Mackay 206; Calder, *People* 389–92). Mackay argues that industrial welfare improved greatly during the war (207), but even factory managers were not always so convinced. One notes that the workers in his factory "feel they are part of a vast machine which runs like a clock, without human personality, never seeing them ... expressing itself impersonally from time to time like a book of rules" (Mass-Observation, *People in Production* 353).

53. Histories often marginalise female conscientious objectors. See Hylton (84–8), Ziegler (76–7), Mackay (58), Calder (*People* 494–8; *Myth* 71–7). Stella St. John describes her experiences as an imprisoned female "conchie."

54. The government tried to remedy such a sense of pointlessness by staging city parades to tempt women into factories, in which women rode on lorries with war *matériel* and the sign "We Made These" (Hodgson 465).

55. For discussion of shell-shock see p.166n33. For discussion of masculinity and war-trauma in First World War writing see Misha Kavka, John Palattella, Gerald Izenberg, Judith Sensibar and John Lowe, as well as literary criticism of Pat Barker's *Regeneration* trilogy (1991–5) including Dennis Brown, Jennifer Shaddock and Laurie Vickroy.

56. World War I saw conscientious objectors suffer public harassment including anonymous mailing of white feathers implying cowardice. The Second World War British home front saw conscientious objectors receive better treatment from government and populace, although "conchies" were still a minority receiving opprobrium (Calder, *Myth* 76, *People* 497; Mackay 58).

57. Rather than use Freud to explain the death craving in these factory novels one can use industrial developments to explain Freud. When industrialisation began in the late seventeenth century, machinery came to inspire new models of human life, implying that "human life was essentially mechanical" (Tropp 31). Freud defines the nervous system as "an apparatus having the function of abolishing stimuli" (11: 116), an apparatus for engineering homeostasis.

5 Elizabeth Bowen's Uncanny Houses

58. Scott MacKenzie, Richard Cook and Hanita Brand examine how this naturalising equation plays out in a variety of national contexts and times, respectively eighteenth-century England, nineteenth-century Scotland and twentieth century Israel.

59. In a similar vein, Lydia Fisher examines how mid-nineteenth- and early twentieth-century American fiction "direct[s] citizens to the gendered roles supported by dominant America's domestic ideology" (4385). Doris Sommer and Margarita Saona analyse how mid-twentieth century Latin American popular romance literature builds a national imaginary through the trope of "natural" heterosexual marriage (Somner 4; Saona 208).

60. The blackout saw traffic fatalities for pedestrians and cyclists increased eight-fold, and a January 1940 poll showed nearly one in five British people had been injured during the blackout (Gardiner 80).
61. Churchill confirmed home's imaginative centrality to the conflict when he renamed the civilian army from the "Local Defence Volunteers" to the "Home Guard" in July 1940.
62. The First World War saw rationing at its close, and as the Second World War approached the government anticipated a broader need for it in the next conflict. Ration books were printed at the end of the 1938 Munich Crisis and food rationing began officially on 8 January 1940 (Gardiner 120).
63. Freud states that the danger we intuit when in the grip of the uncanny stems from sensing our own "compulsion to repeat" (14: 360–1). For discussion of this compulsion, which Freud terms the "death drive," see Chapter 4.
64. In a later article, Ellman reads them as menacing objects with alien life ("Shadowy Fifth" 7–8, 10–11).
65. The Big Houses occupied an ambiguous class position, combining a bourgeois position with a "quasi-aristocratic" quality (McCormack 52). To complicate things further, some became occupied by Catholics after Emancipation (Ingelbien 1105n24).
66. For discussion of the Big House in Irish literature, see Otto Rauchbauer, Claire Norris, Ingelbien and McCormack.
67. Wealthier women were more likely to have the financial resources to leave cities to recover from sleepless nights of raids and visit evacuated children. Working class women were often unable to leave the cities, years going by before many could see their offspring. Furthermore, homelessness was never distributed equally across classes since poorer homes were notoriously flimsy. Finally, the middle-class and working-class had dramatically different experiences of shelter life. For working-class women the war could be a closing down of opportunities rather than a multiplying of them, and any argument that the war advanced a feminist cause must thus grapple with the problematic of class.

6 "The Rubbish Pile and the Grave": Nation and the Abject in Piper, Graham Sutherland and Peake

68. A flourishing industry of mediums sought to deny this after World War I (Plain 71–2).
69. For discussion of olfactory urban geography, in general, see Constance Classen, David Howes and Arthur Synnott, Stallybrass and White, Yi Fu Tuan and Stephen Halliday.
70. The artists today described as "British neo-Romantic" did not use the term themselves and were not an organised group. Raymond Mortimer coined the term in a 1942 review (208) and Robin Ironside developed it in his influential *Painting Since 1939* (1947). Piper preferred the term "contemporary Romantic painting" (Jenkins 42).
71. To appreciate how startling the new wartime enthusiasm for Romanticism was, one must consider the way 1930s British fine art was dominated by

surrealism, abstraction and post-impressionism (Chilvers 2; Watney 3; Yorke, *Spirit* 77; Evans 3).

72. Neo-romanticism arguably saw modernity as as much a threat as war (Harrod 20; Mellor, *Paradise* 34). Neo-romanticism was also criticised for insularity (Grigson 206).

73. Peake's Gormenghast corpus also includes *Boy in Darkness* (1956), an unfinished manuscript for *Titus IV* and a play adaptation. His wife Maeve Gilmore notes that Peake did not intend something "as tidy as a trilogy" (qtd. in Mantrant 74).

74. Sophie Mantrant (71), Yorke (*Mervyn Peake*; "Frankly Missing"), Tanya Gardiner-Scott (*Evolution*) and Moorcock ("Achievement" 80) discuss Peake's relationship to the Romantic tradition.

75. There is controversy over whether Peake's oeuvre can be classified as Gothic. Although Peake uses Gothic trappings complete with mouldering castle, ghosts, and strange rituals, he disapproved when the US edition of *Titus Groan* was subtitled "A Gothick Novel" (Morgan 79), and some critics have objected to the "unhelpful 'Gormenghastly' and 'Gothic' branding of Peake" (Neill, "Frankly" 25; cf. Langdon Jones par. 9). Hugh Brogan notes that Peake's writing is often more jaunty than chilling (39). On the other hand, Peake scholars Winnington, Piette and Yorke find the term useful (Winnington, *Alchemies* 188–9; Piette, *Imagination* 53; Yorke, "Frankly Missing" 22, 24), and almost all Peake's poetry examined in this chapter are relentlessly Gothic in affect, unrelieved by his characteristic whimsy.

76. For discussion of Peake's poetry, see A. T. Tolley (124), Binns (23), Jay Parini, Duncan Barford, Nick Freeman, Winnington ("Parodies and Poetical Allusions"; "Uncollected Poems"), Gardiner-Scott ("'The Consumptive'"), Langdon Jones and Adam Roberts.

77. For analysis of how Peake's experiences in China influence his writing, see Winnington (*Alchemies* 31), Bristow-Smith ("Chinese Puzzle") and Moorcock ("Achievement" 81). For Peake's experiences as a soldier and civilian see Piette (*Imagination* 54), Jamie Hughes (25), Winnington (*Alchemies* 135), Punter (*Terror* 2: 121), Gardiner-Scott ("Memory" 27), Langdon Jones, Piette ("Review of *London's Burning*" 44) and Bristow-Smith ("Review of *Imagination at War*" 47). For Peake's experiences at Belsen-Bergen see Gilmore (51), Moorcock ("Achievement" 83), Pocock (142), Gardiner-Scott ("Memory" 21, 26), Blignaut (112), Mills (*Stuckness* 2), Parini (par. 7) and Roberts (par. 14).

78. Estimating the numbers was difficult given the multitudes and the fact that counting took precious time from succouring survivors. Patrick Gordon Walker records that 35,000 corpses were left unburied (137), but the war crimes trial for Krämer stated 10,000 (Caven 211).

79. For a poignant description of the horror of the bulldozed corpses see Caven (214). The first public use of the footage was in Alain Resnais's documentary *Nuit et Brouillard* (1955) (Haggith 92).

80. Adorno nuanced his position in 1966: "Perennial suffering has as much right to expression as a tortured man has to scream. Hence it may have been wrong to say that after Auschwitz you could no longer write poems. But it is not wrong to raise the less cultural question whether after Auschwitz you can go on living" (qtd. in Linafelt 54).

Afterword: The Politics of Lamentation

81. In different ways, Jahan Ramazani ("Afterword"; *"Poetry of Mourning"*), Rae, Madelyn Detloff, Derrida (*"Fors"*; *Mémoires*), R. Clifton Spargo, Douglas Crimp ("Melancholia"; "Mourning"), David Eng and David Kazanjian, Michael Moon and Ranjana Khanna either depathologise melancholia or argue for the ethical necessity for non-normative mourning. Celebrating melancholia itself is problematic, since Freudian melancholia is a selective forgetting of the dead rather than more accurate remembering (Forter; Mitscherlich and Mitscherlich; Santner; Gillian Rose; Horowitz). For this reason, Rae argues for the term "resistant mourning," to denote that mourning is unresolved but not denied (22).

82. Morris Brody and Vincent Mahoney note, "Psycho-analytic literature lacks clarity in both the use and the description of the concepts introjection, identification, and incorporation. Not only are the terms used interchangeably, but often there is a lack of unanimity as to whether they refer to defence mechanisms or to instinctual processes" (57). Sandor Ferenczi coined the term introjection in 1909, defining it as the opposite of paranoid projection (Ferenczi; cf. Hinshelwood 331). Freud adopted the term in "Instincts and Their Vicissitudes" (1915) to describe the way that the ego takes into itself any object that is a source of pleasure. Freud himself describes two forms of introjection, introjection in which the subject identified with the swallowed object and introjection in which the subject feels the swallowed object is a discrete entity within them (Hinshelwood 330). This latter process is renamed "incorporation" in the object-relations psychoanalytic tradition developed by Melanie Klein. Klein argues the child incorporates significant people as "internal objects" which acquire a complex life of their own (Klein 166). Object relations analysts like Klein and Wilfred Bion describe the repertoire of phantastical actions people take in relation to their internal objects.

83. Liss illustrates the oversimplifications of incorporation with reference to the United States Holocaust Memorial Museum's identity card project in which museum visitors were given an identity card at the start of their visit and at the end learned whether that person survived (24).

84. Although I discuss Peake here, the two most famous World War II anti-elegies are Dylan Thomas's "Refusal to Mourn the Death, by Fire, of a Child in London" and W. S. Graham's "Many without Elegy."

References

Ackroyd, Peter. *London: The Biography.* London: Vintage, 2000.

Adey, Peter. "Holding Still: The Private Life of an Air Raid." *M/C Journal* 12.1 (March 2009). 17 July 2009. <http://journal.media-culture.org.au/index.php/mcjournal/article/viewArticle/112>

Aldiss, Brian. Introduction. *Ice.* By Anna Kavan. 1967. London: Pan, 1970.

——. Introduction. *The War of the Worlds.* By H. G. Wells. London: Penguin, 2005. xiii–xxix.

An Airman's Letter to His Mother. Dir. Michael Powell. MGM, 1941.

Anderson, Benedict. "Narrating the Nation." *Times Literary Supplement* (13 June 1986): 659.

——. *Imagined Communities: Reflections on the Origin and Spread of Nationalism.* 2nd ed. London: Verso, 1991.

Anderson, Mary Désirée. *Bow Bells Are Silent.* London: Williams and Norgate, 1943.

Angel, Katherine. "Defining Psychiatry: Aubrey Lewis's 1938 Report and the Rockefeller Foundation." *European Psychiatry on the Eve of War.* Eds. Katherine Angel, Edgar Jones and Michael Neve. London: Wellcome Trust, 2003. 39–56.

Ariès, Philippe. *Western Attitudes Towards Death from the Middle Ages to the Present.* 1974. Trans. Patricia M. Ranum. London: Marion Boyars, 1976.

Auden, W. H. "For the Time Being: A Christmas Oratorio." *Collected Poems.* Ed. Edward Mendelson. New York: Vintage, 1991. 347–400.

Baldick, Chris (ed.). Introduction. *The Oxford Book of Gothic Tales.* Oxford: Oxford UP, 1992. xi–xxiii.

Baldick, Chris and Robert Mighall. "Gothic Criticism." *A Companion to the Gothic.* Ed. David Punter. Oxford: Blackwells, 2001. 209–228.

Bardgett, Suzanne. "What Wireless Listeners Learned." *Belsen 1945: New Historical Perspectives.* Eds. Suzanne Bardgett and David Cesarani. London: Valentine Mitchell, 2006. 123–36.

Barford, Duncan. "'Madness Can Be Lovely': The Range and Meaning of Mervyn Peake's Nonsense Verse." *Peake Studies* 4.1 (Winter 1994): 29–52.

Barham, P. "From the Asylum to the Community: the Mental Patient in Postwar Britain." *Cultures of Psychiatry.* Eds. M. Gijswijt-Hofstra and Roy Porter. Amsterdam: Rodopi, 1998. 221–40.

Barker, Pat. *The Regeneration Trilogy: Regeneration; The Eye in the Door; The Ghost Road.* 1991–1995. London: Viking, 1997.

Barlow, Alan. "Testimony on Behalf of the Treasury Department to the Select Committee on Equal Compensation." 1943. *Britain in the Second World War: A Social History.* Ed. Harold Smith. Manchester: Manchester UP, 1996. 67–8.

Barthes, Roland. *Mythologies.* 1957. Trans. Annette Lavers. London: Granada, 1973.

Baudelaire, Charles. *Les Fleurs du mal/Flowers of Evil.* Trans George Dillon and Edna St. Vincent Millay. New York: Washington Square, 1962.

——. *Paris Spleen.* 1869. Trans. Louise Varese. New York: New Directions, 1970.

Baudelaire, Charles. *Selected Writings*. Trans. P. E. Charvet. Cambridge: Cambridge UP, 1972.

BBC Written Archives Centre, Caversham. E2/131/22. Memo from BBC Assistant Director, European News Directorate, 19 April 1945.

Beaton, Cecil. *British Photographers*. London: Collins, 1944.

Benjamin, Walter. *Charles Baudelaire: A Lyric Poet in the Era of High Capitalism*. Trans. Henry Zohn. London: Verso, 1997.

——. *Illuminations*. Ed. Hannah Arendt. New York: Schocken Books, 1969.

Bennett, Andrew and Nicholas Royle. *Elizabeth Bowen and the Dissolution of the Novel*. New York: St Martin's, 1995.

Berthoud, Roger. *Graham Sutherland: A Biography*. London: Faber, 1982.

Bhabha, Homi. "The World and the Home." *Dangerous Liaisons: Gender, Nation, and Postcolonial Perspectives*. Eds. Anne McClintock, Aamir Mufti and Ella Shohat. Minneapolis, MN: U of Minnesota P, 1997. 445–55.

——. Introduction and "DissemiNation: Time, Narrative, and the Margins of the Modern Nation." *Nation and Narration*. Ed. Homi Bhabha. London: Routledge, 1990. 1–7, 291–322.

Biddle, Tami Davis. *Rhetoric and Reality in Air Warfare: The Evolution of British and American Ideas about Strategic Bombing, 1914–1945*. Princeton: Princeton UP, 2002.

Binns, Ronald. "Situating Gormenghast." *Critical Quarterly* 21.1 (March 1979): 21–33.

Bion, Wilfred. *Second Thoughts*. London: Heinemann, 1967.

Blignaut, E. A. "Mervyn Peake: From Artist as Entertainer to Artist as Philosopher and Moralist in the 'Titus' Books." *English Studies in Africa* 24.2 (September 1981): 107–15.

Bluemel, Kristin. *George Orwell and the Radical Eccentrics*. New York: Palgrave Macmillan, 2004.

Blunt, Alison and Robyn Dowling. *Home*. Oxford: Routledge, 2006.

Bogacz, Ted. "War Neurosis and Cultural Change in England 1914–22." *Journal of Contemporary History* 24 (1989): 227–56.

Booth, Allyson. *Postcards from the Trenches: Negotiating the Space Between Modernism and the First World War*. New York: Oxford UP, 1996.

Botting, Fred. "The Gothic Production of the Unconscious." *Spectral Readings: Towards a Gothic Geography*. Ed. David Punter and Glennis Byron. London: Palgrave Macmillan, 1999. 11–36.

——. *Gothic*. London: Routledge, 1996.

——. "AfterGothic: Consumption, Machines and Black Holes." *The Cambridge Companion to Gothic Fiction*. Ed. Jerrold E. Hogle. Cambridge: Cambridge UP, 2002. 277–300.

——. "*Dracula*, Romance and Radcliffean Gothic", *Women's Writing* 1.2 (February 1994): 181–201.

Bottome, Phyllis. *London Pride*. London: Faber, 1941.

Bowen, Elizabeth. *Bowen's Court* and *Seven Winters: Memories of a Dublin Childhood*. 1942, 1943. Rev. 1964. London: Vintage: 1999.

——. *Collected Stories*. New York: Vintage, 1981.

——. "The Cult of Nostalgia." Ts. Elizabeth Bowen Collection. Harry Ransom Centre for Research in the Humanities. Austin, Texas.

——. *The Death of the Heart*. 1938. London: Vintage, 1998.

——. *The Heat of the Day*. 1949. London: Penguin, 1962.

——. "The Lost Art of Living." Ts. Elizabeth Bowen Collection. Harry Ransom Centre for Research in the Humanities. Austin, Texas.

——. *The Mulberry Tree: Writings of Elizabeth Bowen*. Ed. Hermione Lee. London: Virago, 1986.

Bowlby, Rachel. *Just Looking: Consumer Culture in Dreiser, Gissing and Zola*. New York: Methuen, 1985.

——. *Still Crazy After All These Years: Women, Writing and Psychoanalysis*. New York: Routledge, 1992. 1–33.

Brabon, Benjamin. "'Ghostly National Imaginings: Benedict Anderson and the Gothic Cartography of Great Britain." *The Influence of Benedict Anderson*. Eds. Alistair McCleery and Benjamin Brabon. Edinburgh: Merchiston Press, 2007. 41–58.

Brand, Hanita. "Housing the Other." *The Nation of the Other*. Eds. Anna Branach-Kallas and Katarzyna Wieckowska. Torun, Poland: Wydawnictwo Uniwersytetu Mikolaja Kopernika, 2004. 171–85.

Brandt, Bill. "A Statement." 1970. *Bill Brandt: Selected* Texts. Ed. Nigel Warburton. Oxford: Clio, 1993. 29–32.

Breitman, Richard. "Himmler and Bergen-Belsen." *Belsen in History and Memory*. Eds. David Cesarani, Tony Kushner, Jo Reilly and Colin Richmond. London: Frank Cass, 1997. 72–84.

Briggs, Julia. "The Ghost Story." *A Companion to the Gothic*. Ed. David Punter. Oxford: Blackwells, 2001. 122–31.

Bristow-Smith, Laurence. "The Chinese Puzzle of Mervyn Peake." *Peake Studies* 3.3 (Winter 1993): 25–44.

——. "Review of *Imagination at War* by Adam Piette." *Peake Studies* 4.4 (1994): 46–50.

Brittain, Vera. *England's Hour*. 1940. London: Futura, 1981.

——. *One Voice: Pacifist Writings from the Second World War: "Humiliation with Honour" and "Seed of Chaos."* London: Continuum, 2005.

Brody, Morris W. and Vincent P. Mahoney. "Introjection, Incorporation, and Identification." *International Journal of Psycho-Analysis* 45 (1964): 57–63.

Brogan, Hugh. "The Gutters of Gormenghast." *Cambridge Review* 23 (November 1973): 38–42.

Bronfen, Elisabeth. "Hysteria, Phantasy and the Family Romance: Ann Radcliffe's *Romance of the Forest*." *Women's Writing: The Elizabethan to the Romantic Period* 1.2 (February 1994): 171–80.

Brooking, Julia. *A Textbook of Psychiatric and Mental Health Nursing*. Edinburgh: Churchill Livingstone, 2002.

Brown, Dennis. "The *Regeneration* Trilogy: Total War, Masculinities, Anthropology, and the Talking Cure." *Critical Perspectives on Pat Barker*. Eds. Sharon Monteith, Margaretta Jolly, Nahem Yousaf and Paul Ronald. Columbia, South Carolina: U of South Carolina P, 2005.

Bruhm, Steven. "The Contemporary Gothic." *The Cambridge Companion to Gothic Fiction*. Ed. Jerrold E. Hogle. Cambridge: Cambridge UP, 2002. 259–276.

Bryher [Annie Winifred Ellerman]. *The Days of Mars: A Memoir, 1940–1946*. New York: Harcourt Brace Jovanovich, 1972.

Buck-Morss, Susan. *Dialectics of Seeing*. Cambridge, MA: MIT, 1989.

Buffard, Simone. *Le froid pénitentiare. L'impossible réforme des prisons.* Paris: Seuil, 1973.

Burke, Edmund. *A Philosophical Enquiry into the Origin of Our Ideas of the Sublime and Beautiful.* 1759. Ed. Adam Phillips. Oxford: Oxford UP, 1990.

Butler, Judith. *Bodies That Matter: On the Discursive Limits of Sex.* New York: Routledge, 1995.

——. *Gender Trouble: Feminism and the Subversion of Identity.* New York: Routledge, 1990.

——. *The Judith Butler Reader.* Ed. Sarah Salih. Malden, Massachusetts: Blackwell, 2004.

——. *Precarious Life: The Power of Mourning and Violence.* London: Verso, 2004.

Byron, Glennis. "Victorian Gothic." Jekyll and Hyde Event. Edinburgh City of Literature and Napier University: St Augustine's Church, Edinburgh. 28 February 2008.

Calder, Angus. *The Myth of the Blitz.* 1991. London: Pimlico, 1992.

——. *The People's War.* London: Jonathan Cape, 1969.

Callard, David. *The Case of Anna Kavan.* London: Peter Owen, 1992.

——. "Bitter Pilgrimage." *London Magazine* 29.9 (December 1989): 48–61.

Cannadine, David. "War and Death, Grief and Mourning in Modern Britain." *Mirrors of Mortality: Studies in the Social History of Death.* Ed. Joachim Whaley. London: Europa, 1981. 187–242.

Carpenter, M. "Asylum Nursing Before 1914." *Rewriting Nursing History.* Ed. C. Davis. London: Croom Helm, 1980.

Caruth, Cathy. "Trauma and Experience." *Trauma.* Ed. Cathy Caruth. Baltimore: Johns Hopkins UP, 1995. 3–12.

——. *Unclaimed Experience: Trauma, Narrative and History.* Baltimore: Johns Hopkins, 1996.

Castle, Terry. "The Spectralisation of the Other in The Mysteries of Udolpho." *The New Eighteenth Century: Theory, Politics, English Literature.* Eds. Felicity Nussbaum and Laura Brown. London: Methuen, 1987. 231–53.

Caven, Hannah. "Horror in Our Time." *Historical Journal of Film, Radio and Television* 21.3 (August 2001): 205–53.

Cecil, Mary. "Through the Looking Glass." 1956. *The Inner World of Mental Illness.* Ed. Bert Kaplan. New York: Harper and Row, 1964. 213–34.

Cesarani, David. "A Brief History of Bergen-Belsen." *Belsen 1945: New Historical Perspectives.* Eds. Suzanne Bardgett and David Cesarani. London: Valentine Mitchell, 2006. 13–21.

Cesarani, David and Tony Kushner. *The Internment of Aliens in Twentieth Century Britain.* London: Frank Cass, 2004.

Chappell, Connery. *Island of Barbed Wire: The Remarkable Story of World War Two Internment on the Isle of Man.* London: Robert Hale, 2005.

Cherry, Steven. "Wartime and Post-War Crises." *Mental Health Care in Modern England.* Woodbridge: Suffolk, Boydell, 2003. 208–42.

Chesney, George. *The Battle of Dorking.* 1871. Oxford: Oxford Paperbacks, 1997.

Chessman, Harriet. "Women and Language in the Fiction of Elizabeth Bowen." *Twentieth-Century Literature* 29.1 (Spring 1983): 69–85.

Cheyette, Brian. *Constructions of "The Jew" in English Literature and Society.* Cambridge: Cambridge UP, 1993.

Chilvers, Ian. *Oxford Dictionary of Twentieth Century Art*. Oxford: Oxford University Press, 1998.

Chisholm, Diane. "'The Uncanny." *Feminism and Psychoanalysis: A Critical Dictionary*. Ed. Elizabeth Wright. Oxford: Blackwell, 1992. 436–40.

Chodorow, Nancy. *The Reproduction of Mothering*. 2nd ed. 1999. Berkeley: U of California P, 1999.

Church Bliss, Kathleen. The Papers of Miss Kathleen Church Bliss. Imperial War Museum, London. Department of Documents.

Churchill, Winston. *War Speeches* vol. 1 [3 vols]. Ed. Charles Eade. London: Cassell, 1951.

Ciambezi, Luisella. "The Desecration of Rituals in Gormenghast." *Peake Studies* 3.4 (Spring 1994): 17–20.

Cixous, Hélène. "The Laugh of the Medusa." 1975. Trans. Keith Cohen and Paula Cohen. *Signs* 1 (1976): 875–94.

Clark, Kenneth. "The Artist in Wartime." *The Listener* (26 October 1939): 810.

——. *Landscape Into Art*. London: John Murray, 1949. 2nd ed. 1976.

Classen, Constance, David Howes and Anthony Synnott. *Aroma: The Cultural History of Smell*. London: Routledge, 1994.

Clery, E. J. *The Rise of Supernatural Fiction, 1762–1800*. Cambridge: Cambridge UP, 1995.

Conway, Peter. [George Alexis Bankoff] *Living Tapestry*. 1946. London: Staples Press, 1946.

Cook, Richard. "The Home-ly Kailyard Nation: Nineteenth-Century Narratives of the Highland and the Myth of Merrie Auld Scotland." *ELH* 66.4 (Winter 1999): 1053–73.

Cottrell, Leonard. "The Man from Belsen." 1946. *Belsen 1945: New Historical Perspectives*. Eds. Suzanne Bardgett and David Cesarani. London: Valentine Mitchell, 2006. 142–152.

Crammer, J. "Extraordinary Deaths of Asylum Inpatients." *Medical History* 36 (1992): 430–41.

Cresswell, Tim. *Place: A Short Introduction*. Oxford: Blackwell, 2004.

Crimp, Douglas. "Melancholia and Moralism." *Loss: The Politics of Mourning*. Eds. David Eng and David Kazanjian. Berkeley and Los Angeles: U of California P, 2003. 188–202.

——. "Mourning and Militancy." *October* 51 (Winter 1989): 3–11.

Cuoto, Maria. *Graham Greene on the Frontier*. London: Macmillan, 1988.

Curtis, L. Perry. *Jack the Ripper and the London Press*. New Haven: Yale UP, 2001.

Daily Mail. *Lest We Forget: The Horrors of Nazi Concentration Camps Revealed for All Time in the Most Terrible Photographs Ever Published*. London: Associated Newspapers, 1945.

Dalzielle, Tanya. "Mourning and Jazz in the Poetry of Mina Loy." *Modernism and Mourning*. Ed. Patricia Rae. Lewisburg: Bucknell UP, 2007. 102–17.

Davenport, Gary. "Elizabeth Bowen and the Big House." *Southern Humanities Review* 8.1 (Winter 1974): 27–34.

DeCoste, Damon Marcel. "Modernism's Shell-Shocked History: Amnesia, Repetition, and the War in Graham Greene's *Ministry of Fear*." *Twentieth Century Literature* 45.4 (Winter 1999): 428–52.

DeLamotte, Eugenia. *Perils of the Night*. New York: New York UP, 1990.

Derrida, Jacques. "*Fors*: The Anguish Words of Nicolas Abraham and Maria Torok." Trans. Barbara Johnson. *The Wolf Man's Magic Word: A Cryptonomy.* Ed. Nicolas Abraham and Maria Torok. Minneapolis: U of Minnesota P, 1986. xi–xlviii.

——. *Mémoires: For Paul de Man.* Trans. Jonathan Culler, Cecile Lindsey and Eduardo Cadava. New York: Columbia UP, 1986.

——. *Spectres of Marx: The State of the Debt, the Work of Mourning, and the New International.* 1993. Trans. Peggy Kamuf. New York: Routledge, 1994.

Detloff, Madelyn. "'Tis Not my Nature to Join in Hating, But in Loving: Toward Survivable Public Mourning.'" *Modernism and Mourning.* Ed. Patricia Rae. Lewisburg: Bucknell UP, 2007. 50–68.

Dijkstra, Bram. *Idols of Perversity: Fantasies of Feminine Evil in Fin-de-Siècle Culture.* Oxford UP, 1988.

Doolittle, Hilda. *The Gift.* Ed. Jane Augustine. Gainesville, Florida: UP of Florida, 1998.

——. "May 1943." 1950. *Collected Poems 1912–1944.* New York: New Directions, 1983. 492–501.

Dove, Richard. "Totally Un-English? Britain's Internment of Enemy Aliens in Two World Wars." *Yearbook of the Research Centre for German and Austrian Exile Studies* 7 (2005). Amsterdam: Rodopi.

Drake-Carnel, Francis. *Old English Customs and Ceremonies.* London: Scribner, 1938.

Dryden, Linda. "'City of Dreadful Night': Stevenson's Gothic London." *Robert Louis Stevenson: Writer of Boundaries.* Eds. Richard Ambrosini and Richard Dury. Madison: U of Wisconsin P, 2006. 253–64.

Edwards, Justin. *Gothic Canada: Reading the Spectre of a National Literature.* Edmonton; U of Alberta P, 2005.

Ellis, Kate Ferguson. "Can You Forgive Her? The Gothic Heroine and Her Critics." *A Companion to the Gothic.* Ed. David Punter. Oxford: Blackwells, 2001. 257–68.

——. *The Contested Castle.* Urbana, Illinois: U of Illinois P, 1989.

Ellis, Markman. *The History of Gothic Fiction.* Edinburgh: Edinburgh UP, 2000.

Ellmann, Maud. *Elizabeth Bowen: The Shadow across the Page.* Edinburgh: Edinburgh UP, 2003.

——. "The Shadowy Fifth." *The Fiction of the 1940s: Stories of Survival.* Eds. Rod Mengham and N. H. Reeve. Basingstoke: Palgrave Macmillan, 2001. 1–25.

Eng, David and David Kazanjian. "Mourning Remains." *Loss: The Politics of Mourning.* Eds. David Eng and David Kazanjian. Berkeley and Los Angeles: U of California P, 2003.

Engels, Friedrich. Extract from *The Condition of the Working Class in England.* 1845. Eds. Richard LeGates and Fredric Stout. *The City Reader.* London: Routledge, 1996. 46–55.

Evans, Myfanwy. "Dead or Alive?" *Axis* 1 (1935).

Faviell, Frances. *A Chelsea Concerto.* London: Cassell: 1959.

Ferber, Edna. "Grandma Isn't Playing." 1943. *Wave Me Goodbye: Stories of the Second World War.* Ed. Anne Boston. 1989. London: Virago, 2003. 116–133.

Ferenczi, Sandor. "Introjection and Transference." *First Contributions to Psycho-Analysis.* London: Hogarth, 1909. 30–79.

Ferguson, Helen. [Anna Kavan]. *Let Me Alone.* London: Jonathan Cape, 1930.

——. *A Stranger Still.* London: Jonathan Cape, 1935.

Feudtner, Chris. "'Minds the Dead have Ravished': Shell Shock, History, and the Ecology of Disease-Systems." *History of Science* 31.4 (1992): 377–420.

Fisher, Lydia. "Domesticating the Nation: American Narratives of Home Culture." *Dissertation Abstracts International A* 61.11 (May 2001): 4385.

Fisk, Robert. *In Time of War: Ireland, Ulster and the Price of Neutrality 1939–45.* 1983. London: Paladin, 1985.

Fitter, R. S. R. and J. E. Lousley. *The Natural History of the City.* London: Corporation of London, 1953.

Fitzgerald, Lauren. "Female Gothic and the Institutionalisation of Gothic Studies." *Gothic Studies* 6.1 (May 2004): 8–18.

FitzGibbon, Constantine. *The Blitz.* London: Macdonald, 1970.

Fleenor, Julian. (ed.). *The Female Gothic.* Montreal: Eden, 1984.

Fliess, P. Ms. 85/40/1/. Imperial War Museum, London. Department of Documents.

Fludernik, Monika and Greta Olson (eds). Introduction. *In the Grip of the Law: Trials, Prisons and the Space Between.* Frankfurt: Peter Main, 2004. xiii–liv.

Forter, Greg. "Against Melancholia: Contemporary Mourning Theory, Fitzgerald's *The Great Gatsby*, and the Politics of Unfinished Grief." *Modernism and Mourning.* Ed. Patricia Rae. Lewisburg: Bucknell UP, 2007. 239–59.

Foucault, Michel. "Of Other Spaces." 1984*: Repository of Texts Written by Michel Foucault.* Trans. Jay Miskowiec. 10 September 2007. <http://foucault.info/ documents/heteroTopia/foucault.heteroTopia.en.html>

Fraser, C. F. *Control of Aliens in the British Commonwealth of Nations.* London: Hogarth, 1940.

Freedman, Jean. *Whistling in the Dark: Memory and Culture in Wartime London.* Lexington: U of Kentucky P, 1999.

Freeman, Hugh and German E. Berrios (eds.). *150 Years of British Psychiatry, 1841–1991.* London: Gaskell, 1991.

Freeman, Nick. "'The Cocky Walkers': Youth Crime and Social Comment." *Peake Studies* 8.4 (April 2004): 9–15, 18.

Freeman, Spencer. *Production Under Fire.* Dublin: Fallon, 1967.

Fremlin, Celia. "Lack of Interest in Working for the War Effort.*" Hearts Undefeated: Women's Writing of the Second World War.* Ed. Jenny Hartley. 1994. London: Virago, 2003. 469–471.

Freud, Sigmund. *The Penguin Freud Library.* Trans. James Strachey. Eds. James Strachey, Angela Richards and Albert Dickson. 15 vols. Harmondsworth: Penguin, 1975–1986.

Fuller, Roy. "The Growth of Crime" and "The Middle of a War." *Penguin New Writing* 13 (June 1942): 83–6.

Fussell, Paul. *The Great War and Modern Memory.* 1975. London: Oxford 1977.

Garamone, Jim. "Obama Vows Not to Waver in America's Defense." 20 January 2009. American Forces Press Service News. 25 January 2009. <http://www. defenselink.mil/news/newsarticle.aspx?id=52734>

Gardiner, Juliet. *The 1940s House.* London: Macmillan, 2000.

Gardiner-Scott, Tanya. "Memory Emancipated: The Fantastic Realism of Mervyn Peake." *Mythlore* 14.2 (Winter 1987): 26–9.

——. *Mervyn Peake: The Evolution of a Dark Romantic.* New York: Peter Lang, 1989.

——. "'The Consumptive: Belsen 1945': A Note." *Peake Studies* 1.2 (Summer 1989): 26–8.

Garrity, Jane. "Nocturnal Transgressions in *The House of Sleep*: Anna Kavan's Maternal Registers." *Modern Fiction Studies* 40.2 (Summer 1994): 253–77.

Gaskill, Malcolm. *Hellish Nell: Last of Britain's Witches*. 2001. London: Fourth Estate, 2002.

Gellhorn, Martha. "Dachau." 1945. *Hearts Undefeated: Women's Writing of the Second World War*. Ed. Jenny Hartley. 1994. London: Virago, 2003. 593–99.

Genz, Stéphanie. *Post-Femininities in Popular Culture*. Basingstoke: Palgrave Macmillan, 2009.

Genz, Stéphanie and Benjamin Brabon. *Post-Feminist Gothic*. Basingstoke: Palgrave Macmillan, 2006.

Gilbert, Sandra M. and Susan Gubar. "Charred Skirts and Deathmask: World War II and the Blitz on Women." *No Man's Land*. New Haven: Yale UP, 1994. 211–65.

——. *The Madwoman in the Attic: The Woman Writer and the Nineteenth Century Literary Imagination*. 2nd ed. New Haven: Yale UP, 2000.

Gillman, Peter and Leni. *Collar the Lot: How Britain Interned and Expelled its Wartime Refugees*. London: Quartet, 1980.

Gilmore, Maeve. *A World Away*. 1970. *Mervyn Peake: Two Lives*. London: Vintage, 1999.

Glendinning, Victoria. *Elizabeth Bowen: Portrait of a Writer*. London: Phoenix, 1977.

Goldmann, Lucien. *Towards a Sociology of the Novel*. 1964. Trans. Alan Sheridan. London: Tavistock, 1975.

Goodall, Felicity. *Voices from the Home Front: Personal Experiences of Wartime Britain 1939–45*. Cincinatti, Ohio: David and Charles, 2004.

Gordon Walker, Patrick. "Belsen Concentration Camp: Facts and Thoughts." 1945. *Belsen 1945: New Historical Perspectives*. Eds. Suzanne Bardgett and David Cesarani. London: Valentine Mitchell, 2006. 137–41.

Graham, W. S. "Many Without Elegy." *New Collected Poems*. Ed. Matthew Francis. London: Faber, 2004. 40–1.

Granger, Isabelle. H. Ms. 94/45/2. 17 July 1939. Imperial War Museum, London. Department of Documents.

Graves, Charles. *London Transport at War*. London: Oldcastle, 1989.

Green, Henry. *Caught*. 1943. New York: Augustus Kelley, 1970.

Greene, Graham. "The Conservative." 1941. *Collected Essays*. London: Bodley Head, 1969. 359–61.

——. *The Ministry of Fear: An Entertainment*. 1943. London: Heinemann, 1943.

——. *Ways of Escape*. 1980. London: Penguin, 1981.

Griffiths, Gareth. *Women's Factory Work in World War I*. Stroud: Alan Sutton, 1991.

Grigson, Geoffrey. "Authentic and False in the New Romanticism." *Horizon* 17 (March 1948): 203–11.

Grunenberg, Christoph (ed.). *Gothic Transmutations of Horror in Late Twentieth-Century Art*. Boston: MIT, 1997.

Gubar, Susan. *Poetry After Auschwitz: Remembering What One Never Knew*. Bloomington: Indiana UP, 2003.

Haggerty, George. *Gothic Fiction/Gothic Form*. London: Pennsylvania State UP, 1989.

——. *Queer Gothic*. Urbana, Illinois: U of Illinois P, 2006.

Haggith, Toby. "The Filming of the Liberation of Bergen-Belsen and its Impact on the Understanding of the Holocaust." *Belsen 1945: New Historical Perspectives*. Eds. Suzanne Bardgett and David Cesarani. London: Valentine Mitchell, 2006. 89–122.

Halberstam, Judith. *Skin Shows: Gothic Horror and the Technology of Monsters*. Durham: Duke UP, 1995.

Halliday, Stephen. *The Great Stink of London: Sir Joseph Bazalgette and the Cleansing of the Victorian Metropolis*. Stroud: Sutton, 1999.

Hannan, Martin. "Scot Who Claimed the Holocaust was a Hoax." *Scotsman* (1 June 1998): 22.

Hanson, Neil. *The Unknown Soldier: The Story of the Missing of the Great War*. 2005. London: Corgi, 2007.

Harris, Greg. "Compulsory Masculinity, Britain, and the Great War: The Literary-Historical Work of Pat Barker." *Critique* 39.4 (Summer 1998): 290–304.

Harrisson, Tom. *Living Through the Blitz*. 1976. London: Penguin, 1990.

Harrod, Tanya. "The Mapping of a Gone and Pleasant Land." *Independent on Sunday Magazine* (5 August 1990): 20.

Hartley, Jenny. *Millions Like Us: British Women's Fiction of the Second World War*. London: Virago and Past Times, 1997.

Haskall, A., D. Powell, R. Myers, and Robin Ironside. *Since 1939: Ballet, Films, Music and Painting*. London, 1948.

Haslewood, I. S. "The Blitz on London." Ts. 04/40/1. Imperial War Museum, London. Department of Documents.

Havers, Richard. *Here Is the News: The BBC and the Second World War*. Stroud: Gloucestershire, 2007.

Hellen, Anita. "'Blasé Sorrow': Ultramodernity's Mourning at *The Little Review*, 1917–20." *Modernism and Mourning*. Ed. Patricia Rae. Lewisburg: Bucknell UP, 2007. 118–35.

Hemmings, Robert. "'The Blameless Physician': Narrative and Pain, Sassoon and Rivers." *Literature and Medicine* 24.1 (2005) 109–26.

Hewison, Robert. *Under Siege: Literary Life in London, 1939–1945*. 2nd ed. London: Methuen, 1988.

Hewitt, John. *The Collected Poems of John Hewitt*. Ed. Frank Ormsby. Belfast: Blackstaff Press, 1991.

Hill, Diana Murray. *Ladies May Now Leave Their Machines*. London: Pilot, 1944.

Hinshelwood, R. D. *A Dictionary of Kleinian Thought*. 2nd ed. London: Free Association, 1991.

Hodgson, Vere. "A Munitions Procession." 1941. *Hearts Undefeated: Women's Writing of the Second World War*. Ed. Jenny Hartley. 1994. London: Virago, 2003. 465.

Hoeveler, Diane Long. *Gothic Feminism: The Professionalisation of Women from Charlotte Smith to the Brontës*. University Park: Pennsylvania State UP, 1998.

Hogle, Jerrold. "The Gothic Ghost of the Counterfeit and the Progress of Abjection." *A Companion to the Gothic*. Ed. David Punter. Oxford: Blackwells, 2001. 293–304.

——. "Past, Present and Future." *Gothic Studies* 1.1 (August 1999): 1–9.

Holden, Inez. "Fellow Travellers in Factory." *Horizon* 3.14 (February 1941): 117–22.

——. *The Night Shift*. London: Bodley Head, 1941.

——. *There's No Story There*. London: Bodley Head, 1944.

Holmes, Colin. *Anti-Semitism in British Society, 1876–1939*. London: Arnold, 1979.

Honey, Maureen. *Creating Rosie the Riveter: Class, Gender and Propaganda During World War II*. Amherst: U of Massachusetts P, 1984.

Hooks, Bell. *Yearning: Race, Gender and Cultural Politics*. London: Turnaround, 1991.

Hoover Vacuum Cleaners. Advertisement. *Spectator* (24 November 1944): 490.

Hopton, J. "Prestwich Hospital in the Twentieth Century." *History of Psychiatry* 10 (1999): 349–69.

Hornby, William. *History of the Second World War: Factories and Plant* [sic]. London: HMSO, 1958.

Horner, Avril and Sue Zlosnik. "Skin Chairs and other Domestic Horrors: Barbara Comyns and the Female Gothic Tradition." *Gothic Studies* 6.1 (May 2004): 90–102.

——. "Strolling in the Dark: Gothic *Flânerie* in Djuna Barnes' *Nightwood*." *Gothic Modernisms*. Eds. Andrew Smith and Jeff Wallace. Basingstoke: Palgrave Macmillan, 2001. 78–94.

Horowitz, Gregg. *Sustaining Loss: Art and Mournful Life*. Stanford: Stanford UP, 2001.

Hoskins, Robert "Greene and Wordsworth: *The Ministry of Fear*." *South Atlantic Review* 48.4 (November 1983): 32–42.

Hughes, Jamie A. "'I Have My Battleground No Less Than Nations: Peake's Daydream of Gormenghast." *Journal of Evolutionary Psychology* 25.1–2 (March 2004): 24–31.

Hurley, Kelly. "British Gothic Fiction, 1885–1930." *The Cambridge Companion to Gothic Fiction*. Ed. Jerrold E. Hogle. Cambridge: Cambridge UP, 2002. 189–208.

Hylton, Stuart. *Their Darkest Hour: The Hidden History of the Home Front, 1939–1945*. 2001. Stroud: Sutton, 2003.

"In the Heart of the Empire." *Picture Post* (22 October 1938): 23–7.

Irigaray, Luce. *This Sex Which Is Not One*. 1977. Trans. C. Porter and C. Burke. Ithaca: Cornell UP, 1985.

Ingelbien, Raphael. "Gothic Genealogies: *Dracula, Bowen's Court*, and Anglo-Irish Psychology." *ELH* 70.4 (Winter 2003): 1089–1105.

Inglesby, Elizabeth. "'Expressive Objects': Elizabeth Bowen's Narrative Materialises." *Modern Fiction Studies* 53.2 (Summer 2007): 306–33.

Ingrams, Richard and John Piper. *Piper's Places*. London: Chatto and Windus, 1983.

Ironside, Robin. *Painting Since 1939*. London: Longmans, 1947.

Izenberg, Gerald N. *Modernism and Masculinity: Mann, Wedekind, Kandinsky through World War I*. Chicago: U of Chicago P, 2000.

Jacobs, Carol. *Telling Time: Levi-Strauss, Ford, Lessing, Benjamin, De Man, Wordsworth, Rilke*. 1992. Baltimore: Johns Hopkins UP, 1993.

Jacobs, Jane. *The Edge of Empire: Postcolonialism and the City*. London: Routledge, 1996.

Jacobstahl, R. Ms. 80/2/1. Imperial War Museum, London. Department of Documents.

Jacobus, Mary. *Reading Woman: Essays in Feminist Criticism*. London: Methuen, 1986.

James, F. E. "Insulin Treatment in Psychiatry." *History of Psychiatry 3* (1992): 221–35.

James, Lawrence. *The Rise and Fall of the British Empire*. 2nd ed. London: Abacus, 1998.

Jefferies, Richard. *After London, or Wild England*. 1885. Cirencester: Echo Library, 2005.

Jenkins, David (ed.). *John Piper: The Forties*. London: Philip Wilson, 2000.

Jenks, Chris. "Watching Your Step: the History and Practice of the *Flâneur*." *Visual Culture*. London: Routledge, 1995.

Jentsch, Ernst. "On the Psychology of the Uncanny." 1906. Trans. Roy Sellars. *Angelaki* 2.1 (1996): 7–17.

Jesse, F. Tennyson. "Note to Isolationists." 1940. *Chaos of the Night: Women's Poetry and Verse of the Second World War*. Ed. Catherine Reilly. London: Virago, 1984. 69.

Johnson, Claudia. *Equivocal Beings: Politics, Gender, and Sentimentality in the 1790s*. Chicago: U of Chicago P, 1995.

Johnson, David. *The City Ablaze: The Second Great Fire of London, 29th December 1940*. London: William Kimber, 1980.

Johnson, Robert. *British Imperialism*. Basingstoke: Palgrave Macmillan Macmillan, 2003.

Jones, Kathleen. *A History of Mental Health Services*. London: Routledge, 1972.

——. *Asylums and After*. London: Athlone, 1993.

Jones, Langdon. "A Reverie of Bone: A Review of the Work of Mervyn Peake." 1967. 7 January 2008. <http://langjones.co.uk/bone.html>

Jones, Steve. *When the Lights Went Down: Crime in Wartime London*. Bulwell: Wicked, 1995.

Kahane, Claire. "The Gothic Mirror." *The (M)other Tongue: Essays in Feminist Psychoanalytic Interpretation*. Eds. Shirley Nelson Garner, Claire Kahane and Madelon Sprengnether. Ithaca, New York: Cornell UP, 1985. 334–51.

Kapp, Yvonne and Margaret Mynatt. *British Policy and the Refugees, 1933–41*. London: Frank Cass, 1997.

Katin, Zelma. *Clippie: The Autobiography of a War Time Conductress*. London: John Gifford, 1944.

Kavan, Anna. *I Am Lazarus*. London: Peter Owen, 1945.

——. *Sleep Has His House*. 1948. London: Picador, 1973.

Kavka, Misha. "Men in (Shell-)Shock: Masculinity, Trauma, and Psychoanalysis in Rebecca West's *The Return of the Soldier*." *Studies in Twentieth Century Literature* 22.1 (Winter 1998): 151–71.

Keats, John. "Ode to a Nightingale." 1819. *The Complete Poems*. 2nd ed. Ed. John Barnard. London: Penguin, 1976. 346.

Kee, R. *The World We Left Behind: A Chronicle of the Year 1939*. Weidenfeld and Nicolson, 1984.

Kelly, John. "Time and the Global." *Development and Change* 29.4 (October 1998): 839–71.

Kessell, Mary. "German Diary by a War Artist." 1945. *Hearts Undefeated: Women's Writing of the Second World War*. Ed. Jenny Hartley. 1994. London: Virago, 2003. 600–1.

Khanna, Ranjana. *Dark Continents: Psychoanalysis and Colonialism*. Durham, North Carolina: Duke UP, 2003.

Kilgour, Maggie. *The Rise of the Gothic Novel*. London: Routledge, 1995.

Kittler, Friedrich. *Discourse Networks 1800–1900*. Trans. Michael Metteer and Chris Cullens. Stanford: Stanford UP, 1990.

Klein, Melanie. *The Selected Melanie Klein*. Ed. Juliet Mitchell. New York: Free Press, 1986.

Kochan, Miriam. *Britain's Internees in the Second World War*. London: Macmillan, 1983.

——. *Prisoners of England*. London: Macmillan, 1980.

Kristeva, Julia. *Powers of Horror*. 1980. Trans. Leon Roudiez. New York: Columbia, 1982.

Kushner, Tony, David Cesarani, Jo Reilly and Colin Richmond. "Approaching Belsen." *Belsen in History and Memory*. Eds. David Cesarani, Tony Kushner, Jo Reilly and Colin Richmond. London: Frank Cass, 1997. 3–33.

Kushner, Tony. "The Memory of Belsen." *Belsen in History and Memory*. Eds. David Cesarani, Tony Kushner, Jo Reilly and Colin Richmond. London: Frank Cass, 1997. 181–205.

——. *The Holocaust and the Liberal Imagination*. London: Blackwell, 1994.

Lacan, Jacques. *Écrits*. Paris: Seuil, 1966.

Lafitte, François. *The Internment of Aliens*. 2nd ed. London: Libris, 1988.

Lang, Andrew. *The Poetical Works*. Ed. Leonora Blanche Lang. London: Longmans, 1923.

Laplanche, J. and J.-B. Pontalis, *The Language of Psycho-Analysis*. 1967. Trans. Donald Nicholson-Smith. New York: Norton, 1973.

Lassner, Phyllis. *British Women Writers of World War II: Battlegrounds of their Own*. Basingstoke: Macmillan, 1998.

Last, Nella. "The Changes War Brings to Women." 1940–1942. *Hearts Undefeated: Women's Writing of the Second World War*. Ed. Jenny Hartley. 1994. London: Virago, 2003. 510–12.

Lattek, Christine. "Bergen-Belsen: From 'Privileged' Camp to Death Camp." *Belsen in History and Memory*. Eds. David Cesarani, Tony Kushner, Jo Reilly and Colin Richmond. London: Frank Cass, 1997. 37–71.

Laub, Dori. "Bearing Witness, or the Vicissitudes of Listening." *Testimony*. Eds. Shoshana Felman and Dori Laub. New York: Routledge, 1992. 57–74.

Laurent, Livia. "Internment on the Isle of Man." 1940. *Hearts Undefeated: Women's Writing of the Second World War*. Ed. Jenny Hartley. 1994. London: Virago, 2003. 366–9.

Lawrence, D. H. "The Odour of Chrysanthemums." 1909. *Twentieth Century Short Stories*. Eds. Douglas Barnes and R. F. Egford. Cheltenham: Thomas Nelson, 1990. 64–90.

Lawrence, Margery. *Fourteen to Forty-Eight*. London: Robert Hall, 1950.

Le Cam, Pierre-Yves. "Peake's Fantastic Realism in the Titus Books." *Peake Studies* 3.4 (Spring 1994): 5–15.

Le Queux, William. *The Invasion of 1910, With a Full Account of the Siege of London*. London: Eveleigh Nash, 1906.

Lebzelter, Gisela. "Henry Hamilton Beamish and the Britons: Champions of Anti-Semitism." *British Fascism: Essays on the Radical Right in Inter-War Britain*. Eds. Kenneth Lunn and Richard Thurlow. London: Croom Helm, 1980. 41–56.

——. *Political Anti-Semitism in England 1918–1939*. London: Macmillan, 1979.

Lehmann, John. "The Armoured Writer II." *New Writing and Daylight* (Winter 1942–3): 165–76.

——. "Foreword." *Penguin New Writing* 25 (1945): 7.

Leicester Joint Refugee Commission. "To Rudolf Bamberger." October 1939. Ts. 99/25/1. Imperial War Museum, London, Department of Documents.

Leslie, Doris. *House in the Dust.* 1942. London: Heinemann, 1969.

Lewinski, Tea. Ms. 97/28/1. Imperial War Museum, London. Department of Documents.

Lifton, Robert Jay. *Death in Life: The Survivors of Hiroshima.* 1967. London: Weidenfeld and Nicolson, 1968.

——. *The Future of Immortality, and Other Essays for a Nuclear Age.* New York: Basic Books, 1987.

Light, Alison. *Forever England: Femininity, Literature and Conservatism between the Wars.* London: Routledge, 1991.

Linafelt, Tod. *Surviving Lamentations: Catastrophe, Lament, and Protest in the Afterlife of a Biblical Book.* Chicago: U of Chicago P, 2000.

Link, Alex. "'The Capitol of Darknesse': Gothic Spatialities in the London of Peter Ackroyd's Hawksmoor." *Contemporary Literature* 45.3 (Fall 2004): 516–37.

Liss, Andrea. *Trespassing Through Shadows: Memory, Photography and the Holocaust.* Minneapolis: U of Minnesota P, 1998.

Listen to Britain. Dir. Humphrey Jennings and Stewart McAllister. Crown Film Unit, 1942.

Littlewood, Roland and Maurice Lipsedge. *Aliens and Alienists: Ethnic Minorities and Psychiatry.* 3rd ed. London: Routledge, 1997.

Loewenstein, Andrea. *Loathsome Jews and Engulfing Women: Metaphors of Projection in the Works of Wyndham Lewis, Charles Williams, and Graham Greene.* New York: New York UP, 1993.

Lomax, Montagu. *The Experiences of an Asylum Doctor, with Suggestions for Asylum and Lunacy Law Reform.* London: Allen & Unwin, 1921.

London Can Take It. Dir. Humphrey Jennings and Harry Watt. GPO, 1940.

Loraux, Nicole. *Mothers in Mourning.* Trans. Corinne Pache. Ithaca: Cornell UP, 1997.

Low, David Alexander Cecil. *British Cartoonists, Caricaturists and Comic Artists.* London: Collins, 1942.

Lowe, John. "Fraternal Fury: Faulkner, World War I, and Myths of Masculinity." *Faulkner and War.* Eds. Noel Polk and Ann J. Abadie. Jackson, Missouri: U of Mississippi P, 2004.

Lowe, R. *The Welfare State in Britain Since 1945.* Basingstoke: Macmillan, 1993.

Lubbers, Klaus. "Continuity and Change in Irish Fiction." *Ancestral Voices: The Big House in Anglo-Irish Literature.* Ed. Otto Rauchbauer. Dublin: Lilliput, 1992. 17–29.

Luckhurst, Roger. "The Contemporary London Gothic and the Limits of the 'Spectral Turn.'" *Textual Practice* 16.3 (Winter 2002): 527–46.

Lunn, Kenneth and Richard Thurlow (eds). *British Fascism: Essays on the Radical Right in Inter-War Britain.* London: Croom Helm, 1980.

Lunn, Kenneth. "Political Anti-Semitism Before 1914: Fascism's Heritage?" *British Fascism: Essays on the Radical Right in Inter-War Britain.* Eds. Kenneth Lunn and Richard Thurlow. London: Croom Helm, 1980. 20–40.

Lynd, Sylvia. "The Searchlights." *Collected Poems of Sylvia Lynd*. London: Macmillan, 1945. 4.

Macaulay, Rose. *The Pleasure of Ruins*. London: Weidenfeld and Nicolson, 1953.

Machen, Arthur. *The Great God Pan, and the Inmost Light*. 1890. Boston, MA: Roberts Brothers, 1895.

Mackay, Robert. *Half the Battle: Civilian Morale in Britain During the Second World War*. Manchester: Manchester UP, 2002.

MacKenzie, Scott Richard. "Home and Away: Nation and Home at the End of the English Eighteenth Century." *Dissertation Abstracts International A: The Humanities and Social Sciences* 59.11 (May 1999): 4153.

MacNeice, Louis. "Photographs of London." *Lilliput* (Nov 1943): 407–414.

——. "Refugees." *Horizon* 3.14 (February 1941): 164–5.

Mantrant, Sophie. "Mervyn Peake's Gormenghast Novels: A Baroque Hostility to Straight Lines." *Etudes Britanniques Contemporaines* (June 2005): 71–82.

Martin, Rupert. "War Work." 1983. *Bill Brandt: Selected Texts*. Ed. Nigel Warburton. Oxford: Clio, 1993. 47–50.

Marx, Karl. "Estranged Labour." 1844. *Early Writings*. Trans. Tom Nairn. 1974. Intro. Lucio Colletti. 1974. Harmondsworth: Penguin, 1975. 322–34.

Massey, Doreen. "A Global Sense of Place." *Marxism Today* 35.6 (June 1991): 24–9.

Mass-Observation. "The Tube-Dwellers." *The Saturday Book*. Ed. Leonard Russell. Hutchinson, 1943. 102–12.

——. *People in Production*. London: John Murray, 1942.

——. "Public Opinion and the Refugee." 1940. Ts. File Report 332. Mass Observation Archive. U of Sussex.

——. "Recent Trends in Anti-Semitism." 1943. Ts. File Report 1648. Mass Observation Archive. U of Sussex.

——. *War Begins at Home*. Eds. Tom Harrisson and Charles Madge. London: Chatto and Windus, 1940.

——. *War Factory*. Ed. Tom Harrisson and Celia Fremlin. London: Gollancz, 1943.

——. "Women and Morale." 1940. Ts. File Report 520. Mass Observation Archive. U of Sussex.

Mathews, Cristina Moore. "Home, Nation, and Novels of Domestic History." *Dissertation Abstracts International A* 64.6 (Dec. 2003): 2075–76.

Mazda Light Bulbs. Advertisement. *Lilliput* (Jan 1942): xxvii.

Mazlish, Bruce. "The *Flâneur*: From Spectator to Representation." *The Flâneur*. Ed. Keith Tester. London: Routledge, 1994. 43–60.

McClintock, Anne. *Imperial Leather: Race, Gender and Sexuality in the Colonial Contest*. London: Routledge, 1995.

McCormack, W. J. "Setting and Ideology: with Reference to the Fiction of Maria Edgeworth." *Ancestral Voices: The Big House in Anglo-Irish Literature*. Ed. Otto Rauchbauer. Dublin: Lilliput, 1992. 33–60.

Mellor, David. "Brandt's Phantasms." *Bill Brandt Behind the Camera: Photographs 1928 to 1983*. Oxford: Phaidon, 1985. 71–97.

——. *A Paradise Lost: The Neo-Romantic Imagination in Britain, 1935–55*. London: Lund Humphries, 1987.

Mengham, Rod. *The Idiom of the Time: The Writings of Henry Green*. Cambridge UP; Cambridge; 1982.

Miéville, China. "The Conspiracy of Architecture: Notes on a Modern Anxiety." *Historical Materialism* 2.1 (1998): 1–32.

Middlebrook, M. and C. Everitt. *The Bomber Command War Diaries.* Viking, 1985.

Mighall, Robert. *A Geography of Victorian Gothic Fiction: Mapping History's Nightmares.* Oxford: Oxford UP, 1999.

Milbank, Alison. *Daughters of the House: Modes of the Gothic in Victorian Fiction.* Basingstoke: Macmillan, 1992.

Miles, Robert. "Abjection, Nationalism and the Gothic." *The Gothic.* Ed. Fred Botting. Cambridge: Brewer, 2001. 47–70.

——. *Ann Radcliffe.* Manchester: Manchester UP, 1995.

——. (ed.). "Female Gothic Writing." *Women's Writing: the Elizabethan to the Romantic Period* 1.2 (February 1994).

Miller, Kristine A. "'Even a Shelter's Not Safe': The Blitz on Homes in Elizabeth Bowen's Wartime Writing." *Twentieth Century Literature* 45.2 (Summer 1999): 138–58.

——. "'The World Has Been Remade': Gender, Genre, and the Blitz in Graham Greene's *The Ministry of Fear.*" *Genre* 36.1–2 (2003 Spring–Summer): 131–50.

Miller, Michael. *The Bon Marché.* Princeton, NJ: Princeton UP, 1981.

Millions Like Us. Dir. Frank Launder and Sidney Giliat. Granada International, 1943.

Mills, Alice. *Stuckness in the Fiction of Mervyn Peake.* Amsterdam: Rodopi, 2005.

Ministry of Information. *Front Line 1940–1941.* London: HMSO, 1942.

——. "What do I do, if my job is that of housewife and mother?" *Picture Post* (17 August 1940): 3.

Minns, Raynes. *Bombers and Mash: The Domestic Front 1939–45.* London: Virago, 1980.

Mitchell, Juliet. Introduction. *The Selected Melanie Klein.* Ed. Juliet Mitchell. New York: The Free P, 1986. 9–32.

Mitscherlich, Alexander and Margarete Mitscherlich. *The Inability to Mourn.* Trans. Beverly Placzek. New York: Grove Press, 1968.

Moers, Ellen. *Literary Women.* Garden City, New York: Doubleday, 1976.

Moncrieff, Joanna. "An Investigation into the Precedents of Modern Drug Treatment in Psychiatry." *History of Psychiatry 10* (January 1999): 475–490.

Moon, Michael. "Memorial Rags: Emerson, Whitman, AIDS, and Mourning." *Professions of Desire: Lesbian and Gay Studies in Literature.* Eds. George Haggerty and Bonnie Zimmerman. New York: MLA, 1995. 233–40.

Moorcock, Michael. "The Achievement of Mervyn Peake." *Mervyn Peake: The Man and His Art.* Eds. Sebastian Peake, G. Peter Winnington and Alison Eldred London: Peter Owen, 2006. 80–83.

——. *Mother London.* 1988. London: Penguin, 1989.

Morell, John. "Arnold Leese and the Imperial Fascist League." *British Fascism: Essays on the Radical Right in Inter-War Britain.* Eds. Kenneth Lunn and Richard Thurlow. London: Croom Helm, 1980. 57–75.

Moretti, Franco. *Signs Taken for Wonders: Essays on the Sociology of Literary Forms.* Trans. Susan Fischer, David Forgacs and David Miller. London: Verso, 1983.

Morgan, Edwin. "The Walls of Gormenghast." *Chicago Review* 14.3 (Autumn–Winter 1960): 74–81.

Mortimer, Raymond. *New Statesman* (28 March 1942): 208.

Morton, H. V. *In Search of London*. 1951. London: Methuen, 1988.

Moynahan, Julian. "Elizabeth Bowen: Anglo-Irish Post-mortem." *Raritan* 9.2 (1989): 68–97.

Mumford, Lewis. *The City in History*. Harmondsworth: Penguin, 1961.

Murray, George. "We May Shudder, but We Dare Not Turn Away." *Lest We Forget: The Horrors of Nazi Concentration Camps Revealed For All Time in the Most Terrible Photographs Ever Published* London: Associated Newspapers, 1945. 4–5.

Nairn, Tom. *The Break-Up of Britain: Crisis and Neo-Nationalism*. 3rd ed. Edinburgh: Big Thinking, 2003.

The National Archives (TNA): Public Record Office (PRO) FO 371/25189/462 (W 7984/7941/49). Memorandum by Neville Bland dated 14 May 1940.

——. (PRO) FO 371/30917 (C 7853/61/18). Minute dated 10 September 1942.

——. (PRO) FO 371/24472/11 (C 5471/116/55). Minute dated 21 April 1940.

——. (PRO) INF 1/251, part 4. Papers of the Ministry of Information Planning Committee, 25 July 1941.

Neill, Gerard. "Frankly Disturbing." *Peake Studies* 7.2 (2000–2001): 22–33.

——. "Peake at the Imperial War Museum." *Peake Studies* 1.4 (Summer 1990): 29–34.

Nelki, Erna. "The Internment of Women in England, 1940." 1981. Ts. 84/50/1. Imperial War Museum, London. Department of Documents.

"New York by Night." *Picture Post* (14 December 1940): 12–13.

Nicholson, Jane. *Shelter*. London: Harrap, 1941.

Nuit et Brouillard (Night and Fog). Dir. Alan Resnais. 1955.

Night Shift. Dir. Jack Chambers. Paul Rotha Productions. 1942.

Nordau, Max. *Degeneration*. 2nd popular ed. Trans. anon. London: William Heinemann, 1913.

Norris, Claire. "The Big House: Space, Place, and Identity in Irish Fiction." *New Hibernia Review* 8.1 (Spring 2004) 107–21.

Norris, Pat. *Spies in the Sky*. Chichester: Springer, 2008.

Norton, Rictor (ed.). Introduction. *Gothic Readings: The First Wave 1764–1840*. Leicester: Leicester UP, 2000. London: Continuum, 2000. vii–xiii.

O'Brien, Kate. "Fiction." *Spectator* (24 November 1944): 488.

O'Brien, T. H. *Civil Defence*. London: HMSO, 1955.

Ogbe, Hilda. *The Crumbs off the Wife's Table*. Ibadan: Spectrum, 2001.

Opie, Robert. *The Wartime Scrapbook*. London: New Cavendish Books, 1995.

Orwell, George. "Anti-Semitism in Britain." 1945. *George Orwell's Essays and Articles*. 25 August 2008. <http://orwell.ru/library/articles/antisemitism/english/e_antib>

——. Diary. 8 April 1941. *A Patriot After All: Vol 12 of the Complete Works*. Eds. Peter Davison, Ian Angus and Sheila Davison. London: Secker and Warburg, 1998. 467–8.

Overseas Service. "Polychromatic Bombing." *The Listener* (24 April 1941): 587.

Owen, Wilfred "Mental Cases." *The Wilfred Owen Multimedia Digital Archive*. Oxford University. 7 July 2008. <http://www.hcu.ox.ac.uk/jtap/warpoems.htm#21>

Paget, Guy. *Sporting Pictures of England*. 1945. London: Collins, 1947.

Palattella, John. "'In the Midst of Living Hell.'" *William Carlos Williams Review* 17.2 (Fall 1991): 13–38.

Palmer, Harold D. and Francis J. Braceland. "Six Years Experience with Narcosis Therapy in Psychiatry." *American Journal of Psychiatry* 94 (July 1937): 37–57. 7 July 2008. <http://ajp.psychiatryonline.org/cgi/content/abstract/94/1/37>

Panter-Downes, Mollie. "The Power of Photography." 1945. *Hearts Undefeated: Women's Writing of the Second World War.* Ed. Jenny Hartley. 1994. London: Virago, 2003. 592.

——. "Year of Decision." 1944. (29 April 1944). *Good Evening, Mrs Craven.* Ed. Geoffrey Lestage. London: Persephone, 1999. 155–65.

Parini, Jay. "Far from Gormenghast." 6 September 2008. *Guardian Online.* 7 February 2009. <http://www.guardian.co.uk/books/2008/sep/06/poetry>

Paris, H. J. *English Water Colour Painters.* 1945. London: Collins, 1947.

Parsons, Deborah L. "Souls Astray: Elizabeth Bowen's Landscape of War." *Women: A Cultural Review* 8.1 (Spring 1997): 24–32.

——. *Streetwalking the Metropolis.* Oxford: Oxford UP, 2000.

Pasdermadjan, Hrant. *The Department Store.* London: Newman Books, 1954.

Pond, Oliver and Margarethe. Ms. 96/45/1. Imperial War Museum, London. Department of Documents.

Peake, Mervyn. *Boy in Darkness and Other Stories.* Ed. Sebastian Peake. London: Peter Owen, 2007.

——. *Collected Poems.* Ed. R. W. Maslen. Manchester: Carcanet, 2008.

——. *The Glassblowers.* London: Eyre and Spottiswoode, 1950.

——. *The Gormenghast Trilogy: Titus Groan, Gormenghast, Titus Alone.* 1946–1959. London: Vintage, 1999.

——. *Shapes and Sounds.* 1941. London: Village, 1974.

——. Unfinished Play Manuscript. Peake Manuscripts 7.iii. Held by the Mervyn Peake Estate.

Peake, Sebastian. *A Child of Bliss.* 1989. *Mervyn Peake: Two Lives.* London: Vintage, 1999.

Peake, Sebastian, G. Peter Winningston and Alison Eldred (eds). *Mervyn Peake: The Man and His Art.* London: Peter Owen, 2006.

Philips Wireless. Advertisement. *Picture Post* (10 February 1940): 3.

Philips, Terry. "The Rules of War: Gothic Transgressions in First World War Fiction." *Gothic Studies* 2.2 (August 2000): 232–44.

Phillips, Lawrence. *London Narratives: Post-War Fiction and the City.* London: Continuum, 2006.

Piercy, Marge. *Gone to Soldiers.* New York: Summit, 1987.

Piette, Adam. "Review of *London's Burning* by Stansky and Abrahams." *Peake Studies* 4.2 (1992): 42–4.

——. *Imagination at War: British Fiction and Poetry 1939–1945.* London: Papermac, 1995.

Piper, John. *British Romantic Artists.* London: William Collins, 1942.

——. "New War Pictures." May 1941. *John Piper: The Forties.* Ed. David Fraser Jenkins. London: Philip Wilson, 2000. 50.

——. "Pleasing Decay." *Architectural Review* 102 (Sept 1947): 85–94.

Plain, Gill. *Women's Fiction of the Second World War: Gender, Power and Resistance.* Edinburgh: Edinburgh UP, 1996.

Pocock, Tom. *1945: The Dawn Came Up Like Thunder.* London: Collins, 1983.

Pollak, Ernest. "Dreams" and "Departure to Freedom Curtailed" Ts. and ms. 86/89/1. Imperial War Museum, London. Department of Documents.

Pollock, Griselda. "Vicarious Excitements: *London a Pilgrimage* by Gustave Doré and Blanchard Jerrold, 1872." *New Formations* 2 (Spring 1988): 25–50.

Ponting, Clive. *1940: Myth and Reality*. London: Hamish Hamilton, 1990.

Pool, Phoebe (ed.). *Poems of Death*. Illustr. Michael Ayrton. London: Frederick Muller, 1945.

Poovey, Mary. "Ideology and *The Mysteries of Udolpho*." *Criticism* 21 (Fall 1979): 307–30.

Powell, Anthony. *The Soldier's Art*. 1966. London: Heinemann, 1966.

Pred, Allan. "Place as Historically Contingent Process." *Annals of the Association of American Geographers* 74.2 (1984): 279–97.

Prendergast, Christopher. *Paris and the Nineteenth Century*. Oxford: Blackwell, 1992.

Priestley, J. B. *Daylight on Saturday*. London: Heinemann, 1943.

Pritchett, V. S., Graham Sutherland, Kenneth Clark and Henry Moore. "Art and Life." *The Listener* 26.670 (13 November 1941): 657–9.

Punter, David and Elisabeth Bronfen. "Gothic: Violence, Trauma and the Ethical." *The Gothic*. Ed. Fred Botting. Cambridge: Brewer, 2001. 7–22.

Punter, David. "Hungry Ghosts and Foreign Bodies." *Gothic Modernisms*. Eds. Andrew Smith and Jeff Wallace. Basingstoke: Palgrave Macmillan, 2001. 11–28.

——. "Introduction: The Ghost of a History." *A Companion to the Gothic*. Ed. David Punter. Oxford: Blackwells, 2001. viii–xiv.

——. *Gothic Pathologies: The Text, the Body and the Law*. Basingstoke: Macmillan, 1998.

——. *The Literature of Terror*. 2nd ed. 2 vols. Edinburgh: Pearson Education, 1996.

Rae, Patricia (ed.). Introduction. *Modernism and Mourning*. Lewisburg: Bucknell, 2007. 13–49.

Ramazani, Jahan. "Afterword." *Modernism and Mourning*. Ed. Patricia Rae. Lewisburg: Bucknell UP, 2007. 286–295.

——. *Poetry of Mourning: The Modern Elegy from Hardy to Heaney*. Chicago: Chicago UP, 1994.

Ramsey, Winston G. (ed.). *The Blitz Then and Now*. 3 vols. London: Battle of Britain Prints, 1987–89.

Ratcliffe, Alexander. *The Truth About the Jews*. British Protestant League, 1943.

Rauchbauer, Otto. "The Big House and Irish History: An Introductory Sketch." *Ancestral Voices: The Big House in Anglo-Irish Literature*. Ed. Otto Rauchbauer. Dublin: Lilliput, 1992. 1–15.

Reaveley, Constance. "The Machine and the Mind." Ed. Jenny Hartley. 1994. London: Virago, 2003. 467–9.

Reed, Jeremy. *A Stranger on Earth: The Life and Work of Anna Kavan*. London: Peter Owen, 2006.

Reid, Vera W. "Cameos of 1939–1940." Ts. PP/MCR/88. Imperial War Museum, London. Department of Documents.

Reilly, Jo. "Cleaner, Carer and Occasional Dance Partner? Writing Women back into the Liberation of Bergen-Belsen." *Belsen in History and Memory*. Eds. David Cesarani, Tony Kushner, Jo Reilly and Colin Richmond. London: Frank Cass, 1997. 149–61.

"Review of *Degeneration Amongst Londoners* by James Cantlie." *The Lancet* (7 February 1885): 264–5.

Renan, Ernest. "What is a Nation?" 1882. Trans. Martin Thom. *Nation and Narration*. Ed. Homi Bhabha. London: Routledge, 1990. 8–22.

Return of the Vampire. Dir. Lew Landers. Columbia, 1944.

Richards, Jeffrey and Anthony Aldgate. *Best of British: Cinema and Society 1930–1970*. Oxford: Blackwell, 1983.

Richardson, Dorothy. *Pilgrimage*. 4 vols. 1915–38. London: Virago, 1979.

Ridler, Anne. *The Shadow Factory*. London: Faber, 1946.

Rigby, Mair. "Uncanny Recognition: Queer Theory's Debt to the Gothic." *Gothic Studies* 11.1 (May 2009): 46–57.

Riley, Denise. *War in the Nursery: Theories of the Child and Mother*. London: Virago, 1983.

Roberts, Adam. *"Review of Collected Poems* by Mervyn Peake." 4 August 2008. *Strange Horizons*. 1 March 2009. <http://www.strangehorizons.com/reviews/2008/08/collected_poems.shtml>

Rolt, Lionel. "Hawley Bank Foundry." *Sleep No More*. London: Constable, 1948. 117–42.

Rose, Gillian. *Mourning Becomes the Law*. Cambridge: Cambridge UP, 1996.

Rose, Jacqueline. "Bizarre Objects: Mary Butts and Elizabeth Bowen." *The Critical Quarterly* 42.1 (2000): 75–85.

Rosewarne, Vivian. "Letter from an Unknown Airman." 1940. *Private Words, Letters and Diaries from the Second World War*. Ed. Ronald Blythe. London: Viking, 1991. 306–8.

Rothwell, Stanley. "The Gentle Touch: A Narrative of Civil Defence Activities in Wartime." Microfilm DS/MISC/66. Imperial War Museum, London, Department of Documents.

Rotter, Andrew John. *Hiroshima: The World's Bomb*. Oxford: Oxford UP, 2008.

Royle, Nicholas. "Crypts in London: The Novels of Elizabeth Bowen." *Proceedings of the Eighth International Conference on Literature and Psychoanalysis*. Ed. Frederico Pereira. Lisbon: Inst. Superi Psicologia Aplicada, 1992. 143–7.

Russell, John. *British Portrait Painters*. London: Collins, 1944.

Sage, Victor. *Horror Fiction in the Protestant Tradition*. New York: St. Martin's, 1988.

Salomon, Roger. *Mazes of the Serpent: An Anatomy of Horror Narrative*. Ithaca, New York: Cornell UP, 2002.

Sansom, William. *Fireman Flower and Other Stories*. London: Hogarth, 1944.

——. *The Blitz: Westminster at War*. 1947. Oxford: Oxford UP, 1990.

Santner, Eric. *Stranded Objects: Mourning, Memory and Film in Postwar Germany*. Ithaca, New York: Cornell UP, 1990.

Saona, Margarita. "Do We Still Need the Family to Imagine the Nation? National Family Romances by Latin American Women Writers." *Disciplines on the Line: Feminist Research on Spanish, Latin American, and U. S. Latina Women*. Eds. Anne J. Cruz, Rosilie Hernández-Pecoraro and Joyce Tolliver. Newark, Delaware: Cuesta, 2003. 207–31.

Saywell, Shelley. *Women in War: First Hand Accounts from World War II to EL Salvador*. New York: Viking, 1985.

Schmitt, Cannon. *Alien Nation: Nineteenth-Century Gothic Fictions and English Nationality*. Philadelphia: U of Pennsylvania P, 1997.

Schneer, Jonathan. *London 1900: The Imperial Metropolis*. New Haven: Yale UP, 1999.

Scull, Andrew. "Psychiatrists and Historical 'Facts': The Historiography of Somatic Treatments." *History of Psychiatry* 6 (June 1995): 225–41.

Seaton, Jean. "Broadcasting and the Blitz." *Power Without Responsibilty: the Press, Broadcasting, and New Media in Britain.* 6th ed. Abingdon: Routledge, 2003.

——. "The BBC and the Holocaust." *European Journal of Communication* 2.1 (March 1987): 53–80.

Sedgwick, Eve Kosofsky. *The Coherence of Gothic Conventions.* 1980. New York: Methuen, 1986.

——. *The Epistemology of the Closet.* Berkeley: U of California P, 1990.

Sensibar, Judith. "'Behind the Lines' in Edith Wharton's *A Son at the Front.*" *Wretched Exotic.* Eds. Katherine Joslin and Alan Price. New York: Peter Lang, 1993.

Shaddock, Jennifer. "Dreams of Melanesia: Masculinity and the Exorcism of War in Pat Barker's *The Ghost Road.*" *Modern Fiction Studies* 52.3 (Fall 2006): 656–74.

Shapiro, Stephen. "Transvaal, Transylvania: Dracula's World-system and Gothic Periodicity." *Gothic Studies* 10.1 (May 2008): 29–47.

Sheller, Mimi and John Urry. "The New Mobilities Paradigm." *Environment and Planning A* 38.2 (2006): 207–26.

Sheridan, Dorothy (ed.). *Wartime Women: An Anthology of Women's Writing for Mass-Observation.* New York: Columbia UP, 1985.

Shiach, Morag. "Modernity, Labour and the Typewriter." *Modernist Sexualities.* Eds. Hugh Stevens and Caroline Howlett. Manchester: Manchester UP, 2000. 114–29.

Shields, Rob. "Fancy Footwork: Walter Benjamin's notes on *Flânerie.*" *The Flâneur.* Ed. Keith Tester. London: Routledge, 1994. 61–80.

Shorter, Edward. *A History of Psychiatry: From the Era of the Asylum to the Age of Prozac.* John Wiley, 1998.

Showalter, Elaine. *The Female Malady: Women, Madness and English Culture, 1830–1980.* London: Virago, 1987.

——. *Sister's Choice: Traditions and Change in American Women's Writing.* Oxford: Clarendon, 1991.

Sittner, Friedrich. "To Mrs Annie May Priestley." 9 June 1940. Ms. 95/4/1. Imperial War Museum, London. Department of Documents.

Sitwell, Edith. "Lullaby." *Collected Poems.* 1957. London: Macmillan, 1979. 274–5.

Slobodin, Richard. *W. H. R. Rivers: Pioneer Anthropologist, Psychiatrist of the Ghost Road.* Rev. ed. Stroud: Alan Sutton, 1997.

Smith, Andrew and Diana Wallace. "The Female Gothic: Then and Now." *Gothic Studies* 6.1 (May 2004): 1–7.

Smith, Andrew and Diana Wallace (eds). *The Female Gothic: New Directions.* Basingstoke: Palgrave, 2009.

Smith, Andrew and Jeff Wallace (eds). *Gothic Modernisms.* Basingstoke: Palgrave Macmillan, 2001.

Smith, Andrew. "Rethinking the Gothic: What Do We Mean?." *Gothic Studies* 4.1 (May 2002): 79–85.

Smith, Andrew and William Hughes (eds). *Queering the Gothic.* Manchester: Manchester UP, 2009.

Smith, Harold. *Britain in the Second World War: A Social History.* Manchester: Manchester UP, 1996.

Smith, Malcolm. *Britain and 1940: History, Myth and Popular Memory.* London: Routledge, 2000.

Sommer, Doris. *Foundational Fictions: The National Romances of Latin America.* Berkeley: U of California P, 1991.

Spargo, R. Clifton. *The Ethics of Mourning: Grief and Responsibility in Elegiac Literature.* Baltimore: Johns Hopkins UP, 2004.

Spender, Stephen. Introduction. *War Pictures by British Artists: Air Raids.* Oxford: Oxford UP, 1943.

Spier, Eugen. *The Protecting Power.* London: Skeffington, 1951.

Spurling, John. *Graham Greene.* London: Methuen, 1983.

Stallybrass, Peter and Allon White. *The Politics and Poetics of Transgression.* Ithaca, NY: 1986.

Stansky, Peter and William Abrahams. *London's Burning: Life, Death and Art in the Second World War.* London: Constable, 1994.

Steinert, Johannes-Dieter. "British Relief Teams in Belsen Concentration Camp: Emergency Relief and the Perception of Survivors." *Belsen 1945: New Historical Perspectives.* Eds. Suzanne Bardgett and David Cesarani. London: Valentine Mitchell, 2006. 62–78.

Stevenson, Robert Louis. *The Strange Case of Dr Jekyll and Mr Hyde.* 1886. London: Penguin, 1994.

Stewart, Victoria. "The Auditory Uncanny in Wartime London: Graham Greene's *The Ministry of Fear.*" *Textual Practice* 18.1 (Spring 2004): 65–81.

St. John, Stella. *A Prisoner's Log, Holloway.* London: Howard League for Prison Reform, 1944.

Stoker, Bram. *Dracula.* 1897. New York: Penguin, 1993.

Stone, Martin. "Shell-shock and Psychiatry." *The Anatomy of Madness: Essays in the History of Psychiatry.* Eds. W. F. Bynum, Roy Porter and Michael Shepherd. Vol. 2. London: Tavistock, 1988. 242–71.

Stonebridge, Lyndsey. "Bombs and Roses: The Writing of Anxiety in Henry Green's *Caught.*" Eds. Rod Mengham and N. H. Reeve. *The Fiction of the 1940s: Stories of Survival.* Palgrave Macmillan, Basingstoke, 2001. 46–69.

Stratton, Jon. *Coming Out Jewish: Constructing Ambivalent Identities.* London: Routledge, 2000.

Struther, Jan. [Joyce Maxtone-Graham]. *Mrs Miniver.* London: Chatto and Windus, 1943.

Stuhlmann, Gunther. "Anna Kavan Revisited: The Web of Unreality." *Anais* 3 (1985): 55–62.

Summerfield, Penny. *Women Workers in the Second World War: Production and Patriarchy in Conflict.* 1984. London: Routledge, 1989.

Summers-Bremner, Eluned "Monumental City: Elizabeth Bowen and the Modern Unhomely." *Modernism and Mourning.* Ed. Patricia Rae. Lewisburg: Bucknell UP, 2007. 260–70.

Sutherland, Graham. "Images Wrought from Destruction." 1971. *Sutherland: The Wartime Drawings.* Roberto Tassi. 1979. Trans. and ed. Julian Andrews. London: Sotheby Parke Bernet, 1980.

——. "Thoughts on Painting." *Listener* (6 Sept 1951): 376–8

——. "A Trend in English Draughtsmanship." *Signature* (July 1936): c. 11.

Taylor, A. J. P. *English History, 1914–1945.* Oxford: Oxford UP, 1965.

Taylor, Frederick. *Dresden: Tuesday, February 13, 1945.* New York: HarperCollins, 2004.

Taylor, Philip M. *Munitions of the Mind: A History of Propaganda from the Ancient World to the Present Day.* Rev. ed. Manchester: Manchester UP, 1995.

Tester, Keith. Introduction. *The Flâneur.* Ed. Keith Tester. London: Routledge, 1994. 1–21x.

Thomas, Dylan. "A Refusal to Mourn the Death, by Fire, of a Child in London." *Horizon* 12.70 (October 1945): 223.

Thompson, W. H. *I Was Churchill's Shadow.* London: Christopher Johnson, 1951.

Thomson, James. *The City of Dreadful Night.* 1880. Gloucester: Dodo, 2005.

Thrift, Nigel. *Spatial Formations.* London: Sage, 1996.

Thurlow, Richard. *Fascism in Britain: A History, 1918–1985.* London: Blackwell, 1987.

Thurschwell, Pamela. *Literature, Technology and Magical Thinking, 1880–1920.* Cambridge: Cambridge UP, 2001.

Titmuss, Richard. *Problems of Social Policy.* London: HMSO, 1950.

Todd, Janet. *The Sign of Angelica: Women, Writing and Fiction, 1660–1800.* London: Virago, 1989.

Tolley, A. T. *The Poetry of the Forties in Britain.* Ontario: Carleton UP, 1985.

Treece, Henry and J. F. Hendry. *The New Apocalypse.* London: Fortune, 1939.

Tropp, Martin. *Images of Fear: How Horror Stories Helped Shape Modern Culture, 1818–1918.* Jefferson, North Carolina: McFarlane, 1990.

Tuan, Yi-Fu. *Passing Strange and Wonderful: Aesthetics, Nature and Culture.* Washington DC: Island, 1993.

Uhlman, Fred *Captivity.* London: Jonathan Cape, 1946

United States Office of War Information. *KZ: Bildbericht aus Fünf Konzentrationslagern.* 1945. Wuppertal: Vereinigung der Verfolgten des Naziregimes/ Bund der Antifaschistinnen und Antifaschisten Nordrhein-Westfalen, 2006.

Venturi, Robert, Denise Scott Brown and Steven Izenour. *Learning from Las Vegas: The Forgotten Symbolism of Architectural Form.* 1972. Cambridge, MA: MIT, 1977.

Vickroy, Laurie. "Can the Tide Be Shifted?: Transgressive Sexuality and War Trauma in Pat Barker's Regeneration Trilogy." *Journal of Evolutionary Psychology* 23.2–3 (August 2002): 97–104.

Vidler, Anthony. *The Architectural Uncanny: Essays in the Modern Unhomely.* Cambridge, Massachusetts: MIT, 1992

Walkowitz, Judith R. *City of Dreadful Delight.* Chicago: U of Chicago P, 1992.

Wallace, Diana. "Uncanny Stories: The Ghost Story as Female Gothic." *Gothic Studies* 6.1 (May 2004): 57–68.

"War Doesn't Change." *Picture Post* (19 April 1941): 16–17.

Ward, J. T. *The Factory Movement 1830–1855.* London: Macmillan, 1962

Warner, Sylvia Townsend. *A Garland of Straw and Other Stories.* London: Chatto and Windus, 1943.

Warwick, Alexandra. "Feeling Gothicky?" *Gothic Studies* 9.1(May 2007): 5–19.

——. "Lost Cities: London's Apocalypse." *Spectral Readings: Towards a Gothic Geography: Towards a Gothic Geography.* Eds. Glennis Byron and David Punter. London: Macmillan, 1999. 73–87.

Wasserstein, Bernard. *Britain and the Jews of Europe, 1939–1945*. 2nd ed. London: Leicester UP, 1999.

Wasson, Sara. "'A Network of Inscrutable Canyons': Wartime London's Sensory Landscapes." *The Swarming Streets*. Ed. Lawrence Phillips. Amsterdam: Rodopi, 2004. 77–95.

Watney, Simon. *English Post-Impressionism*. London: Studio Vista, 1980.

Watts, Cedric. *A Preface to Greene*. London: Longman, 1997.

Waugh, Evelyn. *Men at Arms*. 1952. London: Penguin, 1964.

——. *Vile Bodies*. Chapman Hall, London, 1930.

Wells, H. G. *The Fate of Homo Sapiens*. London: Secker and Warburg, 1939.

——. *The Time Machine*. 1895. London: Penguin, 2005.

——. *The War in the Air*. 1908. London: Penguin, 2005.

——. *The War of the Worlds*. 1898. London: Penguin, 2005.

Whalan, Mark. "'How did they pick John Doe?': Race, Memorialization, and Modernism in US Interwar Literature." *Modernism and Mourning*. Ed. Patricia Rae. Lewisburg: Bucknell UP, 2007. 85–101.

Williams, Anne. *Art of Darkness: A Poetics of Gothic*. Chicago: U of Chicago P, 1995.

Williams, Raymond. *The Country and the City*. 1973. New York: Oxford UP, 1975.

Williams, Rosalind. *Dream World: Mass Consumption in Late Nineteenth-Century France*. Berkeley, CA: U of California P, 1982.

Williams-Ellis, Amabel. *Women in War Factories*. London: Gollancz, 1943.

Wills, Clair. "The Aesthetics of Irish Neutrality during the Second World War." *Boundary 2* 31.1 (Spring 2004): 119–45.

Wilson, Elizabeth. *The Sphinx in the City*. Berkeley: U of California P, 1991.

Windholz, G. and L. H. Witherspoon. "Sleep as a Cure for Schizophrenia: A Historical Episode." *History of Psychiatry* 4.13 (March 1993): 83–93.

Winnington, G. Peter. "Parodies and Poetical Allusions." *Peake Studies* 7.4 (April 2002): 25–9.

——. *Vast Alchemies: The Life and Work of Mervyn Peake*. London: Peter Owen, 2000.

——. "Uncollected Poems by Mervyn Peake." *Peake Studies* 2.4 (1992 Summer): 5–17.

Winter, Jay. "Introduction: H. G. Wells and the Nightmare of War." *War in the Air*. By H. G. Wells. London: Penguin, 2005. xiii–xxv.

——. "Shell-Shock and the Cultural History of the Great War." *Journal of Contemporary History* 35 (2000): 7–11.

Wisker, Gina. "Viciousness in the Kitchen: Sylvia Plath's Gothic." *Gothic Studies* 6.1 (May 2004): 103–17.

Wolff, Janet. "The Invisible *Flâneuse*: Women and the Literature of Modernity." *Theory, Culture and Society* 2.3 (1985).

Wolfreys, Julian and Ruth Robbins (eds). *Victorian Gothic: Literary and Cultural Manifestations in the Nineteenth Century*. Basingstoke: Palgrave Macmillan, 2000.

Wollman, Howard and Philip Spencer. "'Can Such Goodness be Profitably Discarded?' Benedict Anderson and the Politics of Nationalism." *The Influence of Benedict Anderson*. Eds. Alistair McCleery and Benjamin Brabon. Edinburgh: Merchiston Press, 2007. 1–20.

Woolf, Virginia. "Street Haunting." *A Bloomsbury Group Reader*. Ed. S. P. Rosenbaum. Oxford: Blackwell, 1993. 317–327.

Woon, Basil. *Hell Came to London: A Reportage of the Blitz during 14 Days*. London: Peter Davies, 1941.

Wordsworth, William. "Intimations of Immortality from Recollections of Early Childhood." *Selected Poems*. Ed. Walford Davies. London: J. M. Dent, 1975. 101–111.

——. *The Prelude: A Parallel Text*. 1805–6, 1850. Ed. J. C. Maxwell. 1972. London: Penguin, 1986.

——. "Tintern Abbey." *Romanticism*. 2nd ed. Ed. Duncan Wu. Oxford: Blackwell, 1998. 268.

Wu, Duncan (ed). *Romanticism*. 2nd ed. Oxford: Blackwell, 1998.

Yannick, Ripa. *Women and Madness: The Incarceration of Women in Nineteenth-Century France*. 1986. Trans. Catherine du Peloux Menagé. Cambridge: Polity, 1990.

Yee, Chiang. *The Silent Traveller in War Time*. London: Country Life, 1939.

Yorke, Malcolm. "Frankly Missing the Target." *Peake Studies* 7.3 (2001): 18–29.

——. *Mervyn Peake: My Eyes Mint Gold*. New York: Overlook, 2002.

——. *The Spirit of Place: Some Neo-Romantic Artists and Their Times*. London: Constable, 1988.

Young, Alan. "W. H. R. Rivers and the War Neuroses." *Journal of the History of the Behavioral Sciences* 35 (1999): 359–378.

Young, Elizabeth. 'Dependencies.' *London Review of Books* (25 February 1993): 22–23.

Young, Iris Marion. "Abjection and Oppression." *Crises in Continental Philosophy*. Eds. Arleen Dallery and Charles Scott. Albany, New York: SUNY, 1990. 201–14.

——. "House and Home: Feminist Variations on a Theme." *Intersecting Voices: Dilemmas of Gender, Political Philosophy, and Policy*. Princeton: Princeton UP, 1997. 134–64.

Z, Mickey. "Forgotten February." 7 February 2007. *CounterCurrents.org*. 27 March 2009. <http://www.countercurrents.org/mickeyz070207.htm>.

Zambreno, Kate. "Anna Kavan." *Context* 18. 17 September 2007. <http://www.dalkeyarchive.com/article/show/186>

Ziegler, Philip. *London at War, 1939–1945*. 1995. London: Arrow, 1997.

Index

A bold page number indicates an illustration.

women, 32–3, 42, 45–9, 61, 70,
    83–129, 165n16, 165n24,
    167n40, 167n44, 167n45,
    167n46, 167n47, 167n48,
    167n49, 167n50, 168n54,
    168n59, 169n67
  iconography of death and, 62–3
  mobile *versus* immobile, 114
  in *flânerie*, 32–3
  see also advertising; domestic
    labour; conscription;
    conscientious objectors;
    narcosis; female Gothic;
    feminism; masculinity;
    mothers
Woolf, Virginia, 32–3
Wordsworth, William
  "Ode: Intimations of Immortality
    from Recollections of Early
    Childhood," 91
  "Tintern Abbey," 74, 118
World War I, 9–11, 53, 54, 57–8,
    86–7, 98–9, 112, 117, 131, 135,
137, 149, 157, 163n4, 164n6,
    165n20, 168n55, 168n56,
    169n62, 169n68
  re-enactment of in World War II,
    10–11, 53, 117, 135, 168n56,
    169n62
  trenches named after London
    streets, 11
  see also air raids; shell-shock

xenophobia, 2, 69, 74–5, 163n5

Yee, Chiang, 33
Yorke, Malcolm, 137, 139, 142,
    164n10, 169n71, 170n74,
    170n75
Young, Iris Marion, 106, 134

Ziegler, Philip, 5, 6, 9, 11–14, 17,
    21, 22, 34, 37, 43, 44, 99, 137,
    151–2, 165n23, 165n25,
    166n30, 168n53
Zlosnik, Sue, 31, 85